# ISLAMIC GOVERNMENT

# ISLAMIC GOVERNMENT

A. H. Qasmi

ISHA

ISHA BOOKS

Delhi-110009

Islamic Government



ISBN: 81-8205-482-6



Published in 2008 in India by
ISHA Books
B-63, 1st Floor, New Gupta Colony,
Near DDA Market,
Delhi-110009
Phone: 9212142040
ishabooks@hotmail.com

*Laser Type Setting by:* Shree Vaishnavi Creations, Delhi
*Printed at*: Vishal Kaushik Printers, Delhi

# Contents

*Preface* (*vii*)

1. **Concept of State** **1**
• The Establishment • The Caliphate

2. **State in Existence** **13**
• The Authority • The Brotherhood • Islamic Morals

3. **System of Government** **55**
• State under Islam • The Fraternity • Lord's Rule • Fundamental Liberties • Legal System • Significant Principles

4. **Charter for Governance** **105**
• Perfect Statute • Lord's Supremacy • No Discrimination • Almighty's Rule

5. **Believers' Rights** **141**
• Original Laws • Law in Force • Centre of Power

6. **Non-believers' Rights** **155**
• All Protections • No Discrimination

7. **Seat of Power** **171**
• Prophet in Town • Peace for All •Movement for Education

8. **No War Pact** 229
• The Attacks • Holy Prophet, Best in the World • Peace Proclaimed

9. **Possession of Mecca** 267
• Final Victory • Peace for All • Beginning of New Age

10. **Law and Order** 285
• Prophet's Words • Rapid Growth • The Ideology

*Bibliography* 333

*Index* 339

# Preface

Man is a social creature. It is the society where he learns how to live in this vast cosmos. Apart from society, people are divided into different castes, cultures and creeds. All these factors go in developing a man's personality. Of all the factors, mentioned above, religion is most important.

There exist about more than two thousand religions in the world today. A religion is regarded as a sacred institution, which governs a man's life here and hereafter and teaches him how to lead a happy and prosperous life.

What's unique to Islam is its endowment to humanity from the divine creator or the Almighty. It is not a set of principles and dogmas scribed by a scholar or thinker. It was sent on the earth circa fifteen hundred years ago, but its principles and preachings hold good even today. Besides showing humanity a straight way to the eternal success, it also has a say in various other walks of human life, such as economy, politics, human rights, social relations, judiciary, marriage and so on and so forth.

Another distinguished feature of Islam is that apart from being the latest religion, it is also the last one. That is to say, whatever is there in Islam, it is valid upto to the doomsday. Now, there will not come any other religion till the Day of Judgement. Therefore, it is the most powerful and as well as the most human-nature-friendly.

Given the present global scenario, there was being felt a dire need to bring out such a mini-encyclopaedia of Islam which may cater to the maximum needs of man in the least possible sheet of paper.

We are sure that the endeavour would prove to be a capsule of treasure of knowledge about Islam, prepared perfectly. Nevertheless, considering the adage 'to err is human', we would be obliged if the readers suggest some improvements for further editions.

**Editor**

# 1

# *Concept of State*

The Ulama, over the centuries, have developed a structure for determining the entire set of rules and regulations arising from the Quran and the Surma (normative practice) of his messenger, Muhammad (PBUH).' This structure is called *fiqh* and is a legal discourse. But this legal discourse has been marginalized and attacked from many quarters, and for that reason few people are aware of the political ideas which the Ulama hold. This chapter attempts to convey certain traditionally held political ideas of the Ulama which will challenge conventional political notions held by some political scientists and students of Islamic civilization.

The Ulama and the Islamic legal discourse *(fiqh)* have been continually and ferociously attacked, even from within the Muslim world, from many quarters from secularists to modernists, reformists to fundamentalists. If these groups have one thing in common, it is a desire for power, and more specifically for state-centred schemes for Muslim progress.

Simply stated, the Ulama stand in their way as modern state centralization has historically been shunned by the Ulama. In fact, the very essence of the Ulama project that edifice erected to determine rules and regulations from the revelation is its decentralization, slow accumulation of positions and argumentation, local dominion, and diffusion. No one person can define and represent the Islamic experience, so the Ulama resist Islam being centralized in the person of the nation-state leader, or in any university or institute. And as for state-centred schemes for progress, in accord with traditional religions, the Ulama do not see progress as a virtue. As Norbert Wiener remarks.

Most of us are too close to the idea of progress to take cognizance either of the fact that this belief belongs only to a small part of recorded history, or of the other fact, that it represents a sharp break with our own religious professions and traditions.

The importance of the nation-state and the concept of progress to the dominant voice of politics in and about the Muslim world, helps explain why the Ulama are portrayed as the enemy or at least as the obstacle, to necessary 'change' and 'development'. But they are not unique in this respect.

Jerry Mander in his book *In the Absence of the Sacred,* quotes Oren Lyons, describing legal procedures of the Iroquois Nation: 'We meet and just keep talking until there's nothing left but the obvious truth, and both (disputing) families agree on the solution'. I was struck by the similarity between this description and that of Lawrence Rosen of a *qadı* (judge) in a Moroccan town.

For rather than being aimed simply at the invocation of state or religious power, rather than being devoted mainly to the creation of a logically consistent body of legal doctrine, the aim of the *qadi is* to put people back in the position of being able to negotiate their own permissible relationships without pre-determining just what the outcome of those negotiations ought to be.

What the Ulama share with other traditional knowledge-elites is a desire to preserve a social realm where law is played out in the communal arena with language (or other discursive formats), where not only contention is resolved, but also societal definition and direction is nurtured. This definition and direction comes from the community itself, and not from a media dominated by huge corporations or the government, or from a priestly class of lawyers who design and prosecute laws. In fact, there seems to be no place in their vision for the totalitarian, corporate, legal fiction called the State which we take for granted.

The word *qadi* recalls the Arabic word's meaning of one who settles the affair *(qada),* and Rosen shows how the discretion given to the *qadi* a discretion typically criticized by Western observers as laxity allows him to make law a 'metasystem which creates order in a universe that is often experienced in a more disorderly way'.' The disputants are facilitated by the *qadi* to continue defining the situation until the solution is obvious to all. Consensus developed over time and not coercion, is the central product of this legal activity.

**The Establishment**

There is a great chasm between a 'traditional' society, which will mean here a society which organizes itself around divine guidance, and a 'modern' society, which means a society with a state. As we shall see, the concept of state which has fully emerged in the last hundred years or so, and which saturates our field of vision, is alien to many traditional societies and to central activities of Islamic civilization. Yet when we want to investigate politics in Islam, we tend to look for states and at monarchical rulers like caliphs, sultans, and amirs; and when fundamentalists dream, they dream of a powerful, Utopian Islamic State. The fact remains that politics in Islamic civilization is located predominately in quite a different arena, and the Ulama, including Ibn-e-Taymiyah, traditionally resisted all kinds of forces which might have potentially led to the kind of state powers which we have seen recently.

The dream of an Islamic State seems to include visions of sticks taken to rebellious Muslims, timorous non-Muslims citizens, and autocratic rulers on white horses solving all the prevailing problems. But the preoccupation with caliphate seems entirely modern, arising especially in the face of the humiliation suffered at the hands of nineteenth and twentieth century imperialist powers. Historically, Muslim communities throughout the world established the *shariah* by themselves, not *ex cathedra,* as the central focus of their community. Glimpses into daily life, chosen from hagiographic accounts of Sufis and their travels, popular poetry, inscriptions, and accounts of peasant revolts, reveal Muslim communities implementing the *shariah* themselves, striving thereby for a just society. In fact, the very word government *(hukumat)* in Arabic,' as recorded by the lexicographer Ibn Manzur below conveys a negative role for government, not a positive one.

The Arab says *hakam-tu,* I prevented someone and *hakam-tu,* I averted someone with the meaning of I prevented someone and I averted someone. In this category, one says about the *hakim* among people that he is *hakim* because he prevents the oppressor from oppression. Al-Mundhiri reported from Abu Talib that he said about their statement *hakama* Allah among us, that al-Asma'i said the root of *hukumat* (government) is averting the oppressor from oppression:'

Here the government's role is simply to prevent oppression, because positive political benefits arise directly from practising the *shariah*. There is no place in this Arab conception of *hukumat* for massive bureaucracies, governmental spending and taxing, standing armies and governments. This conception suggests that government is quite an incidental affair, necessary only to stop the oppressor, and that the real political activity of the community is to be found elsewhere and I suggest that place is the communal arena of the *fiqh*.

***The Fiqh in the Political Realm :*** The Ulama traditionally exercised a distancing from encroaching state power. Indeed, we find great animosity among the Ulama, including fundamentalist favourites like Ibn Taymiyah, for emerging state power." According to Rosen, the law 'provides a context for the peaceable formation by individuals of their own ties,' so in the classical Islamic theory of the state, law and government were kept largely separate from one another ... By remaining resolutely focused on the individual, the legal establishment forsook the politicization of the law; by avoiding inclusion of the law as an instrument of state policy, the political authorities passed up the opportunity to use law as a vehicle of political centralization.

As with primitive people, Muslims traditionally refused state power over their lives. The kind of distinctions we find between 'then' and 'now', between the largely hidden and suppressed alternative political configurations and our contemporary situations, suggest a fundamental dichotomy. This can be variously characterized as the pre-Columbus era, the last five hundred years (for those concentrating on the civilizations of native peoples) and tradition and modernity (for those emphasizing the sacred, such as the perennialists and traditionalists).

But state power is almost invisible, as often is modernity, and so the fundamental dichotomy between anything today (government, media, religion) and then is not always perceived. One way to call attention to modern and state contexts is to draw on analyses which trace the radical changes influencing daily life. Writers like Mumford, Berman, Illich, Feyerabend, and Ellul show us a world where everything is called into question, where the questions of 'why do we do this' and 'why do we think this is normal' assume a particularly poignant note. The popular anti-hero Travis McGee meditates:

I get this crazy feeling. Every once in a while I get it. I get the feeling that this is the last time in history when the offbeats like me will have a chance to live free in the nooks and crannies of the huge and rigid structure of an increasingly codified society. Fifty years from now I would be hunted down in the street. They would drill little holes in my skull and make me sensible and reliable and adjusted."

In Foucault's lecture 'The Political Technology of Individuals'," a fundamental change in politics is seen with the process of defining the 'police' in the seventeenth and eighteenth centuries. He locates a book written in 1779 which is the 'first great systematic program of public health for the modern state'." At the same moment, 'the French Revolution gives the signal for the great national wars of our days ... meeting their conclusion or their climax in huge mass slaughters'.

While for Saint Thomas, the king should imitate God to lead men to the good life, and for Machiavelli, the art of politics is to increase the power of the prince, the aim of the modern state is to 'reinforce the state itself'." This gives rise to a political arithmetic, a statistics which creates a calculus of power, where 'the individual exists insofar as what he does is able to introduce even a minimal change in the strength of the state, either in a positive or in a negative direction ... And sometimes what he has to do for the state is to live, to work, to produce, to consume; and sometimes what he has to do is to die."

Without a calculus of demography, a statistics of population, what we now call politics—state, power, or government—had little to do with the daily life of traditional societies. With the calculus, the individual becomes the business of the state. From before his birth to after his death, the state is concerned with any increase or decrease the individual might confer on its aggregate power. The state has an interest in monitoring and deciding the fate of infants, educating children, intervening to protect them from parental abuse, immunizing them, and so on. What rational opposition can there be, where one must argue today for 'freedom from state interrogation' over 'health' and 'saving lives'?

The desire of the modern state, which is to endlessly interrogate and govern the subject interminably, with forms that need to be filled out, credit card records, and social security numbers, is contrasted with the reticent 'primitive'. Resistance to development is a resistance to this interrogation.

The very idea of 'naked' truth, and truth 'laid bare' rests in a worldview quite opposite to that of the classical Muslim scholars. Now, the truth of someone is that person's failing, sins, and frailties. In the Islamic world, one did not broadcast shortcomings. In his discussion of the metaphor of rinsing the mouth and sniffing water in the process of *taharat* (ritual purity), Ibn al-Arabi reveals the typical emphasis given to this civilizational value. 'Even if his recompense (for speaking of evil),' Ibn al-Arabi comments, 'is in His statement, *[Allah loves not that evil should be noised abroad in public speech, except where injustice has been done]*, [4:148], nevertheless silence about it is most excellent."

The resistance of the primitive is well-illustrated in a passage in Munif's novel about the advent of oil exploration in what is now Saudi Arabia, where the bureaucrats say, 'The information we need is simple and necessary, and it is confidential too.' To their long series of questions about his parents, Ibrahim blurts out 'What do you want with my mothers?' And then after even more questions, 'What's wrong with you—can't you talk about anything but my father and mother?' Finally, he cries out, 'God help me—leave me alone!"'

Communities who refuse statehood and states are found throughout the world, from the Penans in Malaysia to the Aborigines in Australia, from Indian nations throughout North, Central, and South America to Kurds and Pathans in South and Southwest Asia. *Cultural Survival Quarterly* reports that three-fourths of the 120 military conflicts in the world in 1987 were native nations defending themselves against nation-state. The ultimate supremacy of the nation-state is not yet established and many communities throughout the world are struggling against it till death. In a world dominated by state powers, and at least—if not more—as influentially by corporations, it is no wonder that the voice of the Ulama is seldom heard.

## The Caliphate

The classical discussions of caliphate are sparse, overly abstract, and full of hidden agendas. They are not very helpful while questioning how authority is configured in Islamic societies. The voluminous discussions of who is best suited for leadership *(imamah)* during the prayer *(salah),* in contrast, is very helpful.

Should it not then be possible to extrapolate from the discussion of the *salah,* ideas about a larger universe? Is not the ideal leader for the *salah,* the ideal leader for the larger society? Is not the discussion of the criteria for a good leader for the *salah* at the same time a discussion of the good leader of society? If indeed we can examine the *salah* as a microcosm of the Muslim universe, a number of propitious consequences ensue.

What I am proposing here is nothing short of an entire re-evaluation of politics in Islam. The entire fundamentalist discourse on the Islamic state in fact arises from the invisible concealment of a traditional world view having its own kind of politics, by a modern world-view of the sovereign state. Let us therefore delve into this matter of politics, because one of the main reasons of examining the *fiqh* discussion of the *salah* as a microcosm for the larger discourse of Islamic communities, which is so propitious, stems from the reassessment of politics which it occasions.

Historically, there is a noticeable absence of sustained and direct discussion on Islamic leadership. The subject matter of kingship or caliphate tended to create treatises at once highly abstract and overly specific. The works of Mawardi, Nizam-ul-mulk, al-Ghazzali, and Ibn Khaldun, for example, when addressing kingship or caliphate, have quite definite agendas to pursue; attacking amid abstract and idealistic verbiage, a powerful woman behind a would-be leader, or simultaneous caliphates, or justifying pinning one's hopes on converting a ravaging Hun. Arkoun lists what Mawardi overlooks:

> Al-Mawardi talks neither of the Shiite theory of the designation of the caliph based on a text, nor of the great conflict *(al-fitna)* between Ali and Muawiyyah, nor of Yazid who, according to the Shi'ite version, had Hussain assassinated at Karbala, nor of the conditions of civil war which initiated the fall of the Umayyads and the ascendance of the Abbasides, nor of the politics of Mamun toward the Mutazilites and to Shiism, nor that of Mutawakkil for installing Sunnism, nor of the conquest of power by the Buyides.

The actual caliphate was formally abolished by Ataturk in 1925, and even though it was obvious that the caliphate had been an extremely ineffective system for decades, even centuries, the loss of the caliphate had a tremendous impact on Muslims throughout the world. Muslims in India, for example, spontaneously arose and began walking to Turkey to recover their world. Ali Abd-al-Razi's short treatise, published in Egypt in 1933 on government in Islam, arguing that the caliphate is not essential to the Islamic community, quickly brought him major troubles and seemed to many to be salt thrown on their wounds. To this day, many Muslims have put their hopes in a revived caliphate. We have a situation here where there is a dearth of material on Islamic government, together with an inchoate understanding that, against Abd al-Raziq, politics is essential to Islam.

The problem, as I see it, is that there is no state in Islam-state being understood in the Western sense of a sovereign, corporate institution with a reality across time and space, independent of its human constituents or components. When people talk of the 'Islamic theory of state', Ayubi notes,

> They are addressing themselves specifically to the problem of government and especially to the conduct of the ruler, and

not to the state as a generic category or to the body-politic as a social reality and a legal abstraction ... Even when the Islamic bureaucracy developed and became quite complex, officials and other 'public' personnel appointed to certain jobs or dismissed from them, never signed a contract with the 'State' or any other 'moral personality', but simply with a certain individual employer (al-muwalli).

The issue is not one merely of definition. The concept of a sovereign, corporate nation-state entails absolutism and totalitarianism—no matter how much people in liberal democracies want to believe that their freedom and rights are protected. Traditional scholars spoke of this kind of politics as Thoreau did, where the best government is the least government, or none at all. Ayubi writes that neo-fundamentalists 'invoke the text and quote the source, but in doing so they are highly selective and remarkably innovative. Political precedence is of practically no interest to them; neither is the main body of official jurisprudence, apart from a few exceptions such as Ibn Taimiya.

We tend to equate politics with state and government, and thus when we ask about politics in Islam, we are actually asking about states and governments. At that point, we gather the fairly small series of works, like al-Mawardi's, discussing the caliphate and the sultanate, which digress into discussions about intact testicles and other criteria for leadership, and end up with Abd al-Raziq's ultimate destruction of the whole thing, with his persuasive argument that the Prophet left no system of government and Muslim scholarship never actually addressed the entire issue of how people should be governed.

The moment we disengage 'politics' from 'state', an entirely new situation arises. The many Muslims who were appalled at Abd al-Raziq's position, and at all subsequent liberal positions on government, were right but they were inarticulate (the actual official rebuttal to his work seems to have zeroed in on his use of 'Bolshevik' in a long list of possible governmental systems which could be seen as Islamic). If we ask, 'What governmental system did the prophet leave his community?' the answer is 'the *fiqh* of the *shariah*'. If the *shariah* is the politics of the Islamic community, then its entire legal discussion—the *fiqh*—*is* the expression of politics in Islam. And whereas we have a few hundred pages on the subject matter of caliphate and sultanate, we have perhaps a million pages on the subject matter of *fiqh*.

So if we want to examine Muslim views on leadership, power, relations with the other, differences in communities, structures, and institutions, we would do well to pass over the official statements on caliphates and sultanates and turn instead to the actual arena of political contention and discussion—the *fiqh*. Taking the selection of a leader for the *salah* to be a microcosm of political leadership in Islam unleashes a torrent of positions, arguments, ideas, and terminologies which begin to reflect the historical realities of politics in Islam. At the same time, it offers Muslims an authentic discursive format which allows for an Islamic assessment of politics today. The basic need, then, is to re-evaluate this *fiqh*, both for historical understandings as well as for contemporary problems.

***The Jurisprudence :*** What exactly is the *fiqh?* It is perhaps the most concrete and voluminous monument of Islamic civilization, one format of Muslim understanding *(tafaqquh,* f.q.h.) of the *shariah*, the rules and regulations of Islam. Although the *fiqh* can become atrophied and reified, static and full of the weight of authority, it is traditionally the living expression of the Muslim community's commitment to realize the guidance of the *shariah*. For the Muslim, 'right life' is a consequence of right action, and the criterion for right belief is right conduct. Hence the importance of *fiqh*.

The *fiqh* combines concern with both the spiritual and the quotidian, and serves as the arena for political-economic life, regulating activity in the markets, mediating disputes, and determining David Easton's authoritative allocation of value' as well as administering rites of passage (birth, puberty, marriage, death). Its tendency for accumulation means that it preserves centuries of deliberations, discussions, decisions, and debates.

Therefore, the extension of the *fiqh*, and specifically the *fiqh* of *salah*, to the macrocosm allows us to reconstruct a political discourse. The fiqh surrounding the issue of privacy and windows, for example, tells us something about the priorities of Muslim scholars. We can reconstruct that when someone created a window, the neighbour's right of privacy prevailed: the existence of filled-in windows in traditional Muslim cities is the physical sign of the following event. Someone opens up a window to improve his house, and a neighbour begins to worry that the window looks into his house, disturbing his privacy; they take their case to the *qadi* (from the Arabic root q.d.y. as we saw, meaning to settle or resolve). The *qadi* seeks *sulah*, harmony among disputants, and so he brings along a builder to the site. If indeed the window 'harms'—from the axiomatic *hadith* `There shall be no harming, nor being harmed', *la darara wa la darara*—the window is boarded up. I suggest that in this process, the traditional politics for Muslim societies is seen.

In this process, obedience to the revelation is manifested within community relationships. This is why a break between spirituality, as expressed in obedience to the revelation, and politics, as depicted in interactions in communities, is inconceivable in traditional Islam. Let us look now explicitly at spirituality and politics.

2

# State in Existence

Let us now turn to the story of the Prophet's achievements in Medina. Muhammad's mission is spiritual first and spiritual last, his programmes, which to a superficial observer, appear to be "temporal", were fully inspired by spiritual motives. He was the Messenger of God and it was in this capacity as the last of the Messengers that he had transmuted into reality the word of his Creator. All his energies and efforts were directed to his single end. Whatever he thought or planned, whatever he uttered or did was the outcome of the desire that humanity should recognise its Master, i.e. should recognize the perfect guidance vouchsafed by Him and carry out His Will and Commands with full devotion.

### The Authority

The first task to which the Holy Prophet attended on his arrival at Medina was the construction of a mosque. A suitable site was selected for it and the land which belonged to two orphans was purchased for ten gold coins and then donated to the mosque. The ground was cleared of weeds and shrubs, palm trees and rubbish, and the construction of the mosque commenced. The Prophet joined in the work which encouraged the Muslims. Both the Muhajirun and the Ansar laboured hard to complete it as soon as possible. One of the Muslims chanted:

If we sat down while the Prophet worked
This action of ours would be the worst.

As they constructed the mosque the Muslims sang a rajaz

There is no life but the life of the next world,

O God I have mercy on Ansar and Muhajirun.

The Apostle of God, (peace and blessings of Allah be upon him) however, changed its rhythm or order and said:

There is no life but the life of the next world,

O God! have mercy on Muhajirun and Ansar.

This mosque was square in form, each side measuring approximately 50 yards, facing towards the north and having three gates on each of the remaining three sides. The southern door was for public entrance and the western gate was called Bab al-Rahaman and the eastern gate, reserved for the Prophet's household, was called Bab al-Nisa'.

To the north of the mosque, a place was reserved for those companions of Muhammad (peace be upon him) who had neither family nor home. They were known as Ashab al-Suffah (the people of the Suffah). This was a kind of seminary attached to the mosque for those who devoted full time to the study of religion. Adjoining the mosque were erected two apartments for the household of the Prophet. The mosque was a monument of simplicity—the walls were made of mud bricks and the roof supported by trunks of palm trees. Being covered with palm leaves and twigs it could not keep out rain, which sametimes made the unpaved floor muddy. This simple mosque was the venue of glorious scenes. It was here that the Holy Prophet imparted his teachings to the Muslims. It was here that embassies from different tribes were received. It was here that edicts were issued to kings and emperors. The residence of the Holy Prophet was, however, even simpler than the mosque. Some of the rooms were built of raw bricks whereas the others were mere cells made with the twigs of the palm trees. Worn out blankets were used with a view to providing privacy and seclusion to the inmates of the house.

"During the time of the caliphate of 'Uthman," observes Hasan b. 'Ali, "when we visited the residential quarters of the wives of the Holy Prophet, we found their ceilings so low that we could easily touch them." Similarly another observer Daood b. Qays, describing the house of Muhammad (peace be upon him) says, "I have had the good fortune to see with my own eyes the quarters where the wives of the Holy Prophet lived. These were apartments made out to the branches of palm-trees, and blankets of camel-hair hung at their doors. The courtyard was hardly six to seven paces in length and breadth and rooms did not extend beyond ten paces." After the death of the Prophet's wives all these quarters were annexed to the mosque and the land thus acquired was used for its extension. "Were these rooms kept intact, the world would have seen the austere and simple living of the last of the prophets in whose hand had been placed the keys of the worldly treasures", to which the Prophet showed no inclination.

We have noted earlier the persecution of Muslims in Mecca. They could not even perform their prayers openly. Up to that period, these prayers had to be conducted in secret. Every precaution had to be taken not to let it be known that the prayer service was taking place. In the peaceful conditions of Medina, where Muslims enjoyed full religious freedom, the problem which figured prominently was how to summon the Muslims to the mosque. The Jews summoned their congregations to the temple by blowing trumpets, the Christians by striking gongs. Muhammad (peace be upon him) did not feel drawn at all towards these customs and he considered them inappropriate for such sacred purposes. He felt that the human voice could better communicate the inspiration and emotion which should be dedicated to the solemnity of the occasion. It is narrated that when this problem was discussed, one day 'Abd Allah b. Zayd came to the Holy Prophet and told him: I saw last night a visitant in a dream who had a clapper in his hand and I asked him to sell that to me.

When he questioned what I wanted to do with that, I replied that it was to summon people for prayer, whereupon he said: Should I not show you a better way than this? I replied in the affirmative. Upon this he said, say:

Allahu Akbar, Allahu Akbar

Allahu Akbar, Allahu Akbar

Ashhadu an la ilaha illa Allah

Ashhadu an la ilaha illa Allah

Ashhadu anna Muhammad ar Rasul Allah

Ashhadu anna Muhammad ar Rasul Allah

Hayya ala al-Salah

Hayya ala al-Salah

Hayya ala al-Falah

Hayya ala al-Falah

Allahu Akbar, Allahu Akbar

La ilaha illa Allah

(Allah is the Greatest. Allah is the Greatest. Allah is the Greatest. Allah is the Greatest. I bear witness that there is no god but Allah. I bear witness that there is no god but Allah. I bear witness that Muhammad is the Messenger of Allah. I bear witness that Muhammad is the Messenger of Allah. Hearken to prayer. Hearken to prayer. Hearken to salvation. Hearken to salvation. Allah is the Greatest. There is no god but Allah).

The Holy Prophet said: "Your vision, by the grace of God, is true. Go to Bilal and communicate it to him so that he should call to prayer accordingly." When ' Umar heard this in his house, he came there dragging his cloak on the ground and said: "By Him who has sent you with the truth, I have seen precisely the same vision which has been shown to 'Abd Allah b. Zayd." The Holy Prophet said: 'God be praised for that.' For the morning prayer, the following reminder was added:

As-Salatu khayrum min al-nawm,

(Prayer is better than sleep)

Every day, at the five appointed times, this familiar call summoned the people to their devotions. For over thirteen centuries, the same call has continually sounded from myriad minarets.

It is not only a summons to prayer, but also sums up very concisely the teachings of Islam. There is no god but Allah, the Sole Creator, the Master and the Law-Giver. Muhammad (peace be upon him) is His Apostle and it is through him alone that we can find out the will of God which should be followed. Prayer is the basis of religious life and it is through prayer alone that one can find the path of salvation.

## The Brotherhood

Prayers being thus regulated, the Prophet next turned his attention to cementing the ties of brotherhood amongst the Muslims of Medina, who were called Ansar and the Muhajirin, i.e. emigrants from Mecca. It was a necessary step since the refugees who had left their hearths and homes and had said good-bye to friends and relatives were feeling lonely. To raise the spirits of his homesick and suffering followers, to cast off their feeling of loneliness, and to attune them to the changed circumstances, a new fraternity was established amongst the Muslims of Mecca and those of Medina.

This brotherhood was indeed unique in the history of the world. The fellow-feeling and love on which this new relationship was established found a wonderful expression.

For example Saad b. Sabi', a Helper said to his fellow brother 'Abd al-Rahman b. 'Awf, "I am the richest man amongst the Helpers. I am glad to share my property half and half with you. I have two wives, I am ready to divorce one, and after the expiry of 'iddah, you may marry her." But 'Abd al-Rahman b. 'Awf was not prepared to accept anything: neither property nor home. So he blessed his brother and said: Kindly direct me to the market so that I may make my fortune with my own hands. The Helpers were extremely generous to their brethren-in-faith. They once approached the Holy Prophet with the request that their orchards should be distributed equally between the Muslims of Medina and their brethren from Mecca. But the Prophet was reluctant to put this heavy burden upon them. It was, however, decided that the refugees would work in the orchards along with the Helpers and the yield would be divided equally amongst them.

These are not solitary expressions of the spirit of selflessness which the Holy Prophet had infused in his followers. It was a common trait of their character which they had developed under the influence of Muhammad (peace be upon him). So strong and cordial was this relation that it surpassed even the relationship of blood. When either of the two persons who had been paired as brothers, passed away, his property was inherited by his brother-in-faith. This practice continued till the following verse was revealed and the regular rule of inheritance was allowed to take its usual course:

> And those who believed afterwards and emigrated and strove hard along with you, these also are of you, and the kindred by blood are nearer unto one another in Allah's decree. Verily Allah is of everything the Knower.

The atmosphere of brotherhood and fellow-feeling created by the Holy Prophet produced very healthy results. Age-long enmities amongst the different tribes, especially those that had existed between the Aws and the Khazraj were almost forgotten amongst the converts from those tribes. "Acceptance of the faith required that as Muslims they should acknowledge not only the spiritual but temporal authority of Muhammad and, holding subordinate every distinction of race and kindred, regard each other as brethren." The Holy Quran refers to this brotherhood as a great boon:

> And hold ye fast, all of you, to the cord of Allah, and be not disunited, and remember Allah's favour unto you, in that ye were enemies, and He joined your hearts together, and so ye became by His favour brethren, and ye were on the brink of an abyss of the fire, and He rescued you therefrom. (iii: 103)

The pages of history bear testimony to the fact that it was a marvellous and spectacular reform. Before the advent of the Prophet, the Arabs were an uncompromising people, a nation torn into mutually hostile clans and tribes, who were always ready to unsheathe their bloodthirsty sword for petty reasons. It was due to the teachings of Islam and the untiring efforts of Muhammad (peace be upon him) that the spirit of brotherhood began to surge across Arabia.

The entire past of tribal animosities was obliterated and a new society was summoned into existence which had a deep-rooted sentiment for the brotherhood of man, a consciousness of mutual rights and duties and love, and a humane and noble outlook on life. The prophet had in fact eminently succeeded in creating a social pattern "which had none of the features of the ancient cults, no priesthood and no ceremonial, which was based on no forms, but upon a spiritual relationship to an Unseen God. It was not designed to give prestige to a social group but to create a universal brotherhood composed of all men of every race who would accept this God and promise loyalty to His Holy Prophet."

***The Pact :*** Another important task which attracted the attention of the Holy Prophet was to establish friendly relations between the Muslims and non-Muslim tribes of Arabia, particularly those of Banu Nadir, Banu Qurayzah and Banu Qaynuqa. As this was the first political agreement between Muslims and non-Muslims, we mention only a few of its provisions which would clearly give an idea of the rights of non-Muslims in an Islamic state.

In the name of Allah, the Compassionate, the Merciful. This is a document from Muhammad, the Messenger of Allah, concerning emigrants and helpers in which he made a friendly agreement with the Jews and established them in their religion and property and stated the reciprocal obligations as follows:

> They form one group to the exclusion of other people. The emigrants of Quraysh unite together and shall pay bloodwit among themselves, and shall ransom honourably their prisoners. The Banu 'Awf unite together, as they were at first, and every section among them pays a ransom for acquitting its relative prisoners. (This clause is repeated with the same phraseology concerning Banu Sa'ida, Banu al-Harith, Banu Jusham, Banu al-Najjar, Banu 'Amr b. 'Awf, Banu al-Nabit, and Banu Aws). Believers shall not leave any one destitute among them by not paying his redemption money or bloodwit in kind.

Whosoever is rebellious or whosoever seeks to spread enmity and sedition, the hand of every God-fearing Muslim shall be against him, even if he be his son.

A believer shall not kill another believer, nor shall support an unbeliever against a believer. The protection of Allah is one (and is equally) extended to the humblest of the believers.

The believers are supported by each other. Whosoever of the Jews follows us shall have aid and succour; they shall not be injured, nor any enemy be aided against them.

The peace of the believers is indivisible. No separate peace shall be made when believers are fighting in the way of God. Conditions must be fair and equitable to all.

It shall not be lawful for a believer, who holds by what is in this document and believes in God and the Day of Judgment, to help a criminal nor give him refuge. Those who give him refuge and render him help shall have the curse and anger of Allah on the Day of Resurrection. His indemnity is not accepted. Whenever you differ about a matter it must be referred to God and to Muhammad (peace be upon him).

The Jews shall contribute to the cost of war so long as they are fighting alongside the believers. The Jews of the B. 'Awf are one community with the believers. The Jews will profess their religion; the Muslims, theirs. No one shall go forth to war except with the permission of Muhammad; but this shall not hinder any one from seeking lawful revenge. The Jews shall be responsible for their expenditure, the Muslims for theirs, but if attacked, each shall come to the assistance of the other. Medina shall be sacred and inviolable for all that join this treaty.

These are some of the clauses of the famous treaty. "It appears as a tripartite agreement between the Muhajirin or emigrants of Mecca, the Ansar or adherents of Medina, and the Jews. A careful examination of the text shows, however, that it was more than a treaty of alliance. The first part indeed reflects to us more than an attempt at reconciliation between the tribes; it is in fact a convention for fusing all the rival attempts of the Arab tribes in Medina to constitute one nation in distinction from the rest of the people. It is, in other words, a constitution for the Islamic state in its embryo-nic stage rather than a loose alliance of tribes. In this Muhammad (peace be upon him) had attempted to dissolve the narrow tribal loyalties within a superstructure, by shifting their focus of attention to a new religion and state."

Secondly, this treaty sheds a good deal of light on the position of the Prophet as the controller of the affairs in Medina. The constitution states that wherever there is any dispute, it is to be referred to God and to Muhammad (peace be upon him). "It seems likely that it was contemplated in the original agreement between Muhammad and the Medinites that he would be able to act as an arbitrator between rival factions and thus help to maintain peace in the oasis."

The latter part of the treaty, which refers to an alliance between the Arabian tribes constituting one party and the Jews as the other, clearly lays down the broad principles on which cordial relations could be established between Muslims and non Muslims.

This treaty, which owed itself of the efforts of the Holy Prophet for establishing peace, is a landmark in human history. "It guaranteed mankind thirteen hundred and fifty years ago, free doom of thought and freedom of worship. Protection of life and that of the property was recognized and the crime in all its forms was legally banned. These are fact fresh laurels which Muhammad (peace be upon him) eminently won in the realm of civics and politics of that time, for it guaranteed peace and freedom to the people who had been woefully groaning under the heel of tyranny and opression let loose by despotism and autocracy and anarchy of that age."

After having united all the discordant elements of society, Muhammad (peace be upon him) turned his attention towards his household affairs. He had been living at that time with his wife Sawdah and his daughters Fatimah and Umm Kulthum.

'A'ishah, his new bride, was just attaining her puberty and was still in the house of her father. She was a precocious girl and was developing both in mind and body with rapidity peculiar to such rare personalities. At the suggestion of Abu Bakr and his wife, Muhammad (peace be upon him) decided to consummate the marriage.

Like everything else in Muhammad's life (peace be upon him), the ceremony was simple. 'A'ishah was washed and dressed in clean clothes, Umm Ruman, her mother, then took her to a room where some women of the Ansar had been anxiously waiting for the arrival of the bride. The moment 'A'ishah stepped in, they prayed: "May you be blessed, your fortune is enviable."

This marriage is significant in the history of Islam. It further cemented the ties between Muhammad (peace be upon him) and his devoted friend who always stood by him in hours of distress and who sacrificed his all for the cause of Islam. Secondly, by this marriage, a lady of rare qualities, both of mind and heart, was allowed to enter the haram of the Prophet at an impressionable age, and thus got an opportunity to penetrate into the innermost recesses of the life of Muhammad (peace be upon him). She shared his sacred company and was thus able to develop her potentialities and refine her taste.

Even a glance at the life of this eminent lady clearly bears out the fact that her marriage with the prophet was a source of immense good to herself and to the world of Islam at large. She came into direct contact with the Prophet when her sensibilities were just developing. It was the august personality of the last of the Prophets- (peace be upon him) which nurtured them properly and directed their growth to the right channels. This young age was opportune for marriage, as it has been clearly shown in the researches of the psychoanalysts that much of the emotional life of a mature person and most of those seemingly unaccountable leanings, tastes and tendencies comprised in the term idiosyn-crasies can be traced back to the experiences of his highly formative age, either later childhood, or early adolescence.

Moreover, even from the psycho-sexual stand-point, it was a happy union as it is evident from the records of Hadith. "When the difference (in ages)" says T.H. Von De Velde, Director of the Gynaecological Clinic at Harlem, "is great e.g. exceeds fifteen or twenty years, the results may be happier. The marriage of an elderly (senescent)—not, of course an old (senile)—man to a quite young girl, is often very successful and harmonious. The bride is imme-diately introduced and accustomed to moderate sexual inter-course."

Those Western critics of Islam who have criticized this marriage lose sight of the fact that this marriage did not involve sexual consideration alone. There was so many other reasons behind it. Firstly, there was the consideration of Abu Bakr's honour and status and an expression of due recognition of his glorious service. Then there was the problem of training a young girl who was gifted with penetrating intellect and zest for knowledge so that she might be able to guide young women in different spheres of their lives.

The wives of Muhammad (peace be upon him) with the exception of 'A'ishah, were all of advanced age, and thus could neither share the feelings of the younger generation nor could they properly appreciate their point of view. The difference of age always stood as a barrier between them and the ladies of younger ages. The only lady with whom young women could frankly enter into conversation and discuss their problems without any reserve could be none else but young 'A'ishah. Thus, the marriage of the Prophet with 'A'ishah at an age when she was at the threshold of puberty was a great necessity, as it was through her that instructions could successfully be imparted to the young ladies who had newly entered the fold of Islam. 'A'ishah performed this function most eminently and fully justified the choice of the Messenger of God (peace be upon him).

Moreover, this marriage struck at the root of a wrong notion which had taken a firm hold on the minds of the people, that it was contrary to religious ethics to marry the daughter of a man whom one declared to be one's brother. The Prophet, with the help of his personal example, showed to the people that there was great difference between a brother-in-faith and a brother by blood. The marriage which is forbidden in Islam is not that with the daughter of a man who is tied to oneself in the bond of faith, but with one who is one's niece in blood.

The main concern of the Prophet, however, was the spiritual and moral training of his followers. In a relatively free atmosphere though not totally free from the threat of Mecca vengeance and aggression the Prophet began to propound the principles of righteous conduct, including rituals of worship.

***Other Developments :*** At the end of eighteen months after the Hijra, fasting was established as an obligatory ritual for the month of Ramadan. The word *'saum'* which literally means abstinence, is a worship of a very great significance. It serves as an effective means, in the religious system of Islam, for bringing about purification of the souls of Muslim. A Muslim, according to its implication, is strictly forbidden to take food or drink (and even to smoke) or to indulge in sexual intercourse from the moment when the first streak of light on the eastern horizon announces the coming of dawn, until sunset. And this continued for one full month every year. In the words of Muhammad Asad:

> "Twofold, I learned, is the purpose of this month of fasting. One has to abstain from food and drink in order to feel in one's body what the poor and hungry feel: thus, social responsibility is being hammered into human consciousness as a religious postulate. The other purpose of fasting during Ramadan is self-discipline, an aspect of individual morality strongly accentuated in all Islamic teachings (as, for instance, in the total prohibition of all intoxicants which Islam regards as too easy an avenue of escape from consciousness and responsibility). In these two elements—brotherhood of man and individual self-

discipline —I began to discern the outlines of Islam's ethical outlook."

Moreover, fasting is the means whereby our sense of gratitude towards Allah is awakened. We can rightly measure and truly appreciate the countless favours of the Lord when we are deprived of them, even though for a short span of time. Thus, we can thank our Creator for His infinite bounties that He has so benevolently showered upon us. The following verse of the Qur'an makes a pointed reference to this aspect:

> Ye should complete the number and that you should exalt the Greatness of Allah for His having guided you and that you may give thanks. (ii: 185)

It was at this stage that the payment of zakat was made obligatory by Allah upon all Muslims. Islam does not leave the orphans, the infirm and the old to subsist on what is called "charity." By making the payment of zakat obligatory for the rich, Allah has given the poor a right to share in the wealth of the community. The Qur'an explicitly lays down:

> And in their wealth, is the right of the needy and of those who are deprived of the means of subsistence. (ii; 19)

This verse clearly establishes that the portion of the wealth which the Muslims contribute annually in the form of zakat is a matter of duty for them and, on the other hand, whatever the poor receive is not an act of undue favour for which they should hang down their heads in humiliation. The wealth of the rich that they receive is a matter of right for which they have no reason to feel small. Then the Qur'an has also laid down the purposes for which zakat is to be used. It should be paid, according to the Holy Qur'an, inter alia to those who cannot make an independent living (e.g. the orphans, helpless widows, the infirm, the decrepit, the travellers in distress, and people who have been deprived of the means of sustenance or of opportunities of work through natural calamities over which they have no control), the slaves seeking freedom and the debtors who cannot afford to pay off their debts:

> The compulsory alms are only for the poor and the needy and the agents employed therein, and those whose hearts are to be conciliated, and those in bondage and debtors and for expenditure in the way of Allah and for the wayfarer, an ordinance from Allah. And Allah is Knowing, Wise. (ix: 60)

The Qur'an thus makes it obligatory on those who earn or produce wealth to pass on to the state a specific portion of their savings as God's share to be distributed among the above categories of the members of society. "So great is the stress laid on the levy called zakat, that the compulsory injunction of prayer is always clubbed together with the insistence on the payment of this levy; so much so that when in the time of the first Caliph Abu Bakr, some of the Muslim Arab tribes refused to pay zakat to the State Exchequer, he had to wage a jihad against them till they yielded" and resumed the payment of zakat.

It was during this period that a change in the qiblah, was also ordered by Allah. It is significant that while at Mecca and living among the idolaters of Mecca, the Holy Prophet (may peace and blessings of Allah be upon him) used to pray with his face turned to the holy temple at Jerusalem, but when he came to Medina, where the Jewish element was strong and powerful, he was directed by Divine revelation to turn his face to the Ka'bah as his qiblah. This was a change of far-reaching importance, and it had different reactions in different circles. It strengthened the loyalty of the Muslims to Islam and the Holy prophet. They expressed their implicit faith in Muhammad (peace be upon him) as the recipient of Divine revelation and accepted this change most willingly.

The pagans of Mecca said: "The way Muhammad has changed his direction for prayer towards our qibla, gives us reason to hope that he will eventually come back to our faith also." The Jews were very indignant and said tauntingly: "Muhammad has, in this change of direction for prayer, opposed all the earlier prophets. If he were a genuine prophet, he would have never done like that." The hypocrites (i.e. those who falsely pretended to be Muslims) availed themselves of this opportunity to undermine the increasing influence of Islam. They were sarcastic in their remarks and said: "We are not sure in which direction the Prophet wants to turn for prayer. If the previous position was correct he has abandoned that; and if this new position is right, it means that he had erred before."

The Holy Qur'an refers, in its eloquent style, to these different objections raised from the different quarters, and observe:

> And We appointed not the qiblah, which you have had, but that We might distinguish him who follows the Apostle from him who turns back upon his heels, and this was surely hard except for those whom Allah has guided aright. (ii: 143)

> "The change of direction", says Arnold, "has a deeper signifi-cance than might at first sight appear. It was really the beginning of the national life of Islam; it established the Ka'bah at Mecca as a religious centre for all the Muslim people, just as from time immemorial it had been a place of pilgrimage for all the tribes of Arabia."

A few words may now be added as a prelude to the coming events which are connected with the unsheathing of the sword by the Muslims in the path of Allah. Jihad is a matter of great impor-tance in the history of Islam, but it is sad to note that so many doubts and misgivings are centred around it. The true nature and significance of Jihad can be well understood, when it is viewed in the context of the teachings of Islam as a whole as well as the objectives which it seeks to realize. Moreover, we also have to consider the role of war, in other words, that of power, as a means for the establishment of a sound social order.

It should be clearly borne in mind that Islam does not subscribe to the materialistic world-view which is in vogue among the Western nation. "It is an intense God-consciousness that expresses itself in a rational acceptance of all God-created nature: a harmonious side-by-side of intellect and sensual urge, spiritual need and social demand." It is thus clear that Islam, besides, laying a good deal of stress on the problems of belief, ritual and personal morality and as a consequence of that nursing a moral attitude in the individual—the bedrock upon which is raised the superstructure of Islamic society "also aims at translating the moral attitude into a definite social scheme which would ensure to every member of the community the greatest possible measure of physical and material well-being, and thus, the greatest opportunity for spiritual growth."

This important aspect of Islam, i.e. its social aspect, is woefully neglected by Western thinkers, while estimating the role of power in a comprehensive view of life. They lose sight of the fact that Christianity in its early history did not aim at setting up a state, whereas Islam, from the very beginning, was a politico-religious institution. In order to translate into reality, Islam had to contend with those evil forces which knew no reasoning and persuasion.

It should be made clear, however, that war in Islam is not a casual phenomenon of violence; it is one of the phases of man's striving (jihad) against all that is evil, whether in thought or feeling or action. The raising of the sword is only one aspect of the all-round struggle to establish Islam in the world, and it represents in Muslim Law what is known as an 'honest struggle.'

The word (jihad) is derived from the word jahada, which means "he exerted himself." Thus literally jihad means exertion, striving; but in juridico-religious sense, it signifies the exertion of one's power to the utmost of one's capacity in the path of Allah. This is why, the word jihad has been used as an antonym to the word qu'ud in Islam.

> Not equal are the holders-back among the believers save those who are disabled, and the strivers in the way of Allah with their riches and their lives. Allah hath preferred in rank the strivers with their riches and their lives above the holders-back and unto all, Allah hath promised good. And Allah hath preferred the strivers above holders-back with a mighty reward.
> (iv: 95)

The above-quoted verse speaks eloquently of the fact that Jihad (striving) is just the opposite of idleness.

It is necessary to winnow out one mistaken notion which has taken hold of the minds of so many people. The word jihad is often confused with the word qital (fighting) and these are used in one and the same sense, whereas the Qur'an has made a clear distinction between them. Jihad fi Sabil Allah (fighting in the way of Allah) refers to an all-round struggle, while the other signifies only one aspect of that struggle i.e. fighting. The verse iv: 9.3 mentioned above bears ample testimony to this fact. The Holy Qur'an has clearly pointed out that jihad denotes two kinds of striving; striving with the help of God-given faculties, both mental and physical, and striving with the help of resources which he has at his command.

Ibn Rushd maintains that jihad is an all-round struggle and makes it obligatory for a Muslim to exercise all his powers, maybe in the form of intellectual or physical capacities, or his gift of speech or his moral strength, courage and steadfastness in the face of hardship and his worldly riches.

The Holy Qur'an has elucidated this point, i.e. jihad as an all-round struggle in various surahs. We reproduce below a few of them in order to explain the true nature and significance of jihad in Islam:

> The believers are only those who believed in Allah and His Apostle and thereafter doubted not, and struggled hard with their riches and their persons in the cause of Allah. Those, they are the truthful.
>
> And strive hard for Allah, as is due unto Him. He has chosen you, and has imposed no hardship on you in matter of the religion, the faith of your father Ibrahim.
>
> (xxii: 78)

This verse of the Holy Qur'an sums up the spirit of jihad in Islam. It is a striving in the way of Allah, and has far wider scope than mere fighting. The Holy Prophet once explaining the true qualities of mujahid (the one who strives in the path of Allah) significantly remarked:

> The mujahid is one who tries to struggle against his self, i.e. evil self.

Ibn al-Qayyim in his explanation of this aspect of jihad has observed:

> The jihad against the enemies of Allah with one's life in only a part of the struggle which a true servant of Allah carries on against his own evil self for the sake of his Lord. This striving against the evil tendencies which have dominated his mind and heart is more important than fighting against the enemies in the outside world. It is in fact the basis on which the struggle in the path of Allah can be successfully launched.

Since jihad is an all-round struggle, a struggle directed to so many channels, it necessitates the employment of different methods to acquit oneself creditably of its wide and varied responsibilities. According to Imam Raghib, a Muslim is required to fight against three foes:

(1) against the visible enemy;

(2) against the devil;

(3) against his self (nafs).

Ibn Rushd maintains that the believer may fulfil this struggle in four ways; by his heart, by his tongue, his hands, and by the sword. The first of these implies that a Muslim should develop his sensitivities to the point of excellence, so much so that nothing evil should find its way either in his heart or in his mind. He should have a deep-rooted aversion to everything ignoble and a strong desire to fight it tooth and nail, whether it is found in his own self or in the world outside.

Then comes the function of the power of expression which has a vital role to play in the establishment of a sound and just social order, free from all kinds of exploitation. This power has a double responsibility in the sense that it has to clothe in noble words the noble ideals and sentiments which upsurge the mind and heart of man and then by dint of his eloquence, imprint their superiority in the minds of other people. Moreover, this gift of expression is to be used for protesting against evils in human life. The Holy Qur'an shows the way how the powers of expression is to be used for inviting the people to the path of Allah:

> Invite (all) to the way of their Lord with wisdom and goodly exhortation and argue with them with that which is the best. (xvi: 125)

In his characteristic style, the Holy Prophet has explained that jihad consists not only of using the sword, but that even when Muslim uses his tongue for protesting against the atrocities of tyrants, he is waging jihad. He once said:

> Whoever amongst you sees something abominable,

> he should endeavour to change it with his hand, in case he has the power to do it: but if he lacks the requisite power, he should then use his tongue, and if he is powerless in this also, he must then hate it from the heart, and this in fact is the weakest (state) of faith.

Then in other tradition which is narrated on the authority of Abu Sa'id al-Khudri, the Prophet is reported to have significantly remarked:

> The best of jihad is the uttering of the word of truth in the face of a tyrant ruler.

This would make it abundantly clear that jihad in Islam is not an act of violence. It is, in fact, an all-round struggle in the path of Allah.

In this all-round struggle, however, which covers all aspects of life, Islam has assigned a special place to qital (fighting) as well. There do arise such occasions in which the use of arms becomes a dire necessity and even a slight show of weakness under these circumstances leads to disastrous results. Islam has stressed the need of rising to such occasions and has exhorted its followers to face the dangers that might thus beset them bravely and manfully. Thus, the use of force is not only permitted in Islam, but its need has been duly stressed in the Holy Qur'an and the Sunnah. But it should be made clear that even qital in Islam is not an act of mad brutality. "It represents in Muslim law what is known among western jurists as just war."

In order to understand the true nature of qital in Islam, we must first analyse the different motives which incite people to fight:

(1) The desire for material benefits is the principal impulse to warlike aggression: "Territory, with the attendant booty of various kinds, has been the usual stake in war, coveted alike by peoples and by dynasties."

(2) "The fear of injury as well as the resentment due to actual injury has unfailingly prompted to defensive war when resistance was possible and often when it might well be deemed hopeless. The interests which nations have usually prepared to defend at all costs are, in addition to their territory, their jurisdiction and their honour."

(3) The desire for power and glory has been, in the main, dominant motive of the great conquerors and their armies. It is a fact that ambitious men have again and again resorted to the use of force as a means for appropriating territory and increasing their own wealth and of the people whom they represent, but there is no denying the fact that nations as well as individuals find satisfaction in the exercise of power as an end in itself. "This desire manifests itself positively in the attempt of a nation or class to acquire dominion over others. The love of power for its own sake has been an important factor in the movements which established the great empires of history, and it has been not less conspicuous in struggle for a supremacy among allied states as illustrated in the ancient rivalry of Athens and Sparta, and in the modern contest of the German principalities which issued in the hegemony of Prussia."

(4) "The passions of hatred and revenge have also furnished a relatively independent motive. A nation can take up an attitude that is on a still lower plane than brutal selfish-ness; it can become inspired by a hatred of the diabolic kind which makes it disregard even the counsels of self-interest for the satisfaction of inflicting deadly injury on a loathed enemy. The spirit of hatred has sometimes even been engendered by centuries of conflict or oppression. Sometime, it has its spring in deepseated difference of racial character and culture."

Qital in Islam has not evil design behind it. Islam has the greatest respect not only for the lives of human beings but even for those of animals and plants, and it is only for the achievement of some nobler ends and those too, through noble means, that a Muslim has been exhorted to lay hands upon them. There are so many verses in the Holy Qur'an which speak eloquently of the sanctity of life:

> And there is not an animal on the earth, not a bird that flieth with its two wings, but are communities like unto you. Nothing have we omitted from the Book. Then they (all) shall be gathered to their Lord in the end. (vi: 38)

The Prophet repeatedly emphasised the fact that not to speak of the life of man, even the life of a small bird is extremely precious and cannot be taken without sufficient reason: Whoever kills the swallow, or even a more insignificant bird than that, without any reason, shall be answerable to God for this slaughter.

On another occasion he issued a warning to people about the high-handedness that they showed towards animals:

> If Allah in His infinite mercy pardons the maltreatment which is meted out to your animals, at your hands, it means that you have been relieved of the heavy burden of sins.

Such is the value and consideration which Islam shows to birds and other animals. It is due to the result of Islamic teachings that animals have been treated with utmost kindness and love throughout the Muslim world. "Nowhere in Christendom", says Bosworth Smith, for instance, "with the one exception perhaps of Norway, are beasts of burden and domestic animals treated with such unvarying kindness and consideration as they are in Turkey."

Human life is given still greater security and no one is permitted to lay hand upon it without sufficient reason:

> Those who invoke not, with God, any other god, nor slay such life as God has made sacred except for just cause. (xxv: 68)

> On that account; we ordained for the children of Israel that if any one slew a person unless it be for murder or for spreading mischief in the land – it would be as if he slew all human beings. And if any one saved a life, it would be as if he saved the life of all human beings. (v: 35)

The above-quoted verses show in unequivocal terms the value of human life. The life of every person is sacred and thus its safety is one of the primary duties of society. A well-known scholar of Islam has made the following observations with regard to the above mentioned verses:

> On close analysis of these verses of the Holy Qur'an, we find that human life has been made sacred by God and its security is, therefore, the foremost duty of mankind; but this clause is also appended with a certain condition, i.e. "except for just cause". Similarly, along with the words: "If any one slew a person it would be as if he slew all human beings," there occcurs this conditional phrase: "unless it be for spreading mischief in the land." It means that the safety of human life is guaranteed no doubt but with certain conditions. Justice demands that tyranny and oppression should not be allowed to work havoc in the world; that wickedness ought to be restrained and punished in human society in the interests of the peace and prosperity of the human race. Human life is sacred so far as its activities are confined to the reasonable limits, but when these transgress them and become a source of terror and aggression and constant peril to the lives of other persons, then it loses its sanctity and its termination becomes

> indispensable and therein lies the welfare of humanity. That is why, the Holy Qur'an says: "Mischief is more grievous than homicide."

The Holy Qur'an clearly brings out the that fact that qital is not an end in itself in Islam, but a means to a higher and nobler end—the welfare of humanity. That is why, Islam has exhorted its followers to raise arms not in a spirit of brutality but in a spirit of love for humanity—a spirit in which the surgeon applies the knife to the blistering sores of the human body.

An individual or a community is no benefactor of humanity if it becomes a silent spectator to the atrocities which are perpetrated on innocent people by those who have no feeling for humanity and no consideration for moral principles. A person does not fulfil his responsibilities towards mankind if he does nothing to support the moral order which forms the bedrock of justice in the human race. A man, or a nation, who tries to exterminate evil in all its forms is the benefactor of humanity in the true sense of the term, for it is even a greater evil to commit injustice with impunity than to be punished for it. The Holy Prophet has beautifully summed up the responsibility of man towards his fellowmen in the following tradition:

> It is narrated on the authority of Anas (may Allah be pleased with him) that the Messenger of God once said: 'Help your brother whether he is the wrong-doer or the oppressed one.' Thereupon people said to him, "O Messenger of Allah, we can help the man when he is wronged, but we fail to know how a wrong-doer can be helped.' Upon this the Prophet (may peace and blessings of Allah be upon him) replied, 'You can do this by holding his hand from an act of oppression.'

None having a grain of common sense can favour the

granting of licence to the wicked people for committing crimes and then letting them go scot free. It is not love for humanity but act of enmity towards it that the weaker elements of society should be subjected to wrongs and injustices and no check should be imposed upon the wrong-doers.

"It is absurd to maintain," says W. P. Paterson, "that the rulers of a nation are under obligation, not merely to sacrifice themselves, but to take the responsibility of sacrificing others who instinctively look at them for protection, and of abandoning old men, women and children, to privation, sufferings, and moral perils. The Christian spirit was surely better interpreted in the mediaeval code of chivalry."

Herbert Spencer declares:

> The doctrine of non-resistance is anti-social, as it involves the non-assertion, not only of one's own rights, but of those of others, while it holds out no prospect of leading to the desirable end of international peace.

Grotius argues that recourse to war is permitted and approved by the law of nature, by the consent of the manly and of the wise and by the law of nations, as well as by the divine law which was promulgated and attested by the scriptures.

The law of nature has two branches, the course dictated by natural instincts, and the principles approved by reason. This law intimates its permission of war through the universal instinct of self-preservation, accompanied as it is by nature's disclosure of purpose in the provision of means of defence to all creatures and also by the voice of reason which makes it clear that the well-being of society is incompatible with the unchecked reign of violence.

These observations make it abundantly clear that the use of force is essential in certain conditions in order to maintain the sanctity of human life and to preserve the moral order in the world. The very first passage which gave the sanction of qital to the Muslims makes a pointed reference to all these noble ideals:

> Permitted are those who are fought against, because they have been oppressed, and verily to succour them, Allah is Potent. Those who have been unjustly driven forth from their abodes merely because they say: "Our Lord is Allah." And were it not for Allah's repelling or some by means of others, cloisters and churches, synagogues and mosques, wherein the name of Allah is mentioned much, would have pulled down. Surely Allah shall succour whosoever succoureth Him. Verily Allah is Strong, Mighty.
>
> They are those who, if we establish them in the land, establish the prayer and give the poor-rate and enjoin right and forbid wrong, and unto Allah is the end of all affairs. (xxii: 41)

The passage sums up in clear terms the aims and objects of qital in Islam. It is neither the acquisition of land, nor of power, nor yet of privilege. The Muslims were permitted to use force because their very existence had been made difficult due to persecution by the pagans of Arabia. They had been subjected to unspeakable tortures at their hands; beaten and insulted, and then driven away from their homes for no other reason than that they worshipped Allah. They had as much right to be in their native town and worship in the Ka'bah as the other Arabs, but nobody was tolerant towards them.

The animosity of the Quraysh did not end even after having driven the Prophet and his companions out of their native place. The unjust men of Mecca had not only given no ear to the heavenly Message delivered by Muhammad (peace be upon him) but would not even let him live if he kept on preaching it. The pagan Arabs had evil design in their minds to pursue the innocent souls who left for Medina and to exterminate them even in their new abodes.

If one were to reflect calmly over this state of affairs one would be convinced that the verdict of all religions and ethical philosophies, both ancient and modern, has been that under such circumstances war is not only justifiable but a basic necessity, and non-resistance is blameworthy and even immoral. There has been a practical unanimity as to the moral justification of self-defence when one nation is assailed by the ambition and cupidity of another.

**Islamic Morals**

Then the Qur'an also explains the function of war as a moral necessity. It is with the help of force that the ever-mounting evil in human life is curbed, for if it continues to spread unchecked, it would brutally shake the basis of moral order and justice in human society so much so that even the places of worship would not be safe at the hands of the wicked elements of the human race. It deserves to be noted that the Muslims have been asked to lay down their lives not only to save their own skins from the atrocities of the opponents, and to save their own mosques, but to save churches, synagogues, and cloisters as well. This means that Islam wants to protect the moral order vouchsafed to humanity through the Messengers of God at different stages of human history. The same idea has been expressed in another verse:

> And were it not for Allah's repelling people, some of them by means of others, the earth surely would be corrupted but Allah is Gracious unto the worlds.
>
> (ii: 251)

The above verse reveals that the rise and fall of nations is not a mere accident, but that it follows a definite pattern in the moral order of the universe. If some nations are swept out of effective existence, it is because they have been corrupted to the marrow of their bones and their dominance in the world is a terrible threat to the peaceful existence of the human race. They are, therefore, through the efforts of the other groups of human beings, thrown into an obscure background with a view to saving humanity from their corrupt and unhealthy influences.

The human society always contains a number of anti-social elements which need a check even though this check were to be exercised with the help of force. When the evil becomes parasitic upon the good, that is to say, it begins to nourish by preying upon what is good, it becomes the primary duty of humanity to restrain it with all the means at its disposal. "The philosopher", observes Joad, "cannot philosophize while his neighbour is abducting his wife, nor can the artist paint while the burglar is running off with his canvasses.

In this sense, all civilized activity is dependent upon a minimum background of ordered security, and the maintenance of this background is a condition of its continuance." The use of the sword is, therefore, required to put a curb on the anti-social activities of the evil elements of the human race, as with individuals, so with nations. A rabid nation should no more be permitted to hold to ransom the humanitarian activities of peaceful men. The downtrodden people who are subjected to the tyranny and oppression of heartless tyrants are to be helped at all cost, and it is the bound duty of all God-fearing human being to rescue these helpless folk from the clutches of the enemies of humanity:

> And what aileth you that ye fight not in the way of Allah, and for the oppressed among men and women and children who say: 'Our Lord! Take us forth from the town whereof the people are wrongdoers, and appoint us from before Thee a patron and appoint us from Thee a helper'. (iv: 75)

It is significant that the war which is waged for upholding the cause of the oppressed is named by the Qur'an as "fight in the way of Allah". Then, in the succeeding verse a clear distinction is also drawn between the two types of war; the one which is fought for the sake of Allah and the other which is waged in the cause of evil:

> Those who believe fight in the way of Allah and those who disbelieve fight in the way of Satan. Fight then against the friends of Satan; verily feeble indeed is the cunning of the devil. (iv: 76)

A distinct and clear line of demarcation marks off the "just" from the "unjust" war. Those who fight for self-glorification, self-aggrandisement, or for the exploitation of the resources of the weaker peoples, are in the fact the friends of the devil; whereas the persons who raise arms in order to curb tyranny and oppression and to eradicate evil are the blessed souls who fight in the way of Allah. Thus, every war which is waged for personal or national glorification at the cost of others is a war in the way of Satan and is vehemently condemned by Islam. On the contrary, the war which is fought in defence of the oppressed, which aims at the eradication of evils and the suppression of those who spread them is a Holy War which is upheld by Islam for it is essential to strike at the very root of the supremacy of the wicked elements in order to establish peace and justice in the world.

> And fight them until there is no more tumult and oppression and religion should only be for Allah. So if they desist, then verily Allah is the Beholder of that what they do. (viii: 39)

This verse clearly defines the aims and objects of fighting in Islam. Muslims have been asked to raise arms not for any personal end but purely for the love of Allah, so that the rebels, who, by their evil designs, have made life intolerably difficult for the innocent souls, should be forcibly prevented from carrying on their nefarious activities and there should prevail justice, goodwill and fraternity in human society.

The war of Islam has been completely purged of the spirit of self-aggrandisement or that of national dominance. It is narrated on the authority of Abu Musa al-Ash'ari that once a man came to the Holy Prophet and said: "A person fights for booty, another fights with a view to winning fame and still another raises his arms in order to display his courage and bravery—who among these should be considered as fighter for the sake of Allah?" To the question the prophet replied: "He who raises his arm with the sole objective that the Word of Allah should become supreme is the one who fights for the cause of Allah."

Thus in Islam, it is not every war which is sanctified as jihad. It is the noble objectives alone which justify a Muslim to raise arms against the tyrants and the expoliters of the human race. Such is the importance of this objective behind fighting that Bukhari has assigned a separate chapter to it in which it has been clearly laid down that it is not feasible to assert with certainty whether a man killed in warfare, is a martyr or not; since martyrdom of a person depends upon the intention with which he participates in the battle and it is always hidden from the view of human beings. Allah alone is, therefore, the right judge in this matter. The Prophet emphatically said:

> Allah knows fully well who strives in His cause and sustains injury for His sake.

It is narrated that once in an encounter with the enemies the Prophet had on his side a hypocrite who was known as Qazman. He fought desperately in the battlefield. The Muslims were all praising for his valour and one of them said in the presence of the prophet: "No one has proved himself to be so useful as this man has done." Upon this the Prophet remarked: "His abode is the Hell." Badr al-Din al-Ayni the famous commentator of Bukhari, has recorded that when this man was on the point of succumbing to the injuries which he had received, one of the companions of the Holy Prophet, Qutadah b. Nu'man cheered him up and gave him the tidings of martyrdom. Upon this the dying man disclosed the motive of his fighting and said: "By God, I did not fight for the cause of the faith. I was impelled to take arms for the glorification of my tribe and family."

Ibn Hajar al-'Asqalai, while elucidating the implication of relationship between this particular tradition and the section under which it falls in Bukhari, has made the following significant observations:

> Nothing can be said with certainty, except through revelation, whether a man is a martyr or not and that refers to the address of 'Umar when he said: "You call those people martyrs who fight in the battles; I advise you not to make such explicit assertions and say -as the Holy Prophet said: One who lays down his life in the way of Allah or one who is killed for no fault of his own is a martyr." This assertion is authentic and corroborates the words of the Holy Prophet which have come down to us through another source (Abu Dharr). It is narrated that the Messenger of God once asked his companions: "Whom do you count as martyrs?" They replied: "One who is attacked with a weapon and as a consequence of that he succumbs to the injuries," whereupon the Holy prophet remarked: "How many persons receive injuries and die, but they are neither martyrs nor are their sacrifices laudable. On the other hand, many a man courts natural death in the bed but in the eyes of the Lord, he is a champion of truth and a martyr." These words of the Holy Prophet clearly bring out the fact that it is not appropriate to call anyone a martyr with certainty, but we should speak in a general way, as we have been instructed by the Messenger of Allah: "God alone knows the man who fights or receives

> injury for His sake," Imam Bukhari has recorded the tradition relating to the death of Qazman under the section: "None should be called a martyr with certainty", simply because the person concerned did not fight for the sake of Allah alone, but he had in his heart an absurdly extravagant pride in his race or tribe.

Such is the noble spirit which underlies jihad in Islam. It is not an act of aggression for the sake of material interest or a wanton display of national or tribal power, but it is a sacred duty assigned to every Muslim in the interests of humanity so that there should be peace and justice in the world. It is this war, which aims at the achievement of noble ends, that is given the name of 'fighting in the way of Allah'! This alone has been eulogised in the Holy Book.

It is interesting to note that a war which seeks to serve such a sacred objective, has not only been permitted by all other religions but has also been lavishly praised by them. The Christian teaching include precepts which, at the first sight, appear to rule out any kind of engagement in war as inconsistent with its moral ideals, but even a little bit of careful study would convince one of the facts that even the Christian Church does not stand for an unqualified condemnation of war. "The Council of Aries in one of its canons appears to have visited ecclesiastical censure on those who abandoned the army even in time of peace from conscientious scruples. Some even thought that the sword might be drawn in a holy war for the exterpation of idolatry. Ambrose eulogised the warlike courage which prefers death to bondage and disgrace and claimed the O. T. warriors as spiritual ancestors. He even adopted the classical maxim that one who does not defend a friend from injury is as much at fault as he who commits the injury. Augustine was forced to face the question by the havoc of the Teutonic migrations and the peril of the empire and his active mind fully explored the subject."

His observations are very significant:

The war is sometimes lawful on the Christian principles and the grounds are:

> (a) that it has been and may be waged by appointment of God; (b) that the case of wanton and rapacious attack by one nation on another falls under the same category as crimes of murder and burglary, and should presumably be similarly dealt with; (c) that John the Baptist did not require the soldiers to abandon the service, but only exhorted them to do violence to no man and be content with their wages. The implications of the Sermon on the Mount are most fully discussed in the Epistle to Marcellinus which was called forth by the pagan objection that the precepts of non-resistance were inconsistent with public policy and ruinous to the state. The precept to turn the other cheek to the smiter, cannot be taken literally. What it requires is an inward disposition of patient goodwill towards the aggressor, and it does not prescribe any uniform manifestation of the dispositions in act, as appears from the fact that Jesus at least protected himself against violence. We ought always to cherish the spirit of clemency, and be willing to render good for evil, but many things have to be done in which we have to pay regard not to our kindly inclinations but to the real interests of the others and their interests may require that they should be treated much as they may dislike it with a certain benignant asperity.

In the same way, Thomas Aqinas, explaining the viewpoint of Christianity with regard to war, says:

> Jesus said that he who takes the sword shall perish by the sword. But 'to take' means to use without warrant and the words only prohibit unauthorised or private persons from drawing the sword. (b) War is

> inconsistent with the command that we resist not evil (Matt, 5: 38) and avenge not ourselves. "But these injunctions are fulfilled by the cultivation of a placable spirit and cannot require us to do mischief by allowing wickedness to go unpunished. If the peace-makers are blessed, war-makers are accused. But war may be the best or the only means of attaining the end of peace.

Luther held that the Gospel presupposed natural rights and duties, and vigorously defended the Christian soldier. Calvin argued that the war is branch of the work of retributive justice which has been entrusted by God to the civil magistrate, and that it has the same moral justification as the police measures which protect the citizens against the criminal populations. In Calvin's own words:

> Whether it be a king who does it, or a scoundrel who does it on a small scale, he is equally to be regarded and punished as a robber. It is no breach of the command: 'Thou shalt not kill,' the slaying of the authors of the unjust war is an execution, the judge is God, and the fighting men who defend the right are merely God's instruments. If it be objected that the New Testament does not expressly permit Christians to fight, it is to be observed that NT does not undertake to legislate about civil policy, and that it presupposes the Old Testament in which the greatest men of God, like Moses and David, were mighty men of valour in the service of God.

The views expressed by the famous writers of Christianity eloquently speak of the fact that "war is not always sin", contrary to what is commonly imagined by some of the ultrapacifist interpreters of the Christian faith. Such a view rests on a superficial view of the ethical system of Christianity. The doctrine of retributive justice—that wickedness ought to be punished and curbed— fills at least as large a space as the doctrine of non-resistance in the structure of Christian thought.

Since war need not be merely an impulsive outburst of fury and aggression, but can also be a means for the achievement of some lofty ends, it has been completely humanized by Islam. It is not allowed to degenerate into an act of savagery, but is required to be carried on as a noble struggle with human considerations, under the leadership of a responsible and God-fearing man, and directed to weeding out evil and enthroning goodness, charity and benevolence.

Even a cursory glance over the pages of history would reveal, on the other hand, that war has had in the past even as it has today an extremely horrible record. The countries invaded are ruthlessly devastated, the captured cities are sacked and destroyed, and neither age nor sex counts on immunity. Such has been and continues to be the general practice of warfare. If the practice is commonly less than the theory, this is probably due not so much to clemency as to the consideration that a ruined and depopulated country affords less opportunities of exploitation than the populated one. Islam is the greatest religion of the world which makes a strong plea for humane fighting and regulates the conduct of war in such a way that it ceases to be a sheer drive for power, a naked exaltation of the tribal passion for fighting an act of collective gangsterism, but becomes "a thoroughly reformative process."

> And fight in the way of Allah those who fight you, and transgress not the limits; verily Allah loveth not the transgressors." (ii: 190)

The Holy Prophet has clearly set the limits which may not be transgressed in fighting.

Firstly, the belligerents are divided into classes: combatants, who actually participate in the battle, and non-combatants, who do not or cannot take part in actual fighting or who are incapacitated to do so, for example, women and children, the aged and the infirm, the blind, the imbecile, the travellers, and the man devoted to monastic services. Islam has forbidden their killing altogether.

The following instructions of the Holy Prophet lay down the well-defined limits of warfare:

> Neither kill the old verging on death, nor children and babes nor the females. Do not steal anything from the booty and collect together all those things which fall to your lot in the battlefield, and do good. Allah loves those who do good.

It is narrated on the authority of ' Abdullah b. 'Umar that once the Holy Prophet saw the dead body of a woman who was killed in a battle. He admonished his men and warned them against killing women and children.

It is also recorded that the Holy Prophet (peace and blessings of Allah be upon him) once saw in battlefield that people had surrounded something. He sent one of his men to find out what the matter was. The man returned and told the Messenger of Allah that a woman had been slain and the people had gathered around her. Upon this, the Holy Prophet said: "The woman did not participate in the battle, then why was she made a victim of your sword?" The people replied: "Khalid b. al- Walid was in the van-guard of the army." The Holy Prophet sent a man to Khalid and instructed him not to lay hands on any woman or slave. The Prophet also issued a stern warning to his men against the burning of the enemies.

There is a tradition which has been narrated on the authority of Hamzah al Aslami that the Messenger of Allah once appointed him the leader of a battalion and said: "If you find such and such an infidel, kill him, but do not burn him, because it is the Creator of fire alone Who has the right to use it for punishing the wicked people."

It is recorded by Samurah b. Jundub that the Holy Prophet (peace be upon him) exhorted us to give charity and forbade us from mutilation of dead bodies.

It is said that once a news was brought to Abu Ayyub al Ansari that Muslims killed four prisoners after having tied them in their camp. The famous companion of the Holy Prophet listened to this with a sense of anguish and said: "I heard the Prophet forbidding us to kill our enemies in this way." He also added: "By God, in Whose hand is my life, I would never slay like this even if it were a hen."

This, in brief, is the teaching of the Holy Prophet with regard to dealing with the enemy on the battlefield. So great is the respect for humanity in Islam that it has forbidden wanton destruction of even the enemy's crops and property at the time of invasion or at the time of conquest. While describing the traits of the mischief-monger, the Quran explicitly tells us that:

> When he turns his back, his aim everywhere is to spread mischief through the earth and destroy crops and cattle. But God loveth not mischief and disorder.
>
> (ii: 205)

Islam has purged war of all base passions, so that the Muslims have been ordained to refrain from creating noise on the battlefield as far as possible, and only chant the glory of the Lord, the Creator of the universe. It is narrated on the authority of Qays b. Abd, that the companions of the Holy Prophet did not like taking loudly on the battlefield.

This injunction speaks eloquently of the sanctity of the occasion. War in Islam is not the wild expression of the baser elements of man, but a sacred struggle undertaken to achieve some definite noble ends.

The four righteous Caliphs followed closely the teachings of Allah and His Apostle in letter and spirit and did not deviate from the path shown to them by the Holy Prophet. The celebrated instructions which the first Caliph gave to his army while bidding them farewell on their expedition to the Syrian borders are permeated with the Message of Allah.

He said:

> "Do not commit treachery, nor depart from the right-path. Do not mutilate, nor kill a child, nor aged man, nor a woman. Do not destroy a palm tree, nor burn it with fire and do not cut any fruit tree. You must not slay any of the flocks or herds or the camels, save for your subsistence. You are likely to pass by people who have devoted their lives to monastic service; leave them to what they have devoted their lives. You are likely to find, likewise, people who will present to you meals of many kinds. You may eat; but do not forget to mention the name of Allah:"

It is said that once at the time of conquest a singing girl was brought to al-Muhajir b. Abi Ummyyia who had been publicly singing satirical poems about Abu Bakr. Muhajir got her hand amputated. When the Caliph heard this news, he was rudely shocked and wrote a letter to Muhajir in the following words:

> I have learnt that you laid hands on a woman who had showered abuses on me, and therefore got her hand amputated. God has not sought vengeance even in the case of polytheism, which is a great crime. He has not permitted mutilation even with regard to manifest infidelity. Try to be considerate and sympathetic in your attitude towards others in future. Never mutilate, because it is a grave offence. God purified Islam and the Muslims from rashness and excessive wrath. You are well aware of the fact that those enemies fell into the hands of the Messenger of Allah who had been recklessly abusing him, who

turned him out of his home, and who fought against him, but he never permitted their mutilation.

Another letter written by 'Umar the second Caliph which is addressed to Sa'd b. Abl Waqqas, speaks eloquently of the noble spirit with which the Muslims have been exhorted to take up arms:

> Always search your minds and hearts and stress upon your men the need of perfect integrity and sincerity in the cause of Allah. There should be no material end before them in laying down their lives, but they should deem it a means whereby they can please their Master and entitle themselves to His favour: such a spirit of selflessnes should be inculcated in the minds of those who unfortu-nately lack it. Be firm in the thicket of the battle as Allah helps man according to the perseverance that he shows in the cause of His faith and he would be rewarded in accordance with the spirit of sacrifice which he displays for the sake of the Lord. Be careful that those who have been entrusted to your care receive no harm at your hands and are never deprived of any of their legitimate rights.

*Exemplary Behaviour* : Such in fact is the humane and noble attitude which Islam exhorts its followers to adopt on the battlefield when passions are generally let loose. It is an attitude the like of which is not to be found in the history of any other nation. Has the world any code of military ethics more noble and compassionate than this one? "The moral tone adopted by the Caliph Abu Bakr in his instructions to Syrian army was," says a Christian historian, "so unlike the principles of the Roman government that it must have commanded profound attention from the subject people. Such a proclamation announced to Jews and Christian sentiments of justice and princi-ples of toleration which neither Roman emperors nor orthodox bishops had ever adopted as the rule of conduct."

Western scholars have indulged in a good deal of mudslinging on the question of the use of the sword in Islam. But if one were to reflect calmly on this point one would be convinced that the sword has not been used recklessly by the Muslims; it has been wielded purely with humane feelings in the wider interest of humanity. Utmost regard was, always shown to human life, honour and property even on the battlefield. That is why in all the eighty-two encounters between the Muslims and non-Muslims during the life of the Holy Prophet (peace be upon him), only one thousand and eighteen persons lost their lives on both sides.

Out of this, two hundred and fifty-nine were Muslims whereas the remaining seven hundred and fifty-nine belonged to the opposite camp. One wonders at the audacity of these writers when one only compares the religious wars of Charles the Great, in which 4500 pagan Saxons were killed in cold blood, when one recalls the "famous answer by which the Papal Legate, in the Albiqennian war, quited the scruples of a too conscientious general, 'Kill all God will know His own',—when one recalls the Spanish Inqui-sition, the conquest of Mexico and Peru, the massacre of St. Bartholomew, and the sack of Magdeburg Tilly."

This ruthless criticism on the use of sword by Muslims is a matter of great surprise for us when we find that it emanates from those whose hands are soiled in the blood of countless innocent human beings, by those who exult in the techniques of homicide, who have depersonalized warfare to such an extent that millions of innocent men and women are put to death and numberless are thrown into concentration camps and flogged with steel rods and oxidized whips, and all this is done without any qualm of conscience. As human beings, we hang our heads down in shame when think of the horrifying atrocities which have been perpetrated by the modern civilized man. It is estimated that in the World War I, ten million soldiers were killed and an equal number of civilians lost their lives, and twenty million died on account of widespread epidemics and famines throughout the world as an aftermath of this war. Economic costs are estimated at $ 398,000,000,000 of which 186,000,000,000 were direct costs.

The losses in the World War II were staggeringly greater as compared with the first one. Twenty-two million persons were killed and thirty-four million were wounded. The estimated cost of war was $ 1,348,000,000,000 of which 1,167,000,000,000 consisted of direct military costs.

It is significant that in the Korean War, the first instance in which an international organization for establishing peace utilized military force to suppress aggression, more than one million persons were killed which added to the civilian deaths in Korea and totalled about five millions.

3

# *System of Government*

The modern concept of state is, that it is an organised institution, which is run by the people through their elected representatives for the collective welfare of the people, residing in a specified territory. The ultimate power vests in the people, who are real sovereign and, therefore, masters of their destinies. They are free to legislate and enact any law, following their own desires. The constitution of the state is moulded according to the history, belief, customs and ideology of its people. All the secular states of the world, whether Democratic or Socialistic are administrated by man-made laws, and institutions, and are based on the theory of material advancement, and utilitarianism.

The concept of state in Islam is altogether different from the present-day concept of state. In modern times when territorial nationalism is the order of the day and material and economic considerations almost wholly shape peoples' outlook and policies, the making of an Islamic State stands out as the triumph of an ethical concept. But the Western observers may question: firstly, what the character of Islamic State is and, secondly, as to how an Islamic State can be realised in a democracy in the twentieth century. In this context it becomes necessary for us to ascertain as to what the true form, character and nature of an Islamic State is and how far it can be realised in the structural pattern of a modern society.

In this context, it should be kept uppermost in the mind that Islam is not merely a religion in its narrow import. It is not a set of dogmas, mythological beliefs or mere rituals. It does not divide life into water tight compartments. There is no dichotomy in Islam between the temporal and spiritual; the structure of Islam is essentially religio-political. In this system the state forms an integral part at the apex and as Dr. Muhammad Iqbal points out "is only an effort to realise the spiritual in human organisation". *(Lectures on Reconstruction of Religious Thoughts in Islam,* page 155). Thus, Islam presents the whole of reality to man and wants to give him guidance in every walk of life. It requires him to discriminate between the right and wrong and to accept a path because it is right and not because it is secular or non-secular. It attempts to bring the realities of this world in harmony with the ideals that provide security for this world and the Hereafter. It is a complete code of conduct. It is a way of life and a philosophy of life. It is a social, economic and political system. Hence, it is a statecraft.

It is in this context that the whole outlook and effort for raising the edifice of the state has to be different from the lines on which people ordinarily pursue the task of state building. Thus spiritual and ethical values of Islam have played a decisive role in this regard. This has been embodied in the concept of Islamic State—a state patterned on the socio-moral, religio-political principles of Islam. It is not torn by the dualism of state and church whose separation has been deemed an absolute dogma in Western Political Science. The church is not recognized in the genuine Islamic State as an exclusive institution representing religion. The concept of state religion or the Papacy or theocracy cannot give a correct picture of the character of the Islamic State. In a theocracy, the Pope assumes a special intimacy with God and nobody can reach God except his intermediary. This concept is alien to Islam. The criterion of an Islamic State is not union of the ruler and the government, but the principle of justice and religion combined with social action. Thus, in order to understand the concept of state in Islam, let us examine the essentials of the state.

To constitute a state four elements are essential: (i) territory; (ii) population; (iii) organization; and (iv) sovereignty. In regard to the fourth element, the Islamic State differs fundamentally from all other states, and in that occupies a unique position.

No state can be termed independent unless it enjoys sovereign power i.e. the absolute right to make laws for people within its jurisdiction. This gives rise to the question, who should possess such right? In ancient times, when *might is right* was the rule the most powerful individual, through sheer brute force, used to conquer certain territories and instal himself as the ruler of the people. He called himself king and arrogated to himself the absolute right of law making and the right to set up any form of government that suited his convenience. Being himself the chief law-giver for his people, he was considered above law, and, as such, not bound by any law, not even his own. And in consequence of the enjoyment of this and other exclusive rights and privileges, he regarded himself as God incarnate. As an obvious corollary of this belief, he had full control over the life and death of his subjects who are required to give him unquestioning and unconditional obedience and to serve him blindly. The people were, thus, reduced to the position of mere serfs and chatties: they enjoyed no fundamental rights, nor could they claim, freedom of expression or liberty of conscience.

Later in history, when feudalism became the order of the day, a few feudal lords joined the monarch in claiming the right to make laws for the country, but the people remained where they were earlier so far as their rights and privileges were concerned. The monarchs along with those few lords enjoyed innumerable exclusive privileges and all that at the cost of those whom they ruled by virtue of being the law-givers for the land.

During the mediaeval period, the ecclesiastical authorities in Christian Europe tried to set up theocracy i.e. the rule based upon divine laws; but as the few Commandments which were regarded as infallible could not cover all aspects of human activities, the priests found an excuse to arrogate to themselves the right of making additional laws for the people. They also put themselves above the law, and as such enjoyed exclusive privileges, depriving the people of their just and inalienable rights. Following the pattern of theocracy and in order to assert their so-called inalienable hereditary rights and infallibility, the mediaeval English monarchs claimed the 'Divine Right of Kings' the traces of which theory are still to be found in England, the most democratic country in the world. For that matter, the maxim "The King can do no wrong" still holds as good in England today as it was during the mediaeval and post-mediaeval period.

Even in Greek democracy, which is regarded by some as an ideal institution, the people were divided into two classes: the free (men) and the slaves. The latter, in the opinion of Aristotle, were not fit to participate in government. Their position was like that of animals whose only duty was to serve their free masters who owned them. They had none of the rights of citizens. Nor were women given any right and, so much so that Aristotle would confine to more domestic duties. The philosophers who called the Greek democracy into existence because the sole law-makers for the country and their antipathy towards women and healots resulted in social inequality. In other words, Greek democracy assured freedom only for the free, male Greeks, and was confined to Greece.

Rousseau, the well-known French philosopher, was, however, the first to enunciate the idea of popular sovereignty, and it was after the French Revolution that attempts were made to found state on this basis in Europe.

## State under Islam

The Islamic State, as is well-known, was founded by the Holy Prophet in the seventh century of Christian era; and continued with full vigour during the period of first four Caliphs *(Khulfa-i-Rashidin)*. But soon enough, its complexion changed owing to certain variations in its ideals. However, certain basic ideals like equality, liberty, justice and even toleration remained in force to a certain degree in the post-Rashidin period.

But owing to the existence of institutions like monarchy and feudalism, the fundamentals of Islamic State, could not find a foothold in European countries, although a very energetic, glorious Islamic State was in existence in Spain for several centuries. The abolition of the institutions of monarchy and feudalism in the wake of French Revolution, however, paved the way for the reception of these ideals into Europe.

Even in modern democracies which are based upon popular sovereignty, equality, liberty, justice and toleration are rarely to be found. Strange though it may sound, this contention is nevertheless based on facts. No doubt, in modern state laws are made by the representatives of the people, yet they are made in such a way as to suit the interests of either a class or a party at the cost of the opposition or they remain so defective that different interpretations are put for different sections of the people. They are so nicely twisted that they always favour the "sovereign" class. In all modern democracies, from the President or the King down to the legislature, they are all allowed, in the first instance, to enjoy some sort of exclusive privileges, for instance, exemption from taxation, exemption from appearance in the court or immunity of arrest (while performing their official duties), reservation of seats in trains or planes, or other priorities in several other respects. Secondly, the ruling party makes such laws which could suit and advance its own interest, although it may adversely affect the opposition e.g., if the Labour Government is in power, it will promulgate laws suiting the labourer and normally at the cost of the capitalists and *vice versa.*

The most flagrant example of discrimination in this respect can be found in South Africa where the original, native inhabitants were deprived of their inalienable right to franchise by the foreign ruling class. This racial discrimination was also to be found on another level in one of the most democrative countries of the world viz., the U.S.A.

Even in the most democratic country of the world, viz., England, one finds the same phenomena of inequality although little in comparison to above mentioned countries in operation: For instance, one does find discrimination, though in a lesser degree, so far as the interpretation of law and dispensation of justice are concerned.

Even in the eastwhile communist states which are regarded more advanced in this respect than their capitalist counterparts, the same phenomena of inequality, injustice and intoleration prevails on account of the same defect. The heads of communist states along with their lesser party bosses, were all above the law; nay, they imposed themselves on the people through the force of an election. As there is no check on the sovereign powers of the legislators, they deprived the people even of their liberty of conscience; and by putting an end to private enterprise and initiative, they reduced human beings to the position of an inconsequential part of a huge machine.

This defective system of law-making is primarily due to the fact that the right of sovereignty has been entrusted to human agency without any divine restriction. And it is because of basic human weakness that men when they are entrusted with the law-making power, more often than not misuse it in their own favour or in favour of the party or class which they represent. In other words, unrestricted sovereign powers have been assumed by human beings, in all the states from time immemorial resulting in exclusive privileges for the ruling authorities and deprivation of inalienable human rights of the people as a whole.

In an Islamic State, on the other hand, sovereignty belongs to God, the Almighty Allah. This does not, however, mean that in an Islamic State, all the laws are to be made by God Himself or that the Quran provides all possible positive laws and that people have nothing to do with sovereign functions. On the other hand, the laws, enacted in an Islamic State are, to be made by the people of the state, but in the light of the Quranic fundamentals. Thus, in an Islamic State, the people enjoy a partial and restricted right of law-making. They cannot, of course, make any law which runs contrary to the Quranic instructions, meant for universal application. In this sense, the people who make the laws, are not really law-makers. Nor are they above the law; they are only the executors of law and they stand at par with ordinary citizens.

***First Source :*** There are two kinds of verses in the Holy Quran, namely decisive and allegorical, the latter being those which are capable of different interpretations. The decisive verses are the basis of the Book, and contain the fundamental principles of religion. So that whatever may be the differences of interpretation over allegorical verses, the fundamentals of religion are not affected by them.

***Second Source :*** The *Sunnah* or *Hadith* (the tradition of the Prophet) is the second, and undoubtedly a secondary, source from which the Islamic laws are drawn. *Sunnah* literally means a way, rule or manner of acting. In its original sense, therefore, *Sunnah* indicates the doings, and *Hadith* the sayings of the Holy Prophet, but in effect both cover the same ground and are applicable to his actions, practices and sayings; *Hadith* being the narration and record of the *Sunnah,* but containing, in addition, various Prophetical and historical elements of Islam.

As the Holy Quran generally deals with the broad principles or essentials of Islam the details are generally to be supplied by the *Sunnah* of the Holy Prophet. Even for the two important religious institutions of Islam, viz., prayer and *Zakat,* no details are to be found in the Quran.

The details about these injunctions were only supplied by the practice of the Holy Prophet. These are but two examples: but since Islam covered the whole sphere of human activities, hundreds of points had to be explained by the Holy Prophet by his example in word and deed, while the moral side, his was the pattern which every Muslim was required to follow. The persons, who embraced Islam, thus, stood in need of both the Holy Quran and the *Sunnah.* And it was because the *Sunnah* occupied such a tremendous though a secondary place in the super-structure of Islam that the early Muslims devoted themselves so assiduously and so energetically to collecting all traditions with every possible care that was humanly possible. In judging whether a certain *Hadith* was spurious or genuine, the collectors not only made a thorough investigation regarding the trustworthiness of the transmitters but also applied other tests for its acceptance. No *Hadith* was to be accepted, if it was opposed to or was against the plain teachings of the Quran. Being the secondary source of law, *Hadith,* is, however, to be judged by the Quran. If it agrees with the Quran, it should be accepted; if it runs counter to the spirit of a Quranic injunction, it should be rejected.

***Third Source :*** *Ijtihad* is the third source from which the laws are drawn. The word itself is derived from the root *"Jihad"*, which means exerting oneself to the utmost or to the best of one's ability, and *Ijtihad,* which literally conveys the same significance, is technically applicable to a lawyer's exerting his mental faculties to the utmost for purposes of solving difficult problems. Reasoning or the exercise of judgement, in the theological as well as in legal matters, plays a very important part in Islam. The Quran does recognise revelation as a source of knowledge higher than reason. But it also admits that the truth of the principles established by revelation may be judged by reason, and in doing so, it repeatedly appeals to reason and denounces those who do not use their reasoning faculty. It also recognizes the necessity of the exercise of judgement in the formulation of a decision. *Ijtihad* or the exercise of judgement is expressly recognised in the *Hadith* as the means by which a decision may be arrived at when there is no direction in the Holy Quran or the *Hadith.* The following *Hadith* is regarded as the basis of *Ijtihad* in Islam:

On being appointed Governor of Yaman, Muadh Bin Jabal was asked by the Holy Prophet as to the rule by which he would adjudicate. He replied "by the law of the Quran". "But if you do not find any direction in the Quran, how would you decide", asked the prophet. He replied, "I will apply the *Hadith* and Sunnah". "But if you don't find any guidance in the *Hadith* as well?" He was again asked. "I will then exercise my judgement and act on that," came the reply. The prophet raised his hands and said, "Praise be to Allah who guides His Messenger as He pleases".

This *Hadith* shows not only that the Holy Prophet approved of the exercise of judgement but also that his companions were well aware of the principles, and that *Ijtihad* was freely resorted to by his followers, when necessary, even in the Prophet's lifetime.

***Fourth Source*:** The fourth source of Islamic law is *Ijma.* The word *Ijma* is derived from *jams* which means collecting or gathering together, and *Ijma* carries the double significance of composing and settling a thing which has been unsettled and hence determining and resolving upon an affair, and of agreeing or uniting in opinion. In the terminology of the Muslim jurists, *Ijma,* means a consensus of opinion of the Mujtahids, or an agreement of the Muslim jurists, of a particular age on a point of law. *Ijma,* however, is not an independent source of law; it is only *Ijtihad* on a wider basis and like *Ijtihad,* it is always open to revision.

In the second century of the *Hejira* arose the famous schools of the great jurists who codified the Islamic law according to the needs of the time; and this codification became, the chief basis of Islamic law at that time. However, owing to the degeneration that presently set in the Muslim society (in consequence of which it could not produce jurists of the calibre of the famous four *Imams),* the community as a whole began to believe that the codification, as done by those great *Imams,* was final; and that there was no scope for further *Ijtihad* in *Shariat.* Whatever may be the justification, this belief was nevertheless contrary to the very teachings of Islam.

Since the Islamic laws are to be derived from the Quran which is regarded as a universal guide for all time, it is inevitable that *Ijtihad* should continue to be exercised. It is, therefore, a mistake to suppose that the door of *Ijtihad* was closed after the four *Imams.* It has already been shown that the Quran and the *Hadith* have both directions to the effect that the Muslim world should continue to exercise its judgement in making laws itself. Since the ultimate test of the correctness of *Hadith* is the Quran itself, the conclusion is evident that Islam allows independence of thought, subject only to one thing—that the principles laid down in the Quran are not contravened.

It will thus be seen that the Muslim community possesses the partial and restricted right of law-making. It is this restriction imposed upon the framers of law in an Islamic State which has created a world of difference between this state and all other states. The beauty of the Quranic principles is that they, being of divine in origin, are equally applicable to the whole mankind, irrespective of a person's status, position, colour, race, sex, language or nationality. If a thing is declared legal, it is legal for all in any shape or form. There are to be no exceptions; and even if they are allowed, they are allowed for all under certain conditions and circumstances. We can, therefore, conclude that owing to the restricted right of legislation entrusted to the most learned scholars among the Muslim community, nobody is regarded as a legislator (in the modern sense of the word) in an Islamic State. The authority or authorities in such a state can only be regarded as the executor.

**The Fraternity**

In accordance with the famous verse of the Holy Quran "The believers are but a single brotherhood". The first characteristic of the Islamic state is fraternity. This verse asserts that Muslims, whatever, be their country, race, colour, or language, are members of a single brotherhood. Among the believers white and black, rich and poor, master and servant, Arab and non-Arab, stand together and enjoy equal rights and bear equal responsibilities in running the state.

Such is the force of Islamic brotherhood that even blood relationship counts for nothing. An unbeliever, even if connected with a believer by blood ties, falls into a totally different category of citizenship. As regards the division of the Believers into nations and tribes, the Holy Quran says, "We made you into nations and tribes so that you may recognize each other. Verily the most honoured of you with Allah is he who is the most righteous of you" (XLIX). This verse emphasises that all regional and tribal distinctions are merely for the sake of convenience. Neither can they form the basis for the classification of rights of status of human beings nor should the separation or fusion of nationalities depend upon them.

Among the Believers if any distinction is to be made at all, it should be on the basis of *Taqwa* or piety. The flowering of Islamic fraternity perhaps, reached its climax on the occasion of *Hijrat* when the prophet knitted one *Muhajir* and one *Ansar* together in the brotherhood of Islam and they both lived under the same roof as brothers.

## Lord's Rule

Since sovereignty in an Islamic State is restricted to the four corners of the *Shariah,* whose principles are universal and equally applicable to all, the obvious resultant characteristic of such a state is equality. It is, however, a mistaken notion that Islam sanctions absolute equality among its votaries. Absolute equality is denied by nature, as no two persons are equal in every respect. Any amount of effort on the part of a state to equalise the mental faculties or even physical gifts of different persons will prove fruitless. Consequently, a well-known verse of the Quran says: "Verily, We have given preference to some over others". However, the question arises, "What is the concept of equality in Islam"?

It means equality before law and in matters of civic rights and obligations to the state. Above all, it means affording of equal opportunities to all, irrespective of caste, colour, race or birth; it also connotes social equality, a principle which even some of the most progressive and democratic states in the world have not been able to enthrone even in the present age. Only merit, character and devotion to the cause of Islam should enable a person to occupy the highest position in the state. A person's worth should not be judged by birth, but by efficiency, character and services to the cause of Islam.

## Fundamental Liberties

The third characteristic of an Islamic State is liberty, which in its true perspective was, for the first time, presented by Islam to humanity. The greatest character of individual liberty is involved in that very *'Kalima'*. "There is no god but one God" excluded all other authority but that of God. A Muslim is free as he is not required to obey any other authority, but that of God. In other words, this would mean that he is only free within the limits, prescribed by the *Shariah.* None can encroach upon the rights of others, but at the same time can feel free within his or her own rights. Freedom of expression and liberty of conscience are the two cornerstones of Islamic polity. Even an ordinary citizen of the state can criticise the highest in the state and call him to account. However, licence in the name of liberty is not allowed; none enjoys the right of slandering people or to make fun of the authorities. It is, however, the obligation of the Islamic State not to deprive any citizen of the liberty Islam confers upon him without proving his crime in the court of law and without giving him full opportunity and facilities for his defence.

## Legal System

The fourth characteristic of an Islamic State is justice. Justice in an Islamic State, should be impartial and no respector of persons, whether high or low, prince or peasant, white or black, Muslim or non-Muslim. The Quran enjoins upon Muslims to decide a case on the basis of equality, justice and upright testimony. As such, the entire Muslim community is to be held responsible for the administration of justice. The following verses of the Holy Quran sum up the conception of justice in an Islamic State: "O ye who believe be (firm) maintainers of justice, bearers of witness for Allah's sake, even though it be against your own selves, or your parents or your kins and whether it be against rich or poor; for Allah can best protect both. Follow not the lusts (of your hearts), lest ye swerve; and if ye distort (justice) or decline to do justice, verily Allah is well-acquainted with all that ye do". (IV: 135). "If (O Muhammad;) thou judges concerning the affairs of non-Muslims, judge in equity between them (however hostile may be the attitude towards thee).

For Allah loveth those who judge in equity", (V: 45). Thus the Holy Quran has emphasised again and again that however hostile, mischievous or cruel may be the person with whom the authorities have to deal, it is not permissible for them to deviate even slightly from the path of justice. In the light of the above Quranic injunctions, it becomes incumbent upon the head of the state to provide free impartial justice to all irrespective of caste, creed, colour, nationality, race, status or sex.

According to Islamic notions, the head of the Islamic State has a two-fold judicial function, one positive and the other negative. His positive functions related to the establishment of peace in the state, maintenance of concord among the various sections of the people and the protection of the weak against the strong. His negative functions concern punishment of the evil-doer and the restitution of the rights of the injured. For the dispensation of justice, the head of the state has to appoint *Qadis,* well versed in *Shariah law.* God-fearing and of irreproachable character and sterling piety. The *Qadis* who apply divine law, consider themselves responsible not only to the head of the state but also to God Almighty and, as such, dispense justice equitably and speedily. Since the *Qadis'* court is regarded as God's court, no preferential treatment is to be given even to the highest in the state.

"The King can do no wrong", does not hold good in an Islamic State so far as the dispensation of justice is concerned. No one can claim exemption from appearance in the court or even a preferential seat in the court. Recording of deposition of influential persons through commission is not allowed by Islamic law. The Islamic law lays down easy procedure for the conduct of cases and cheap and speedy justice is to be meted out to rich and poor alike free of cost. However, Islamic State lays greater emphasis on the prevention of crimes than on punishing the culprits after the offences are committed.

Seeking legal opinion from well-known scholars has been in vogue since the very inception of Islam. The authorities allowed learned scholars to give free and legal advice to all and sundry. This institution enabled the state to assume that every citizen know the law, for it gives an equal opportunity to every person to know such legal details which he or she did not already know. Often *Qadis* who were not quite sure about some legal point, referred the case to *Mufti* and took a *Fatwa* from him.

***Dual Responsibility*** **:** The fifth characteristic feature of the Islamic State is that everyone from the Caliph to an ordinary citizen is doubly responsible, viz., to God and to some sort of earthly authority. The fear of God and the punishment in the hereafter being common to all, the people are responsible to the head of the state, who, in turn, is himself responsible to the former. Hence, there is a double check upon the actions of all the citizens in an Islamic State. In public, they do not commit any act of omission or commission for the fear of the state officials, in private, they also abstain from committing any wrong as they are conscious of the presence of Almighty.

Thus, the dichotomy of distinction between the public and private life of a citizen in an Islamic State disappears altogether. The absence of the fear of God is the weakest point in all modern states, particularly in a communist state, where people, devoid of moral conscience, as they are, can commit any wrong, unnoticed by the state officials; whereas people in an Islamic State dare not do any such act of omission or commission as they are conscious of the fact that their God is having a vigilant eye over them and they shall not escape punishment.

In accordance with a verse of the Quran "We created believers" and unbelievers, the population in an Islamic State is divided between believers and unbelievers. Among the believers, there are two kinds: first those who believe in all the revealed religions and their prophets and also in Islam as the last religion and Prophet Muhammad (peace be upon him); and, secondly, those who believe in their own revealed books and prophets, but not in Islam or its Prophet Muhammad (peace be upon him). Since the Islamic State is an ideological state, it is but natural that its administration should primarily be entrusted to those who believe in its ideology and agree to sacrifice their all in running the state and making it a success.

In order to defend the frontiers of the Islamic State and to promote the cause of its ideology, military service is made compulsory upon all the able-bodied Muslims without any exception; in return, they are guaranteed maintenance allowance from the state. The second group of believers, viz., the followers of the revealed books who believe in the existence of the God but do not believe in Islam or its ideology when such people agree to live within the jurisdiction of an Islamic State, their relations are guided in accordance with the famous verse of the Quran, "No compulsion in matters of faith".

The Islamic State regards them as *Zimmis* or its own responsibility; and guarantees them full liberty of conscience protection of property, life and freedom of religious belief. Nay, it goes one step further and provides full scope for the growth of their culture and traditions and the administration of their civil affairs in accordance with their own religious laws. An Islamic State does not believe in forcing its own culture and traditions on others or in adopting coercive measures to get the culture of the *Zimmis* submerged into that of the Muslim, as it is usually seen under a nationalist disposition. As the *Zimmis* are not obliged to defend the Islamic State, they are required to pay a small tax in return, known as *Jizya:* in case they offer themselves for military service, they are exempted from the tax too. No distinction is made between the Muslims and the followers of other revealed books in matters of the civic rights and the latter could qualify themselves for all offices of the state except the religious ones. Thirdly, the unbelievers are those who either do not believe in the existence of God Almighty and in the Hereafter or associate other partners with God.

The followers of this Godless cult are fundamentally opposed to all the believers of God; and are at the perpetual warfare with them. Islam which believes in the establishment of peace by liberating mankind from all shackles of slavery is the worst enemy of the Godless cult. So long as this cult survives, Islam cannot flourish and will not be able to achieve its ideals;

and, therefore, as a moral force, it is directly opposed to this evil force. As such, this Godless cult has been described in the Holy Quran as *fitna* (mischief) which must be rooted out from the Universe so that the faith of God may flourish.

***Guiding Principles :*** As all the guiding principles of the Islamic State are derived from the Quran which, according to Muslim belief, is a divinely revealed book, some people assert that it (the Islamic State) is a religious institution. In reality, the Islamic State is not a religious institution in the sense of medieval Christian theocracy in which certain ecclesiastical authorities claimed for themselves the right of law-making. Others assert that the Islamic State is temporal as it is required to administer affairs which are temporal in character and not spiritual.

It is, however, not temporal in the modern sense of the term, since the modern state is not guided by religion, and it usually lacks moral conscience and a moral basis for administration and application of its laws. Since the fundamental ingredients of an Islamic State are derived from the Quran, it becomes a little difficult to separate religion from temporal function. And since its chief function is to protect Islam and to promote its cause, both within and without and to administer both religious and temporal affairs. In accordance with the Quran and the *Sunnah,* this state may be regarded as both religious as well as temporal. It should, however, be made clear that the state religion of Islamic State must be Islam for whose protection and maintenance, it is called into existence and continues to exist.

It will be a fallacy to compare the Islamic State with any modern state, as it fundamentally differs from all of them and stands as a class by itself. Since it is based on Quranic principles and has a definite mission to perform, it may be regarded as an ideological state. It may, however, be termed as theo-democracy, for, in such a state, under the sovereignty and paramountcy of God, a limited popular sovereignty has been conferred on the believers.

Since the Islamic State encompasses both the religious and the temporal spheres, and come into existence through a contract between the (elected) *Ameer* and the general *Ummah* (community), it is nothing if not a devise to fulfil the aspirations of the individuals themselves collectively and, to a certain extent, individually. The state is thus not marked by any suicidal controversy between the state and the individual. According to the Islamic polity, the state, the *Ameer* and the *Millat* are all animated by an ethical ideal, and it is the duty of each one of them to strive after and towards this ideal. Accordingly, the personal liberty of the individual is guaranteed to a very large extent under this system; and political power is not concentrated in the hands of one person.

Yet another feature of the Islamic State is to carry on the administration through mutual consultation. The Quran says, "those who (conduct) their affairs by mutual consultation" *(Amr a him Shura Beina Hum);* and "(O Muhammad) consult these (i.e. in the affair. Then when thou hast taken a decision put the trust in (Him)" (Ill: 150). Thus, there should exist in an Islamic State a Majlis-i-Shura or Council consisting of representatives of the people, reflecting the total legal wisdom of the entire country. The appointment of this council is made by the *Ameer* himself from among various sections of the people; the only criteria for appointment being their intimate knowledge of the *Shariah,* their character. The Ameer-in-Council is to legislate in consultation with the *Majlis* and administer the state with their consent. Since the final authority is the Quran and the *Sunnah,* pleas should be based on, and in accordance with them. The decision is to be unanimous and the *Shura* feels collective responsibility.

The Islamic State is noted for separation of powers. Although the *Qadis* are to be appointed by the *Ameer,* the highest executive head in the state, in consultation with Shura, yet judiciary is completely independent of the Executive. The fact that *Qadi* can accept a suit against the very person of the *Ameer* without any previous permission and can try him in an open court—this feature of Islamic judiciary is an index to the independence of judiciary in an Islamic State. Nor is the *Ameer* exempted from personal appearance or to be given any preferential seat, in the court. The question of taking deposition of great and prominent personalities by means of commission does not arise in an Islamic State.

***The Centralization :*** Another feature of the Islamic State is centralization in matters of legislation. The nature of the Islamic state which is based on Quranic principles, demands that there should be uniformity in legislation. It is only the Central Legislative Assembly which could legislate in connection with matter touching the religious aspects of life or the common problems of the state for instance, foreign policy, taxation, justice and constitution. However, in matters of temporal administration, much can be left with the provincial authorities. In case of provincial revenues and expenditure, the provincial treasuries can work as independent units; the Provincial *Baitul Mal* is to receive and disburse the amounts realized. In early Islam too, *Zakat* realized from a certain place was used to be spent on the needs of the local people; balance, if any, in the Provincial Treasury used to be deposited with the Central Treasury, whereas deficit, if any, in the Provincial Treasury met from the Central *Baitul Mal.* The whole empire is to be divided into provincial units. The Governors, appointed by the Caliph in consultation with the *Shura* and the local people, could be transferred and dismissed from their posts.

The economic policy of the Islamic State is to be based on some positive injunctions in the Quran. It lays down, "So that the wealth should not circulate only among the rich from among you". Hence, the distribution of wealth among all classes of believers has been emphasised by the institution of property tax, known as *Zakat,* to the extent of 2½ per cent on surplus property, each hoard as well as commercial capital; and restrictions on the process of testamentary disposition, laws of inheritance and the prohibition of usuary. The Islamic State believes in the imposition of minimum taxation and the provision of maximum comforts for the people.

The believers who are supposed to pay less than the *Zimnis* could, however, be required to pay all their surplus wealth to the state in case of emergency. Since the believers have to stake their lives and property for the defence and the maintenance of the state, they are secured due provision for their food, shelter and other necessities of life. Islamic State does not believe in class war nor does it undertake a complete socialization or democrative management of the basic instruments of production and distribution.

It does allow the individuals to acquire private property so that their incentive may not be lost; but, on the other hand, it does not allow the concentration of wealth into few hands in order to perpetuate capitalism in its naked form. The economic system in an Islamic State thus stands midway between the two antagonistic systems in the present world capitalism and communism.

The objective of the Islamic State is to "establish prayer and pay *Zakat;* and enjoin good upon the people and to restrain them from committing wrong "(XXII: 41). The Quran also refers to Muslims as the best people sent down to Universe in order to do good and prevent others from committing wrong. These verses are very significant and sum up the chief objectives of the Islamic State regarding the duties of the Muslims. The first part of the first verse relates to prayers and *Zakat* which enable Muslims to practice in actual life the principle of equality, liberty, fraternity, justice and obedience to the *Imam.* The first part of the second verse regard the Muslims as the best people and as such incapable of doing wrong. They are, therefore, required to persuade others to do good as also restrain them from committing wrong. This express Quranic injunction entails enormous responsibilities upon the head of the state as well as its people. This obligates the state not only to carry out these orders within its own jurisdiction but also beyond it if occasion arose.

It is, thus, that the Islamic State is to be at perpetual war with forces of tyranny, wickedness, and godlessness. In order to emancipate mankind from bondage, whether physical or intellectual, the Islamic State is required to wage *Jihad.* But *Jihad* or holy war is not to be fought for personal aggrandisement or national glorification. It is to be waged only for the establishment of the rule of God and for ending man's tyranny over man and man's injustice to, and man's inhumanity to man.

The first Islamic State was set up by the Holy Prophet (peace be upon him) in the city of Yathrib, later named Medina-tun-Nabi, which ultimately became shortened into Medina. This should be our model, because it is our belief that whatever the Holy Prophet (peace be upon him) did was perfect as he was not only a living embodiment of the Holy Quran but also acted under Divine guidance through revelations.

The State came into existence after the *Hijrah* from Mecca, but before that the Holy Prophet had entered into a compact with the leaders of *Banu Aws* and *Banu Khazraj,* two leading tribes of Yathrib who had embraced Islam and invited him to shift to their town. This pact was made at a place called Aqaba and was in the nature of a bilateral treaty under which the Medinites on their part, accepted the Holy Prophet (peace be upon him) as their religious and political leader and undertook to protect him from all his enemies, and in particularly the *Quraish,* and the Holy Prophet (peace be upon him), on his part, bound himself never to forsake them or to return to Mecca. The words used translated into English read:

> "Nay in life and death I am with you and you are with me. I will fight whom you fight and I will make peace with whom you make peace."

The formula adopted for the oath of allegiance taken by the Medinites at the hands of the Holy Prophet (peace be upon him) was to the following effect:

> "We pledge that we will hear and obey you, in times of our distress and in times of our plenty and shall stand by you whatever may befall us of happiness and of anguish, and that we will speak the truth wherever we be not fearing the censure of the censurers in the path of Allah."
>
> *(Bait-i-Aqaba Thani).*

***City of the Prophet :*** The conditions prevailing at Medina at that time were one of utter chaos. Not only was there no administrative machinery to bind the tribes together but they were actually weary of their traditions of unending tribal wars. *Banu Aws* and *Banu Khazràj* were divided into twelve clans and the Jews into ten and each clan was fully autonomous. The first task, therefore, was to teach the new converts the principles of the new faith. Hence, the first thing undertaken was to construct a mosque where the community could be collected and taught the practical lessons of fraternity, equality, liberty and justice. Thus, the new community was welded into a disciplined group with a common ideology.

Having got the followers together, the Holy Prophet (peace be upon him) gave practical shape to the injunction of the Holy Quran that "the believers are but a single brotherhood, so make peace and reconciliation between your (contending) brothers and fear God that ye may receive mercy" (XLIX: 10) by obliterating the distinction between *Quraish, Aws* and *Khazraj* and pairing them together as brothers in Islam. Each of the 150 *Muhajirs* adopted by an *Ansar* as a brother with whom he was even agreeable to share his wealth but, the *Muhajirs,* not wishing to be a burden on their hosts, were content to engage themselves in various trades with the help of their *Ansar* brothers and this brought prosperity to them and really integrated themselves with the *Ansars.*

After organising his followers into a social polity the Holy Prophet (peace be upon him) applied his mind to the essential task of providing protection to the newly formed community from the *Quraish* who were still bent upon destroying the Muslims. To meet this external threat it was found necessary first to consolidate the position of the community within Medina itself which was then in habited by a large number of Jews also. The hand of friendship was extended to them and treaties of mutual security and defence were entered into guaranteeing them equal civil rights, freedom of religion and mutual protection against external aggression in return for their recognition of the Holy Prophet (peace be upon him) as the paramount executive, military and judicial authority. The Jews willingly accepted this condition and became as a body the allies of the Muslims and thus the city state of Medina came into existence as a political entity.

The Holy Prophet (peace be upon him) was not content to leave all this in a nebulous state; so a charter was drawn up meticulously recording the terms of agreement and the rights and obligations of the respective contracting parties. This became the constitution of Medina and is, perhaps, the first written constitution to be drawn up in the world. It was drawn up in two parts. The first part consisted of 23 articles dealing with matters concerning the *Muhajirs* and *Ansars* and those who were "attached to them and crusaded with them", while the second part dealt with the relationship between the Muslims and the Jews. The basic concept of this charter was that all would accept the Holy Prophet (peace be upon him) as the Paramount Authority in all matters administrative, judicial and military, and obey his lawful orders. He was to be the commander of the combined army, the executive head of the state and the final court of appeal but not a ruler in any sense of the term as the sovereignty over the universe, according to Islam, vests in Allah alone and all without any exception are subject to His laws.

The next main concept was that the Muslims were to form a single unit of this political community, separate and distinct from the rest, and the Jews as a body were to constitute the other unit. The two together were to form a federation for the purposes of war and peace and the defence of Medina. In all other matters each federating unit was to be completely autonomous but subject to the paramountcy of the Holy Prophet (peace be upon him). Each unit was to enjoy complete freedom of religion and governed by its own laws, customs and traditions except that the practice of blood-revenge and counter-revenge was to be totally banned and no interference on the basis of kinship or tribal affinity was to be permitted in the affairs of the state, and particularly, in the administration of justice.

This compact did not extend to purely religious wars *(Jihad)* but the Jews expressly undertook that they would not in any event grant protection to the *Quraish* or their allies.

So far as the Muslims were concerned the number of *Ansar* tribes was fixed at ten and the *Muhajirs* were declared to be one tribe. Each tribe was to be treated on a par with the other in respect of their rights and duties. War and peace and the administration of justice were to be matters of common or federal concern and were to be the concern of the clan, tribe or individual.

This put an end to tribal anarchy and gave birth to a sense of collective responsibility. Henceforth, everyone was to be a party to peace and war and, therefore military service was compulsory for all. In the same way, all were collectively responsible to see that no one dared harm or encroach upon the rights of others and that everyone, according to the teachings of the Holy Quran, acted with absolute fairness, free from any bias or partiality, fear and favour, even though it be against one's own interest or the interest of one's parents, kinsmen or tribesmen (IV: I 35). Tribal affiliation was recognised only to the extent that the tribe was saddled with the responsibility of ransoming its own captives from the enemy and the payment of a debt was made obligatory on the debtors' kinsmen as well.

***The Protection :*** The right to grant protection was to be enjoyed by everyone, high or low, and the pledge given even by the lowliest was to be binding on the entire community but no Muslim was entitled to grant protection to a *Quraish* to Mecca or to prevent anyone from taking revenge from such a *Quraish* for the cruelties perpetrated by them upon the Muslims in Mecca.

If to these we add that the entire Muslim community was already firmly pledged to believe in one God, accept His sovereignty over the universe, follow His Commandments as revealed to the Holy Prophet (peace be upon him) and to obey the latter's lawful commands, then the pattern that emerges is of a community organised on the basis of the cherished principles of equality, liberty and fraternity in the real sense.

The main characteristics of this state that can be gathered from the above are:

- That it was an institution established through a democratic process namely, the free will and accord of the people desiring to form the same and to accept the Holy Prophet (peace be upon him) as the paramount authority (Pledge of Aqaba Thani and Agreement with the Jews).
- That it was a constitutional organisation set up under a written charter (Charter of Medina).
- That it was a federal structure comprising two communities, the Muslims and non-Muslims, and not two territories.
- That it was an ideological state based on the concepts and fundamental principles embodied in the Holy Quran.

What these fundamental principles are is well-known not only to every Muslim but also to the entire world, for the simple reason that Islam is a living force and a world order. Although the fundamental principles of Islam are universally known, yet it would not be out of place to recount them here.

*Concept of Sovereignty:* The concept of human sovereignty is completely absent from the political philosophy of Islam. The Holy Quran proclaims: "It is only for Allah to command" (XII: 40) and "to Allah belongeth the dominion of the heavens and the earth (II: 107). This has been repeated often in the Holy Quran: "To Allah alone belongeth the dominion of the heavens and the earth and all lies between" (V: 17); Knowest thou not that Allah hath power over all things" (II: 106). Next to Allah sovereign power resides in the people, as in respect of Adam.

Allah announced to the angles that He is going to create a *Khalifa* on the earth (II: 30). Again Allah said: "Oh David, We did indeed make thee a *Khalifa* on earth—so judge thou between men in truth and justice" (XXXVIII: 27). This introduces the concept of *'Niabat-i-Ilahi'* and from this flow the following consequences:

- That next to Allah the sovereign power resides in the people. As Sir Abdur Rahim put it in his book on *'Islamic Jurisprudence'* (p. 62), Islamic law does not admit of "the sovereign power being dissociated from the people howsoever they might choose to exercise it".
- That all are equal before the law.
- That the exercise of power is a trust.
- That power has to be exercised in accordance with the Commandments of Allah and in His name.
- That everyone vested with power is accountable for his actions.
- That no one is above the law; none not even the *Khalifa,* enjoys any immunity.

This puts an end to the concept of divine origin of kings hithertofore adopted by the Hindus, the Pharoahs of Egypt, the

Sassanians of Iran and the Christians of Europe. Under this concept, the sovereign was the source of law and it was religious duty to obey his commands; but under the Islamic system, the king was not the source of law and, therefore, not above the law.

**Significant Principles**

***Liberty:*** The Principle of *Tauhid* is the fundamental principle of Islam and the *Kalima-i-Tauhid* is the greatest charter of individual liberty. When a Muslim declares that "there is no god but one God", he at once excludes all other authority but that of God, because this demands "loyalty to God and not to thrones" as Allama Iqbal puts it *'Lectures on the Reconstruction of Religious Thoughts'* (p. 147). This also implies that in Islam there is no room for kingship or dictatorship. There is no ruler and no ruled.

Everyone is *free* within the limits of the divine law. Freedom of expression and liberty of conscience are the cornerstones of Islamic polity and even an ordinary citizen could differ from the opinion of the Holy Prophet (peace be upon him) himself and voice his own views. Liberty did not, however, mean anarchy, for one could encroach upon the rights of others or refuse to obey those in authority or revolt if those in authority were acting within the limits of the divine law. Allah ordains:

> "Oh ye who believe: Obey Allah and obey the Apostle and those charged with authority from amongst you. If ye differ in anything among yourselves, refer it to Allah and His Apostle." (IV: 59).

***Justice:*** Islam seeks to set up a just society and, therefore, attaches the highest importance to justice, equity and fair dealing. The Holy Quran says:

> "Oh ye who believe; stand out firmly for justice, as witnesses to Allah, even as against yourselves or your parents or your kin and whether it be against the rich,

> or poor; for Allah can best protect both. Follow not the lusts of your heart lest ye swerve. If ye distort justice or decline to do justice, verily Allah is well acquainted with all that ye do." (IV: I 35).

Justice is placed next to piety (V: 9). God is also the fountainhead of justice and the doing of justice is a religious duty. The entire community is also made responsible for seeing that none dares harm or encroach upon the rights of others. The entire community was, therefore, involved in the administration of justice. There was no immunity from the law for anyone. The Holy Prophet (peace be upon him) himself never claimed any such immunity. Indeed in his last *Khutba* at the *Hajja-tul-Wida* he publicly declared that if he owed anything to anyone or had deprived anyone of his property or had done any harm to anyone's life or reputation, he was present there to pay his legal dues or recompense any such claimant as he was bound to do under the law. It is reported that of the whole assembly only one person stood up and claimed a few *dirhems* which were promptly paid.

Two important constitutional principles are founded on this:

(i) that everyone is equal before the law and enjoys equal opportunities; and

(ii) that in an Islamic State even the head of the state can be sued not only as a private individual but also in respect of his public acts. The rule of law was a reality under such a system and this is what led German historian Von Hammer to say that under the Islamic system the "law rules through the utterance of justice and the power of the governor carries out the utterance of it" quoted by Syed Ameer Ali in *"A Short History of the Saracens"* (p. 62).

Another consequence of such strict adherence to justice was that all appointments to state offices were made only on the basis of merit and the seeking of office was considered to be a disqualification.

The Holy Prophet (peace be upon him) was always recognised as a truthful, honest and absolutely impartial person, so much so that even non-Muslims used to bring their disputes to him for decision, yet he himself never claimed infallibility. He did not hesitate to point out that he decided the cases brought him on the evidence adduced and that, like any other human being, he was liable to *err* in forming his judgement. Error on his part was, however, unthinkable, because whenever he was in doubt he received a revelation giving him the solution of his doubts.

The classical instances of such revelations are the verses of *Surah Nisa* dealing with the inheritance of female heirs and a *Kalalah* (issueless person), and the verse of *Surah Nur* dealing with the punishment for adultery and false imputation of unchastity against a female.

***The Charter :*** Under the Charter of Medina, the prophet was the court of final appeal but the services of the savants of Medina, chosen from amongst the senior companions, were also utilised for acting as a court of first instance. In the provinces, however, the judicial power was at first vested in the governors but later the practice grew up of appointing, in addition, a separate *Qadi* as an independent functionary.

The Holy Prophet (peace be upon him) had in his lifetime also introduced a department of *'Al-Mazalim'*, which had a wide and general jurisdiction both correctional and remedial in nature. Under this, persons doing wrong to each other could be compelled to do mutual justice and even litigants could be restrained from falsely refuting just claims by inspiring awe into them. This was the basis on which the criminal jurisdiction later developed.

The procedure was naturally simple but even at that early stage the rules had been laid down that parties must be present at the time of the hearing of the disputes, that the burden of proof lay upon the party asserting a claim and the defendant had to deny the claim on oath. If he did so, then the plaintiff was called upon to adduce his evidence; but if the defendant refused to take the oath, the case could be decreed against him straightaway. The number of witnesses required was usually more than one. In certain cases, however, the number was prescribed in the Holy Quran as in the case of marriage, divorce, theft, imputation of unchastity and adultery.

***Concept of Fraternity:*** Fraternity was the fourth fundamental principle embodied in the Holy Quran on which was based the ideological State of Medina set up by the Holy Prophet (peace be upon him). "The believers are but a single brotherhood" (XLIX:10), declares the Holy Quran and then describes them as "friends and protectors of one another" (VIII: 72), with the warning that unless they protect each other there will be "tumult and oppression on earth" (VIII: 73).

The Holy Prophet (peace be upon him) has explained this concept thus: "The *Ummat* (Community) is a single fold in which each is a shepherd unto the other". This, at once, eliminates all differences and distinctions on the basis of caste, colour, creed, race or birth. All—whether black or white, master or slave, rich or poor, Arab or non-Arab—stand on the same footing and equally share the responsibility of running the affairs of the state. The Holy Prophet (peace be upon him) himself removed any possibility of doubt or misconception with regard to this when he declared in his last Sermon at the *Hajja-tul-Wida:*

> "Oh people, listen and obey, even though a mangled Abyssinian slave is appointed your *Amir* provided he executes the Book of Allah among you."

This principle of egalitarianism is not only the foundation of the body-politic of Islam but also its greatest strength. It is on this principle that the *Muhajirs* and the *Ansars* were united together in a bond that was stronger than blood relationship and enabled the Muslims to grow from strength to strength.

Another political consequence which flows from this principle is that in an Islamic State the non-believers form a separate category but not necessarily an inferior one. They were guaranteed protection of property, life and honour, granted freedom of religion and liberty of conscience and assured of non-interference with their culture and traditions or their religious laws. Religious tolerance is inbuilt in the teachings of the Holy Quran and the traditions of Islam. Had it been otherwise, there would have been no Jews left in Asia Minor or Hindus in India or Christians in Spain.

The non-Muslim citizens were called *'zimmis'*. They enjoyed the same rights as the Muslim citizens except that they were exempt from participation in any religious war *(Jihad)* and the payment of poor tax *(Zakat)* but they paid a special tax called *Jizya,* for the protection given to them. Their constitutional position can be best gathered from the following declaration made by Hadrat Ali:

> "Their life is my life, their blood is my blood and their honour is my honour. See that none ill-treats them, for they are your *'zimma'*, your responsibility from God."

***The Democracy :*** Democracy comes next. The affairs of the state were not only required to be regulated in accordance with the laws of the Holy Quran but had also to be decided by mutual consent. The Holy Prophet (peace be upon him) himself was advised by Allah to "consult them (the believers) in all matters of administration and when thou art resolved, then put thy trust in Allah" (III: 159). This verse and verse 38 of *Surah Al-Shoora* lay down the basic principle which should guide the Muslims in the transaction of their national affairs. This principle was followed by the Holy Prophet (peace be upon him) in all matters not covered by a revelation and he never sought to impose his will upon anyone. It is reported in the *'Fatuhul Bari'* (Vol. 7) that on the occasion of making preparations for the Battle of Uhud there was a difference of opinion between the Muslims on the strategy to be adopted. The Holy Prophet (peace be upon him) accepted to follow the majority view that the Muslims should go out and give battle instead of defending Medina from within.

***The Accountability :*** Last but not least, comes the concept of accountability. Authority or power to rule, according to Islam, is a trust– *'Amanat'* – of the people and not the birth right of anyone. The Quran says: "Verily Allah commands you to give over the trusts to those entitled to them and that when you judge between men, you judge with justice" (IV: 58). The nature of this trust is later indicated thus: "Establish regular prayer, pay *Zakat,* enjoin good upon the people and restrain them from doing wrong" (XXII: 41). These are the objectives of an Islamic State, to achieve which those placed in power or authority must strive. This concept of trust automatically brings in that of accountability, because a trustee is in law liable to account. Under the Islamic system this liability extends to rendering account not only to the people who appoint him but also to God as it is also a Quranic injunction.

In the light of these principles, therefore, the final picture that emerges of this first Islamic State is that it is an ideological state set up by the free will of the people in a constitutional manner and following the democrative principle of decision-making in which every citizen has an equal right to participate. Governance in this state is a trust which has to be discharged with due regard to the principles of justice, equality, liberty and fraternity for the welfare of the entire community and in such a manner that the basic needs of all are satisfied and everyone enjoys equality of opportunity without distinction of race, caste, creed, colour, faith, birth or rank.

This was a unique welfare state for which no parallel can be found in the history of the world. In this state, the Government was really a social service designed for evolving a polity based on social justice under which there was no difference between even the head of the state and an ordinary citizen. They observed same laws, had the same obligations and shared the same simple and frugal life. It would be futile to compare this state with the modern states because it differs fundamentally from all of them. The people in it are not confined to any territory nor is sovereignty vested in any human agency. "Islam is non-territorial in its character," says Allama Iqbal, "and its aim is to furnish a model for the final combination of humanity". The entire *Ummat* is a nation no matter where located and that is why as the *Ummat* increased territorial limits of the state also expanded.

The state was divided into provinces for administrative reasons but Medina remained the capital. The concept of state sovereignty is non-existent as sovereignty in Islam vests in Allah. Similarly, the concept of government is also different because government is a trust from the people and has to be exercised in accordance with law and justice for the welfare of the people. Above all, in this ideological state the bifurcation of the unity of man into temporal and spiritual is done away with. The Christian doctrine of "give unto Caesar what is Caesar's and unto God what is God's" is replaced by the thesis propounded by the Holy Prophet (peace be upon him) that "the whole earth is a Mosque". In Islam, the Church and the state constitute one indissoluble whole and, until the very essence of Islam passes away, this unity cannot be relaxed. The state, according to Islam, is only an effort to realise the spiritual in a human organisation, as Allama Iqbal maintains and it is not an end in itself but only a means to an end.

This was the model given us by the Holy Prophet (peace be upon him) himself and after him the next model for us is the structure of the state prevailing during the period of the *Khulafa-i-Rashi-deen*. The basic structure, of course, remained the same but certain changes had to be introduced to meet the changed circumstances as a result of the expansion of the state for beyond the sandy dunes of Arabia to Palestine, Syria, Iraq, Egypt and even further. The first elated to the selection of a *Khalifa.* According to a *Hadith* (confirmed by both *Bukhari* and *Muslim),* the Holy Prophet reported to have said:

> "The affairs of the state of the Bani Israel used to be in the hands of their prophets and when one prophet died another succeeded him; but since after me there is no other prophet so in the near future there will be *Khalifas* after me and many of them". When asked if he would like to give any instructions about them, he said: "Take the oath of allegiance at the hands of him who is chosen as the first (the most fit), by the *Jamhoor* (People)."

The method suggested by the Holy Prophet (peace be upon him) was, thus, the democrative method of election by the people. But since the *Khalifa* had to be a person of undisputably high qualifications, the method adopted for the selection of the first *Khalifa* was first to get the approval of the council of senior Companions of the Holy Prophet (peace be upon him) and then to put him up for election by the entire community. In the council, the *Ansars* wanted the *Khalifa* to be chosen from amongst them but after Hadrat Umar pointed out that the community was one and the fittest person is that community was Abu Bakr (the senior most and most venerated among the Companions of the Holy Prophet whom he himself had in his lifetime during his last illness, assigned the task of leading the congregational prayers), the proposal of the *Ansars* was withdrawn. Thereafter, Hadrat Umar was the first to take the oath of allegiance at the hands of Hadrat Abu Bakr. He was followed by Abu Obaidah, the *Ansar* nominee, and the rest of the council. On the next day, the entire community assembled in the mosque at Medina, and unanimously approved the selection with acclamation and took the oath of allegiance. It should be noticed that the method very closely approximates to the modern method of nomination and election, with a salutary variation of nomination by a high-powered select committee of elders. Since the seeking of office was a disqualification, it was necessary that knowledgeable persons should select a man of unimpeachable character and unquestionable capability.

Hadrat Abu Bakr, in turn, during his last illness, proposed the name of Hadrat Umar before the council of prominent Companions. When he found that they unanimously agreed, he convened a general assembly of the people and made known the unanimous view of the prominent Companions. This, too, was accepted with acclamation and all the people present took the oath of allegiance.

Hadrat Umar was stabbed by a slave of Mughira bin Shaaba and it was felt that he might not survive; he was accordingly approached by the prominent Companions to nominate his successor. He, however, refused to do so. It was actually suggested that he may consider his son, who was duly qualified, as his successor. He replied that he had no power to do so but if he had the power he would have nominated Salim, a manumitted slave, who was no longer alive. He, however, set up a council of regency consisting of the six most important Companions (including his son) and asked them to select one from amongst themselves (but not his son) within three days of his death. The choice fell upon Hadrat Uthman and the people again accepted him unanimously. By this time, the state had spread beyond Arabia and so the oath of allegiance was also taken in each province in the presence of governors.

Hadrat Uthman was murdered by a rebel group and Hadrat Ali was selected as *Khalifa* by the people of Medina, including the rebel group, but the principle of unanimity was unfortunately lacking in his case. There was difference of opinion even among the prominent Companions. The provinces of Syria and Iraq, which were governed by Muawiyyah, did not accept his *Khilafat*.

This led to war with the Iraqis and opened the floodgates of dissension. The Iraqis were defeated and forced to accept the *Khilafat*. Some well-meaning Companions then attempted to bring about a reconciliation but their attempts were thwarted by the assassination of Hadrat Ali. On his death-bed Hadrat Ali refused to nominate his son, Hasan, as the next *Khalifa* but, unlike Hadrat Umar, he did not debar him from being elected.

The result was that Imam Hasan was, in fact, elected by the people. Muawiyyah, who had earlier refused to take the oath of allegiance to Hadrat Ali, did not accept the *Khilafat* of Hasan as well and proclaimed himself the *Khalifa*. After a brief tussle Hasan abdicated in the interest of general peace, but was soon poisoned to death. Muawiyyah, thereupon became the undisputed ruler of the entire Muslim empire. By nominating his son, Yazid, as the next *Khalifa* during his lifetime he laid the foundations of the Umayyed dynasty. Yazid succeeded his father and imposed his *Khilafat* by force. His armies sacked Medina, laid sieze to Mecca and brutally murdered Imam Hussain, the second son of Hadrat Ali, who had been invited by the treacherous Kufans to deliver them from unjust rule of Yazid. The Umayyed dynasty ruled from Damascus till A.D. 749 when they were supplanted by the Abbasids.

It will be futile to delve any further into the tragic history of the succeeding periods as the republican era of Islam ended with Hadrat Ali, except to point that the rulers of the Umayyed and Abbasid periods did not adopt the title of King nor was the hereditary principle of kingship ever fully accepted. Although each nominated his successor from amongst the members of his family the rule of primogeiture was not strictly adhered to. Of the fourteen rulers of the Umayyed dynasty only four had their sons as successors. The practice was to nominate the eldest and fittest member of the royal family.

The principle of election of the *Khalifa* was adhered to right up to the days of the Ottomans even though it had been reduced to mere formality. The Ottomans, even though they had adopted the title of *Sultan*, preserved the idea of free election. Each new Sultan was solemnly elected by the *Ulama* and divines of Constantinople, who claimed to act in the capacity of representatives of the *Ummat*. Thus theoretically, at least, the broad characteristics of free election were all along maintained till the Turks, after the First World War, abolished the institution *of Khilafat*.

The conclusion that emerges from the above is that election of the head of the state is the recognised principle but since he has to be a person of high qualifications the election is preceded by a preliminary selection and nomination by a recognised body of knowledgeable persons. It is for this reason that in the early period only the prominent Companions of the Holy Prophet (peace be upon him) were considered suitable. But this was not an essential condition; had that been so Hadrat Umar would not have mentioned the name of Salim, a liberated slave in connection with this high office.

Muslim jurists like Al-Mawardi, Qadi Baidhawi and Al-Ghazzali have laid down elaborately the qualifications necessary for being eligible for election to the office of *Khalifa*. He was expected to be free from physical infirmities, profoundly knowledgeable both in theology and statecraft, capable not only of leading congregational prayers but also in the field of battle, courageous and, above all, indisputably pious and dedicated to the service of the *Ummat* according to the injunctions of the Holy Quran and the *Sunnah* of the Holy Prophet (peace be upon him).

Al-Mawardi also prescribes qualifications for the electors. He suggests that they must at least be adults, literate, intelligent and of known integrity, because Islam enjoins upon them to exercise their franchise honestly, freely and intelligently in favour of the right person regardless of kinship, tribal affiliation or any other consideration. This is in no way opposed to the practice of general *Baiyat* (allegiance) on the hand of the elected *Khalifa* as the *Baiyat* follows their decision and is its manifestation. If one did not agree to accept a nominated person, he could refuse to take the oath of allegiance as Muawiyyah did in the case of Hadrat Ali.

After the choice of the *Khalifa,* the next important variation introduced in the model state left by the Holy Prophet (peace be upon him) was the establishment of a *Majlis-i-Shoora,* or Advisory Council for meeting the Quranic injunction to act only after consultation. Although the members of the *Shoora* were chosen by the *Khalifa* from amongst both the *Muhajirin* and *Ansars* they did not change with the *Khalifa* as the selection was based on no other consideration but merit. This made the *Shoora* a very important body, more or less of a permanent nature, which was in no way subordinate or subservient to the *Khalifa.*

The *Shoora,* it appears, could initiate proceedings for the impeachment of the *Khalifa.* S. Khuda Buksh, however, in his book 'The *Orient under the Khalifas"* (p. 268) says that "for deposing a Sovereign the people generally met in the chief mosque. Some men of position addressed the assembly when charges were formulated and made against the ruling *Khalifa* and his deposition was declared in the interest of Islam. "History does not record any account of the deposition of any *Khalifa* but the very fact that Muslim jurists unanimously accept that a *Khalifa* could be deposed again affirms the principle that the only and exclusive source of sovereignty and power in Islam was election by the assembled community".

All matters of administration had to be placed before the *Shoora* which decided by a majority of votes after full discussion. The voting was not on any party basis but each member tried to convince the others by his arguments supported by Quranic injunctions and *Hadith.* The endeavour was always to attain unanimity which was more often than not obtained because all acted with a sense of collective responsibility and with an open mind.

The *Shoora* was in effect also the legislature of Islam. No law could, of course, be made which was opposed to the Quran and the *Sunnah* or not in conformity with the principles that could be deduced therefrom but even within this limit no law-making was possible unless approved by the *Shoora* in coming to a decision the *Shoora* followed the democratic method of majority voting which was based on two *Ahadith* to the following effect: "It is incumbent on you to follow the most numerous body"; and "My followers will never agree upon what is not right". This is the principle that later developed into the doctrine of Ijma a which is now unanimously accepted as one of the source of Islamic law.

Originally, it was in fact a referendum of the entire Muslim polity; subsequently it came to be confined to the concensus of the juris-consults or *'Faqihs'* after the end of the republican era on the pretext that since the limits of the state had spread far and wide the referendum of the entire polity had become an impossibility. The learned jurists claimed to act as the representatives of the Muslim world.

Maulana Shibli Nomani maintains that under the *Majlis-i-Shoora* there was another body which discussed problems of day-to-day administration while the Shoora deliberated upon policy matters or rather dictated the policy of the *Khalifa.* Be that as it may, the importance attached to it was so great that Hadrat Umar used to say that "the institution of the *Khilafat* is void without the deliberative council (the *Shoora)*".

The third important change introduced was the complete separation of the judiciary by Hadrat Umar. Having regard to the importance Islam attached to the principle of equality before law and its insistence on absolute fairness in the administration of justice this separation of powers was considered essential. He felt this to be necessary from the very nature of things so that power should be a check to power and all power should not be concentrated in one hand. Thus, it was not Montesqueu or Hallam who conceived of the doctrine of separation of powers and the theory of checks and balances in the distribution of the powers of the state considered so necessary by present day political theorists.

In addition to the above, Hadrat Umar also set up the institution of jurisconsults called *Ifta* to advise the executive and assist the judges as well as the lay public. This body consisted of capable and trustworthy scholars of law *(Muftis)* who could give legal opinions *(Fatwas)*. They were not only legal advisors of the state but also a body which gave legal aid to the lay public on the salutary principle that no one should suffer due to ignorance of law. This principle has only in the twentieth century been recognised in the Western World.

Under the *Umayyads* the *Muftis* were permitted to charge a fee for the services rendered by them. They were also permitted to represent lay clients before the judges by filing a *Tawkel Nama* and from this developed the institution of *vakils* or advocates.

Under the Ottoman Sultans the *Ifta* became a department of state with the *Mufti-e-Azam* as its head. Some idea of the importance of this official can be gathered from the fact that during the days of the Crusades, Sultan Salahuddin Ayubi sought a *Fatwa* from him permitting the killing of a non-Muslim wherever found but the *Mufti-i-Azam* refused to issue such a *Fatwa* as it was opposed to the injunctions of the Quran to the following effect:

> "And fight in the way of Allah against those who fight against you but begin no hostilities. Surely Allah loves not aggressors" (11-91).

> "So if they keep aloof and fight you not, and make you an offer of peace, then Allah has allowed you no way of aggression against them" (IV: 91).

Hadrat Umar also divided the administrative functions of the state into the following departments, each under a Companion of the Holy Prophet (peace be upon him) whose position could be likened to that of a Minister of State under the American system:

(i) *Bait-ul-Mal* or Treasury;

(ii) *Mahasil* or Board of Taxes and Revenue;

(iii) *Jund* or Military Department;

(iv) Educational and Religious Instructions Department;

(v) *Darul-Qada* or Judicial Department;

(vi) *Ahdas* or Police Department;

(vii) *Mazalim* or the Board of Inspection; and

(viii) *Ihtisab* or the Department of Public Censor.

The state, as already mentioned, was divided into Provinces, each headed by a Governor and a *Qadi.* The administrative set-up in the Provinces followed the same republican pattern as in the Centre and enjoyed a considerable amount of autonomy subject to the superintendence of the Centre. Hadrat Umar even gave to the Provinces the power to elect their own governors subject to confirmation by the *Khalifa.*

The sources of revenue at that time were (i) *Zakat,* (ii) *Ganimat,* (iii) *Jizya* – payable by non-Muslims, (iv) *Khiraj* – share of produce of land left with non-Muslims in conquered territories, (v) *Fey* – income of state lands and (iv) *Sadaqat* – contributions in times of need. To these Hadrat Umar added (vii) *Ushr* or *Zakat* out of agricultural produce payable by Muslims. In addition to the above, there was a levy called *jul* or compensation for not being able to participate in *Jihad.* It was the duty of every Muslim to provide his own equipment and weapons when taking part in *Jihad* and as such if he was unable to do so and had the means to provide the same he had to pay for equipping a substitute.

Lastly, to overcome the difficulty felt for meeting new situations arising out of growing problems now covered by Quranic injunctions or *Hadith.* Hadrat Umar developed the practice of *Ijtihad* or analogical deduction. This became necessary due to the extremely limited legislative powers of the Islamic State. Like *Ijma* the doctrine of *Ijtihad* is also based on Quranic texts and traditions of the Holy Prophet (peace be upon him) particularly, the one who to his conversation with Muaz bin Jabal approving of the latter's proposal to decide cases on the basis of *Qiyas* where neither the Quran nor the *Hadith* provided any direct solution. This *Hadith* is reported both in Abu Daud and Tirmidhi. It is on this basis that Hadrat Umar introduced the institution of imprisonment and transportation, banned the sale of a slave girl who had given birth to a child from her master, suspended the *Hadd* punishment for theft in times of scarcity of food, stopped the practice of distribution of lands of non-Muslims in conquered territories, and granted maintenance allowance to an irrevocably divorced woman.

This is comparable to the modern judge-made law. The judges never claim to make law but only to interpret it, yet that interpretation sometimes alters the law itself. The same principle is followed in *Ijtihad* but its importance cannot be minimised if the Islamic law is not to become static. Instances are not wanting of attempts to creatively interpret the Quranic teachings and the *Sunnah* of the Holy Prophet (peace be upon him) to meet the new impacts on the growing Muslim society. But, unfortunately, the introduction of the condition by the *Faqihs* of later periods that *Ijtihad* was only permissible by *Mujtahids* possessing special qualifications led to the misconception that the doors of *Ijtihad* had been closed. Be that as it may, the fact remains that it has not been restored to for more than 700 years now. This is what led Allama Iqbal to lament that the decadence of Islam was largely due to the discontinuance of the practice of *Ijtihad,* which seems to have dulled the capacity of original thinking among the Muslims.

Notwithstanding the separation of the judiciary, the distribution of executive power and the grant of a measure of autonomy to the Provinces, the *Khalifa* retained in his hand the power of superintendence and revision of the work of all authorities through the *Mazalim* jurisdiction. At first during the *Hajj* gathering which was attended by all functionaries, anyone could complain before the *Khalifa* against any authority and the complaint was immediately dealt with in the presence of the person concerned; later such a complaint could be filed at any time. This was a very important jurisdiction which made accountability really effective so far as officials of the state were concerned. This can well be compared to the Writ Jurisdiction of the present times except that it was wider and free from the restrictions with which the modern system is circumscribed.

Under the Islamic system, even the *Khalifa* was responsible to each and every citizen no matter where located and held, himself also equally accountable and open to correction. Two every interesting stories about the first two *Khalifas,* credited to be authentically reported, may give some idea of how these two treated their responsibilities. The first is about a blind widow who had no one to look after her. Seeing her plight, Hadrat Umar thought of helping her by doing her household chores but when he got there the next morning he found her place tidy and done up. The same thing happened the next day and the day after. So he sat watching throughout the next night to find who the mysterious helper was. At break of dawn he saw a person enter the widow's house and clean it up. He waited outside for the person to come out and lo! who should he find coming out? None other than Hadrat Abu Bakr the *Khalifa* himself. On another occasion Hadrat Umar coming to know that a man was dying in one of the bye-lanes of Medina rushed there to find a crowd already collected and an old woman roundly abusing the Khalifa. Finding that he had not been recognised, he tried to plead for the *Khalifa* (himself) and to point out how difficult it was for the *Khalifa,* who was but an individual, to keep information about everyone. The woman replied that if he could not do so, then he should not have become the *Khalifa.* Hadrat Umar admitted his lapse and ordered the man to be removed to the mosque for proper treatment.

Remarkable indeed is the relationship between the nation and the *Khalifa.* The latter never considered himself to be the master but always the servant of everyone in the state and carried on the governance under what Al-Mawardi calls a Bilateral Contract and Rousseau, the modern propounder of the constitutional theory of the state, Contract Social. It will be worth reproducing here the words of the Khutba given by the first *Khalifa* immediately after his election. He declared:

> "O people, I swear by Allah that I never coveted the office either by day or night nor had I any inclination towards it. I never prayed to God openly or in secrecy to confer the same on me. But I certainly feared that some mischief might arise. In fact, a tremendous amount of work has been assigned to me which is beyond my power to fulfil except with the help and guidance of Almighty Allah. I wished to see the strongest of men in my place. Now, it is beyond doubt that I have been elected your *Amir,* although I am not better than you. Help me if I am right. Set me right if I am in the wrong. Truth is a trust, falsehood a treason. The weak among you shall be strong with me till his rights have been vindicated and the strong among you shall be weak with me till, if God will, I have taken what is due from him. Obey me as long as I obey Allah and his Prophet. When I disobey Him and His Prophet then obey me not."

This is the social contract par excellence to which, authorities maintain, no parallel can be found in the history of the world. It defines the relationship between the *Khalifa* and the people who elect him, lays down the limits of his authority, and gives the people the right to remove him if he departs from the right path. Every subsequent *Khalifa* adopted the same formula in his first *Khutba* after election. Even after the end of the republican period of Islam the formula was adhered to, because it was in accord with the essence of the nature of an Islamic State which in theory never changed.

The concept of Islamic State, as discussed above, reveals that most of the modern theories of constitutional government—like social contract, separation of powers, checks and balances, rule of law, natural justice, equality before law, government as a trust, sovereignty of the people next to God, and welfare of the people—were known to Muslims from the earliest times. It is, therefore, considered that there can be no great difficulty in setting up an Islamic State within the framework of a modern democracy based on political theories of the present-day statecraft. But the difficulties that arise are with regard to the institutions similar to those set up by the Holy Prophet (peace be upon him) and the *Khulafa-i-Rashidin*. Let us now consider how, in what manner and to what extent those institutions can be reconstituted in the present day conditions.

The political theorists will pose the question: Can they be re-introduced in the present changed conditions? Take, for instance, the institution of the *Khilafat*. The unity of the state and the *Ummat* has now, of course, disappeared along with the concept of the *Khilafat* and the Universal State. The Muslim world is now divided into several independent states each claiming separate identity. This happened several hundred years ago when at one and the same time there were three Muslim *Khalifas* in three different regions and each was equally great. During the time of the *Abbasids* there were actually three *Khilafats*, one in Asia *(Abbasid)*, another in Africa *(Fatimidi)* and a third in Europe *(Umayyads* in Spain). Thereafter, the Ottomans, after the conquest of Egypt, obtained the surrender of the *Khilafat* in their favour from the Fatimidi Khalifa Salim and retained it till it was abolished by the Turks after the First World War. Even during this later period, other independent Muslim States existed in the subcontinent, Malaya and Indonesia. The idea of a Universal *Khilafat* having eased to be operative and found unworkable as a living factor in the organisation of modern Islam. Allama Iqbal thought that "for the present every Muslim nation must sink into her own deeper self, temporarily focus her vision on herself alone, until all are strong and powerful to form a living family of republics (Lectures *on Reconstruction of Religious Thoughts in Islam,* p. 159).

If the republican form of government is not inconsistent with the spirit of Islam and the *Khilafat* forms the Islamic system of government, then is it not possible to institutionalise the *Khilafat* by vesting it in a body of persons or even an elected body? This was the view of the Turkish Grand National Assembly after the deposition of Sultan Abdul Hamid, the last *Khalifa.* The Turks argued that after the Holy Prophet (peace be upon him), who was the last Prophet, the concept of *Niabat-e-llahi* had ceased to be operative and, therefore, keeping the *Khilafat* indivisible thereafter was purely a matter of expediency. It worked as long as the Empire of Islam was intact, but after the break-up of the Empire its utility had not only disappeared but it had in fact become a hindrance in the way of reunification of independent Muslim States.

The fallacy in this reasoning lay in equating the *Khilafat* with *Niabat-i-llahi.* The *Khalifas* themselves never claimed this right; they only claimed to act as *Khalifa-i-Rasool.* Indeed, Hadrat Umar considered it presumptuous to even assume this title. He, therefore, introduced the title of *Amir-ul-Momineen* and this was the title adopted by subsequent *Khalifas* right up to the time when the Ottomans adopted the title of *Sultan* and considered themselves to be the Shadow of God on Earth—*Zill-e-llahi*—a concept totally opposed to the spirit of Islam.

Notwithstanding the innovations it seems that if we return to the pristine form of Islamic republicanism and institutionalise the concept of Universal *Khilafat* there can be no serious objection, Allama Iqbal also took such a view when he said:

> "It seems to me that God is slowly bringing home to us the truth that Islam is neither nationalism nor imperialism but a league of nations which recognises artificial boundaries and social distinctions for facility of reference only and not for restricting the social horizon of its members". (*Lectures* on the *Reconstruction of Religious Thoughts,* p. 159).

However, even if it is not possible to have a Universal *Khilafat* or to vest the *Khilafat* in a Council of an Islamic League of Nations, there can be no serious objection to the head of each independent Muslim State being vested with the attributes of *a Khalifa* provided he fulfils the qualifications required for the post. The important thing is not whether we call the head of a modern Islamic State a *Khalifa* or not but whether he can act like Abu Bakr or Umar.

So far as his election is concerned, the Islamic polity can well adopt the procedure laid down by Hadrat Umar, namely, initial selection or nomination, if the legislators wish to use the modern terminology, by an electoral college or council or regency consisting of highly qualified persons, to be followed by a general election. The qualifications can be prescribed by the Constitution to ensure that only capable persons are elected and the Electoral College itself should consist of both elected and ex-officio members so that all shades of public opinion are represented and, in order to be successfully nominated, the candidate should obtain a majority of votes from each section, namely, elected and ex-officio members.

Let us now discuss the legislature. *Majlis-i-Shoora* can easily be expanded and adopted to become a modern legislature. Of course, it will have no power to legislate in a field or in respect of a subject already occupied by or provided for in the Quran and Sunnah, but it should be capable of exercising the powers of *Ijma's* and *Ijtihad*. It is, therefore, necessary that they should also be persons possessing special qualifications needed for this task and these should also be carefully laid down in the Constitution. Once elected, they should function as independent members and not be tied to any political party or its programme. They should vote on the questions laid before them on the basis of their own honest conviction. No other consideration ought to be allowed to prevail.

The *Shoora* once elected should not be at the mercy of either the Head of the State or the Prime Minister. Once elected, its members should hold office for their full term unless earlier impeached by the *Shoora* by a special majority. The Council of Ministers should be appointed by the Head of the State and be removable by him. They should be members of the *Shoora* but should be appointed purely on the basis of merit. The Head of the State himself should also be removable by impeachment by the *Shoora* and that too only if a special majority of votes is cast in favour of such impeachment. Alternatively, impeachment should be by a vote of censure passed at a joint sitting of the Electoral college and the *Shoora* by a special majority of both.

It will, thus, be observed that there is no scope for the Anglo-Saxon type of democracy or the parliamentary form of government in the Islamic system. The presidential system appears to be more akin to it. For the successful operation of the parliamentary system it is necessary that there should be only two major political parties opposing each other. Whenever this is not so and there are a number of small parties in the field, the parliamentary system has not worked satisfactorily. Even in the United Kingdom, with the emergence of the Liberal

Party as the one which can effectively tilt the balance, the British are themselves having a second look at their system. Indeed if we look around we shall find that the parliamentary system has not proved successful in any Muslim country, the main reason being that it is entirely foreign to our concepts.

So far as the judiciary is concerned, there is no difficulty at all in adopting the Islamic pattern because the concept of an independent judiciary, even though appointed by the executive, is our special contribution to the world. It has in fact been prevailing from the very infancy of Islamic State. Our system of administration of justice is far superior to that of any other system. Delay and dilatoriness in the process of administration of justice now prevailing are due largely to the importation of British concepts into it which have resulted in encouraging the giving of false evidence and the adoption of dilatory tactics in litigation. These should be removed and the power should be given, at least to the superior courts to strike down laws repugnant to the Quran and the *Sunnah.* Muslims have from the earliest of times established very high traditions of complete impartiality and equality in the administration of justice and there is no doubt that given the proper facilities the judges in the present-day Islamic State can acquit themselves equally well. It is, however, suggested that an *Ulama* Council should also be set up in modern times to bring back the old *Ifta* jurisdiction and to assist the judges in solving complicated questions of *Fiqah.* It should be obligatory for judges to consult them before striking down any existing law on the ground of repugnancy to the Quran and the *Sunnah.* The legislature should also have the right to consult them whenever any question arises regarding the validity of law proposed to be passed by it.

***Revisional Jurisdiction*** : The re-introduction of the revisional or correctional jurisdiction of the Head of the State on the pattern of the *Mazalim* jurisdiction on the executive side is also suggested. A Board or *Nazir-ul-Mazalim* can be set up to advice the Head of the State who should be the Chairman of this Board having a number of Ombudsmen under it. The Ombudsmen should act as courts of first instance from whose decisions there should be an appeal to the Board, whose decision should be final. It is only in this way that principle of accountability of the executive can be made meaningful and effective.

Some machinery like that of the *Muhtasib* should also be devised for enforcing religious duties and obligations and preventing encroachments on the rights of others, which come under the category of *Huquq-ul-lbad*. This will prevent unnecessary litigation by making the people respect each other's rights. Nothing has been said about sovereignty, because the concept of state in Islam is unique in this respect as the sovereignty over the universe vests in Allah Almighty.

To put it in a nutshell, what has been discussed above is a bare outline of the pattern that it may be possible to adopt in the light of modern conditions to bring the system of government into line, as far as practicable, with the essential characteristics of the Islamic pattern. It should be pointed out that unless we accept the unity of the *Ummat* as a cardinal principle of our faith, the super-imposition of a pattern based on this foundation will not be of much use. We must eschew the notions of nationalities within the nation and false concepts of the state as a federation of several nationalities. The Islamic State is a unitary state wherein brothers-in-faith reside and enjoy equal rights without any distinction of caste, colour, creed or race. In unity lies the strength of the Islamic State and in the pursuit of the welfare of the people its greatness. Its aim is to create dynamic social order based on the principle of justice cooperation, brotherhood and self-sacrifice for the welfare of all. In such a society there should be no scope for disharmony or discord and the changes of conflict would be reduced to the minimum, for if everyone behaves in this spirit no one should have any grievance against the other.

4

# *Charter for Governance*

A modern writer defines constitution as "codes which aspire to regulate the allocations of functions, powers and duties among the various agencies and offices of the government...." When we apply it, to a document which was signed within a few months of the Hijrah of the Prophet (PBUH), fourteen hundred years ago, we do not get the exact sense and meaning given to it by either the Prophet (PBUH) himself or those to whom the document was being given. He had called, the Document under study, as:

"A Writing from Muhammad, the Prophet of Allah."

It could also mean a letter and a document, the last being the most appropriate. This settles one thing. It was neither a 'treaty' nor an agreement; because it was "From Muhammad, the Prophet of Allah," and not an agreement between him and others. They had no objection in receiving it as a Charter laying down the Code of Life for Yathrib. They also accepted his position as "The Prophet of Allah," even though some of them desired to retain their attachment to the religion they already professed. They had, as a matter of fact, no option but to accept it or else live in Yathrib as aliens.

A few points need to be borne in mind while studying this Document. First, that the Document must be placed chronologically before any of the other objects is studied. This is necessary, because of two reasons. The first reason is that unless its period is determined it will not be possible to determine the object for which it was promulgated.

We have referred to the immediate object of this Document as the Defence of Yathrib in the last Chapter. The Document is of a permanent nature. There must, therefore, have been other reasons which are of a lasting nature. The Constitution, if we consider it as such, of the first Islamic State, brought into existence by the Prophet (PBUH) himself has to remain, in most respects, if not all, a model Constitution for all states established by Muslims. We, therefore, feel that it needs studying from a number of angles.

It is important to bear in mind that the Document was dictated by the Prophet of Allah (PBUH). He had been receiving Sublime Guidance, for thirteen years, from Allah. A person of his calibre would not issue a document of this nature without an adequate and a set purpose. Furthermore a person of his knowledge, experience and capabilities would not issue a self-contained document piece meal. If a document is issued by installments it loses consistency and results in being misunderstood. His actions subsequent to the issue of this Document have also great relevancy. They show, if he was in the habit of tackling problems in a consistent or a disjointed manner.

It must be kept in mind that he is The Law Giver and laws given by him have stood the test of time. Persons who create and promulgate laws have to consider problems from all angles, otherwise their laws fail to receive such reception as desired. There has to be logic and consistency in the words and actions of men placed in the position he occupied. Written documents become out of date if they are void of consistency. Lastly, it has to be borne in mind that this Document was issued under certain conditions. Therefore, to gauge its proper importance we. must bear in mind all the time, the circumstances which necessitated its issue. These have been discussed briefly.

We have referred to the Document as a Constitutional Charter.

"The form and nature of a constitution are dictated by the relationship prevailing among the various sections or classes of people." There was no organized group with whom the Prophet (PBUH) could have executed a treaty or an agreement. Hence we find that it was neither a treaty nor an agreement. It is important to bear in mind its heading, which also forms the very first Clause.

The heading needs to be given in full.

> "This Document (writing) is from Muhammad The Prophet of Allah (PBUH) to Quraysh and Yathribite Believers and those who will follow them and fight alongside with them. They will form ONE UMMAH to the exclusion of others."

Primarily the Document has been issued to administer the affairs of Muhajir and Ansar Believers. Its jurisdiction is then extended to those who live and fight Jihad under the leadership of these Muhajir and Ansar Believers. Leadership has been given to the entire Muslim community. The Prophet (PBUH) has not spoken of his leadership. This point has great significance for future generations of Believers.

**Perfect Statute**

The manner of promulgation of the Charter may also have a bearing on the circumstances at the time of its issue and the keenness of the recipients to be favoured by inclusion in the Ummah. From the wording and placing of concessions to various tribes, it creates the impression that the dictation of the Charter took place in an open Darbar, and as the Arab custom was and still is, those to whom a clause did not apply they spoke up to be included and at once another clause was dictated for inclusion.

The Document was issued within a few months of the Hijrah of the Prophet (PBUH) which took place in July or August 622 A.C. This is the period when, "a few years earlier, the reign of the grandson of Nousherwan was extended to the Hellespont and the Nile, the ancient limits of the Persian monarchy; the Christians of East were scandalized by the worship of fire and the impious doctrine of the two principles; the Magi were no less intolerant than the bishops, and the martyrdom of some native Persians, who had deserted the religion of Zoroaster was conceived to be the prelude of a fierce and general persecution. The oppressive laws of Justinian, the adversaries of the Church were made the enemies of the state; the alliance of the Jews, Nestorians and Jacobites, had contributed to the success of Chosroes, and his partial favour to the sectaries, provoked the hatred and fears of Catholic clergy."

The Persian monarch was so full of arrogance that, as his predecessors used to carry away the gods of the defeated, back to Persia, he carried away to his capital the Holy Cross from Jerusalem. The situation, however, altered, within a few years as predicted in the Quran. Byzantium, "rallied under Heraclius, who had led his troops in 624 A.C., into the heart of Iran. Chosroes was deposed and executed by his own subjects, and Heraclius recovered the Cross".

It meant a great deal for the prestige of the Emperor. To have brought back Holy Cross, the symbol of true Christianity, to Jerusalem, where the Jews were supposed to have been instrumental in having Jesus Christ crucified, was a great achievement. Syria, at that time was a truly Christian land. "In fact this is the only period in which Syria has been a fully

Christian country..... Not only was the country Christian, but the age was an ecclesiastical age".

It was in this age of persecution, religious prejudices, taboos, ethnical differences, and acute hatred resulting in mass killings, when this Document was dictated to an assembly of Believers, Mushrikeen and Jews, not far from a totally Christian land, where at about the same time controversies raged, which ended in a, "sentence of excommunication on the tomb of St. Peter; the ink was mingled with the sacramental wine, the blood of Christ; and no ceremony was omitted that could fill the superstitious mind with horror and affright".

It was the same period, when in India, Harsha ruled and according to a Chinese pilgrim, "The penalty of imprisonment, inflicted after the cruel Tibetan fashion, which left the prisoner to live or die was freely awarded and mutilation was often adjudged".

In spite of it all we are told that in every one of these lands their particular civilization was at its peak and yet man was in bondage and writhed with pain at the feet of other men. Man had forgotten that he and other men were all descended from Adam and Adam had been created from clay:

"He it is Who hath created you from clay".

6: 2

How unnatural that men should be regarded as unequal and yet inhabit the same planet. Many prophets had come and tried to teach men and women that they were equal as human beings, but it was left to the Last Prophet of Allah to establish complete equality in those who believed in Allah and him as His Messenger and Servant.

While he was dictating this Document of great consequence he was observing the principle of equality. It would take centuries for mankind to realise the effect and importance of this principle.

## Lord's Supremacy

The ultimate destination of mankind, while on this planet is the mastery of elements of nature. He has to achieve vast knowledge of nature of things and elements to an extent that very few can imagine. Acquisition of knowledge at the level of entire humanity demands peace, justice and equality among mankind. This will come about when mankind rises above the level of present ignorance and becomes one Ummah. This is the most important lesson taught by the Last Prophet of Allah, while dictating this unique Document. Universal peace will be achieved when the principle of equality of man is universally accepted. The Prophet (PBUH) when dictating this Document brought the level of all men on an equal pedestal. Jews who, at the time, were looked down upon, except may be in Iran were given equality with Arabs of Quraysh and Ansar origin. Equality of man appears to be one of the main features of his Mission, and, "It is difficult to portray the events of the life of the Prophet (PBUH) unless we first understand the nature of the Mission entrusted to him"."

This Mission, according to the Quran is complete guidance of mankind in all walks of life. Man has to enter Islam completely.

> "O ye who believe! Come, all of you, into submission".
> 2: 208

And the Prophet has to bring mankind into Islam-submission to the Will of Allah.

> "(This is) a Scripture which We have revealed unto thee (Muhammad) that thereby, thou mayst bring forth mankind from darkness unto light, by the permission of their Lord, unto the Path of the Mighty, the Owner of Praise". 14: 1

The Eternal Message of Allah happens to be placed in a world which, in certain respects, alters with changes in time and geography. And yet this Eternal Message guides men to the straight path. "The glory of Islam is that it distinguishes the universal from the changing particulars".

If we study the Quran and try to locate Eternal Commandments we will find that these happen to be all in respect of those aspects of human life and nature, which remain constant and are not subject to any great changes as a result of time and place. Those aspects of life whether at the level of an individual or at the collective level of society, which are subject to changes due to change in surroundings, have been left to the individual or the society, as the case may be, to find the best solution as long as no other Commandment is violated in the process. This means that no restrictions have been placed on "the changing particulars."

It is the same with the Sunnah of the Prophet (PBUH). He has set precedents in all walks of life but restrictions are placed only in the field of universals and particulars are left to be decided by the individual and the society, as the case may be. He was the Messenger of the Code of Life Revealed by Allah. He was not sent as a military commander and yet he demonstrated the "why, when and how" of war, because the Ummah needed guidance in it. He was not a statesman and yet he demonstrated how justice tempered with mercy was to be administered in a society of equals. He led his army to many a battlefield, keeping in view the principles of war and compulsions of strategy and tactics dictated by geography and other factors and demonstrated all the qualities of a great commander.

His critics fail to keep his Mission in view when commenting on his activities as a soldier or as a statesman because their view of a Way of Life is limited to acts of prayers only. To say that, "Muhammad (PBUH) himself was not a warrior and had few military gifts. In battle he invariably followed behind the front line, never, if avoidable, himself engaged in hand to hand fighting", amounts to disregarding his role as a guide of commanders. The writer forgets that commanders do not engage, normally, in hand to hand fighting. They have to direct, control and deploy troops as the situation may demand.

This vague statement of a British general does not mention those qualities of martial nature which in his opinion were absent in the Prophet (PBUH). He would have probably liked to see in him qualities displayed by British generals like Kitchner, who, "sword in hand and Bible in pocket he enjoyed a career of spectacular warfare in Russia, China, India, and Africa...." Kitchner's enjoyment of war amounted to perversity, when he had defeated Mehdi's Army he arranged a victory parade, on 10th of April 1898, in which, he treated the captured enemy commander Amir Mahmud in the most cruel manner. "Dragging chains which were riveted round his ankles, and wearing a halter round his neck the defeated army commander was made to walk, and sometimes run, behind the cavalry. His hands were bound behind his back, and he was driven forward by Sudanese guards who lashed him with whips when he stumbled. Kitchner rode on a white horse in triumph". What a spectacle of British chivalry and martial excellence during the closing years of nineteenth century when European civilization was at its height.

This British general of whom many generations spoke with admiration, gave orders, that the tomb of Mehdi be razed to the ground and his bones to be cast into the Nile. Mehdi's skull which was unusually large was kept aside to be used as inkstand. One suggestion was to use it as a drinking cup. He had ordered Wingate, another famous British soldier, to "loot like blazes. I want any quantity of marble stairs, marble payings, iron railings, looking glasses and fittings, doors, windows, furniture of all sorts". A victorious general who pardoned his life-long enemies must have appeared to General Glubb, to lack martial qualities common among European generals and conquerors. The objective of the Prophet (PBUH) was to establish peace as a precedent for Believers until the end of Time. He had to demonstrate what was an ideal life. This included both war and peace. It included the life of a labourer and also that of a ruler. He demonstrated the life of a man of all walks of life, when he was being persecuted and we find no change in the way he lived, when he was the ruler of entire Arabia and his army had a successful round of exchange of arms with the Byzantian Imperial Army, at the battlefield of Mowta. As a general his strategy was not only to win the war but to succeed in the days after the war as well, and his war stands alone in the annals of military history, which brought happier days both for the winner and the vanquished although a winner in earlier battles he had accepted armistice on the enemy's terms.

It has been recorded by his biographer "When there was peace and war was abolished and men met in safety and consulted together none talked intelligently about Islam without entering it. In these two years double as many or more than double as many entered Islam as before".

Throughout his life he was keen to use all his resources to bring about peaceful atmosphere in which his Message could be understood and accepted. Today, fourteen centuries after him, the world has accepted the point of view that peace alone can solve mankind's problems. A modern writer has said, "In an age of Total War we will need Total Peace". War, however, has to be catered for." Wars do not break out of themselves, but they may change the course of history and the fate of mankind.... War has, therefore, become the greatest of social problems". For him and for Islam war had become the greatest of not only social but also political problem. He gave to the world, Islam—The Message of Peace-when war had been brought to his doorstep. This Document is of great consequence as it gives an answer to a multi-national Ummah, as to how they should face an aggressor and survive. One of the outstanding features of this Document, which cemented the citizens of Yathrib was justice with Equality for all. Peace within communities and, at international level, cannot be established without equality and equal status to men and groups of men—the nations. This equality was not acceptable either within Arabia or at the international level at that time. The Arabs of Mecca, steeped in the idea of racial superiority, their minds clouded with racial prejudices, and having a class ridden society, were in no mood to accept equality between Abu Jehl, the high born Quraishi chief and Bilal the Negro slave.

### No Discrimination

It was the principle of equality of man which evoked the animosity of the two neighbouring mighty empires of Iran and Byzantine, towards Islam and Muslims. The ruling classes of both these empires were securely entrenched as the high born elites, who held the birth right of princely and regal positions. The birth of an Ideology of "Equality before the Eyes of Allah," both in this and the next world, was a revolutionary reality which had to be nipped in the bud. The rest of the world was to array itself on the side of these to Empires, one after the other. The prophesy of Abbas bin Ubada was fulfilled soon enough but it was to continue being fulfilled for ever.

It was during the Second Bayah at al-Aqaba that Abbas bin Ubada al-Ansari, said to the Ansars who were swearing allegiance to the Prophet (PBUH), "O men of Khazraj, do you realise to what you are committing yourselves in pledging your support to this man? It is to war against all and sundry. If you think that if you lose your property and your nobles are killed you will give him up, then do so now, for it would bring you shame in this world and the next. But if you think that you will be loyal to your undertaking even if you lose your property and your nobles are killed, then take him for by God. It will profit you in this world and the next".

The men from Khazraj and many others who followed their footsteps are still being challenged by the enemies of Justice and equality for all. It is, outwardly, that people oppose Islam, while their real opposition is against the principle of equality of man, by those whose vested interest are in danger or being jeopardised. It was a question of life and death in that age. Religion during that age made men of religion oblivious of cruelties perpetuated in the name of religion. Minor differences or even suspicion of minor differences led men to throw others into flames. As has been remarked, "It remained for the Medieval Church, however, to put cruelty and burning and gruesome public executions on the firm popular basis of exalting religious spectacles".

There can be no peace in the world unless the world led by Muslims observes laws relating to Jihad on the Path of Allah and in conducting their foreign affairs as ordained in the Quran. This Document was the first writing, directing towards the principles and the policy according to which human societies should conduct their affairs. It has been universally accepted that in the world of today there is no international law, relating to the conduct of states in matters of conflict or mutual interest, obligations and the making and breaking of treaties. There have been usages in various parts of the world, which have been overlooked more often than not and in all conflicts national interests have prevailed. "International Law, so called, is in reality national law regulating international relations of those states".

***Prefect Document*** : Islam has a complete Code of International Law. It, however, operates at the level of the Millah of Islam, on the principle that Believers are an Ummah when considered with respect to the rest of humanity. If Muslim States observe in their inter-state relations, the Commandments of the Quran, the super powers will find it difficult to drive humanity in World Wars, as they have done twice during twentieth century. These Quranic Injunctions dictate relations between Muslim states and also between Muslim states and others. Islamic Law is the only Law which forbids states to undertake aggression of any kind; not even for the spread of religion.

This Document, apart from being the Constitutional Charter of the state of Yathrib was at the same time the document on the authority of which this state had come into existence. The person proclaiming the coming into being of this new state was Prophet Muhammad (PBUH), the last of the line of prophets, who had received Revealed Word of Allah. As a result of the contents of this Document, the state of Yathrib received all those elements which add up to the formation of a state. "A state exists as soon as the four formal elements (a people, a territory, a government and the characteristics of sovereignty) can be found in it and that recognition by other states merely recognizes the social fact", and non-recognition does not alter its status. The newly created state of Yathrib was, however, recognized soon after its establishment.

The Prophet (PBUH), immediately after the promulgation of this Document went out of Yathrib, stayed with various tribes, each of which held sovereign status within its tribal territory, and executed friendly treaties with them. Apart from establishing treaty relations with neighbouring tribes, these journeys of the Prophet (PBUH) fixed approximate limits of the territory of Yathrib. The boundaries of an Islamic State, cannot be a permanent feature. Islam cannot have and does not have fixed boundaries. Islam attracts people because of principles of justice and equality. It spreads and with its spreading are extended its boundaries. Islam has not remained static even during its days of political eclipse. The spread of Islam in Africa has been when a greater part of Africa had been occupied by European Colonial powers.

In Malay Archipellago Islam was spread by Muslim merchants at a time, when Spain held sway over the area. "They did not come as conquerors, like the Spanish in the sixteenth century, or used the sword as an instrument of conversion; nor did they arrogate to themselves the privileges of a superior and dominant race so as to degrade and oppress the original inhabitants".

It is said of Al-Mamun that when a certain Yazdan bakht a leader of the Manichaean sect came on a visit to Baghdad and held a disputation with the Muslim theologians, in which he was utterly silenced, the caliph tried to induce him to embrace Islam. But Yazdanbakht refused saying, "commander of the faithful, your advice is heard and your words have been listened to: but you are one of those who do not force people to abandon their religion".

It was the same in Eastern Europe where, "The Calvinists of Hungary and Transylvania, and the Unitarians of the latter country, long preferred to submit to the Turks rather than fall into the hands of the fanatical house of Hapsburg; and the Protestants of Silesia looked with longing eyes towards Turkey...." The writer speaks in the same vein of other countries and other lands. "Even in Italy there were men who turned longing eyes towards the Turks in the hope that as their subjects they might enjoy the freedom and the toleration they despaired of enjoying under a Christian government".

As said earlier, this toleration of Muslims, in all the then known lands of the Globe, was the result of magnanimity shown by the Prophet of Islam (PBUH) when dictating this Document in Yathrib, at the time, when the first state of Yathrib was coming into existence. The Muslims have honoured the spirit of this Document throughout these fourteen centuries, which is not a mean achievement. In spite of it, and may be because of it and the resulting popularity of Islam, it "inspires perfidy of the Balkans, the hate of the Jews, the apprehension of the Hindus and the animosity of the Russians".[1] The remarks of Abbas bin Ubada Ansari have been referred to above. His prediction continues to come true and may continue much longer. The basic reason for this opposition is the fear of loss of vested interests of the ruling classes and the religious hierarchy, of many faiths which upholds these classes and are a hindrance towards universal equality of man and the resultant justice and fairplay for the masses.

The tenacity with which Muslims have held on to the principle of equality is due to the fact that, they believe staunchly in the Sovereignty of Allah, which is the core and basis of all Islamic teachings. Islam stands for the Sovereignty of Allah alone and of none else. This, in practice, means that the Eternal Laws enjoined by Allah cannot be altered. If this principle was accepted by the ruling classes they would, after that, not be able to frame laws as and when it suited their vested interests. They desire to keep the framing of laws in their own hands and thus they and their institutions set aside for framing and promulgating laws retain Sovereignty in their own hands.

***People's Power :*** The law assures that Parliament is omnipotent and paramount. It can make or unmake laws on any matter whatsoever.... The power and jurisdiction of parliaments, says Sir Edward Coke, is so transcendent and absolute, that it cannot be confined, either for causes or persons, within any bounds.... It hath sovereign and uncontrollable authority in making, confirming, enlarging, restraining, abrogating, repealing, reviving and expounding of laws, concerning matters of all possible denominations, ecclesiastical or temporal, civil or military, maritime or criminal. This fact is contained in their Constitutions, whether written or based on practice, precedence and legal judgements.

Speaking of the Constitution of England (which included English possessions in Scotland, Ireland and Wales) Dicey, an eminent lawyer, has mentioned "three leading characteristics in the existing Constitution of England; they are now generally designated as the Sovereignty of Parliament, the rule of law and the convention of the constitution"." If a similar analysis was to be made of the Constitutional Charter of Medina, its leading characteristics, that would emerge would be firstly, the "Sovereignty of Allah and His Prophet" (PBUH), secondly, "The Rule of Law" and thirdly, "The Equality of Man." As composed to the Sovereignty of Parliament which means sovereignty of man made laws, and Convention of the Constitution, these characteristics certainly carry more weight. Mankind has, time and again, failed to convince itself that it can successfully conduct its affairs, without Guidance from Allah. Mankind, in nearly every land, "has been the victim of disastrous illusion—the illusion of our ability to emancipate ourselves from natural laws".

Whether we call them as Natural Laws, (Revealed to prophets of earlier eras) or openly admit that they are Laws given by Allah who alone is our Creator and Sustainer and Knows our needs far better than us, makes no difference. These are laws which are based on Truth from Him, who has set a destination for mankind which cannot be arrived at except by conducting ourselves in accordance with these Laws. Man has been given knowledge and intelligence, but both these qualities are limited as compared to the knowledge and Power of Allah. "It is evident that human intelligence has not increased simultaneously with the complexity of the problems involved." Today, as much as in the past, civilized humanity has shown itself incapable of directing either its individual or collective affairs. The modern world, like the Quraysh of Mecca, needs to be bold and pay homage, to the basic principle of the acceptance of the Sovereignty of Allah.

This Document, The Constitutional Charter of Medina, laid down, in no uncertain terms, that Allah alone wielded Supreme Power and that the method of invoking that power is Allah Himself and His Prophet (PBUH) is the interpreter of His Laws. This Document also lays down priorities to be adopted for the security and defence of states established by Muslims. The test of Constitutions whether they are capable of meeting the needs of their respective states has been suggested by a modern American writer as follows:

> "How effective is the constitution in enabling us to come to grips with periodic crises? What are the principal objectives of our national institutions? What service do they render? What are the rights and obligations of American citizenship"?

The Constitutional Charter of Medina, as a Document, is fourteen hundred years old. If modern constitutions are examined in the light of the above mentioned questionnaire it would clearly come out that human mind has not made any perceivable advance in this respect. The history of events in Medina, subsequent to the issue of this Constitutional Charter, has been recorded in greatest possible detail. We can, as a result of its perusal, say that the periodic crises that occurred, in Medina, after the promulgation of this Document, were conveniently solved through actions based on it.

There is no doubt about the fact that at the time of its promulgation, the entire population of Yathrib had rejoiced about it and had unanimously accepted to live under its protection and abide by its laws.

This Document, "brought into existence a voluntary association of all sections of Medinites-Muslims and non-Muslims, emigrants and locals, principals and clients,..." Aus and Khazraj, the two Arab tribes, were the only people who could claim that Yathrib belonged to them. They had been at war with one another but had settled their differences, lately. An agreement had been reached tentatively that in order to give the place semblance of an organized community they should choose a king. Abdullah bin Ubay the leader of Khazraj was being talked of as the future king of Yathrib when Bait-e-Aqba Thani took place. Soon after this, Muhajirs started arriving in Yathrib. They and the Ansars were a far more organized group, than any tribe could be, and Abdullah bin Ubay's crowning ceremony was soon forgotten.

There were Jews also in Yathrib. They were all engaged in trade and commerce and being rich had built themselves strong forts outside the main city of Yathrib. The Jews, however, did not either own or belong to the place. A number of theories have been advanced, but the most plausible theory is that they were immigrants from Syria as a result of one of purges that used to be carried out from time to time, to rid the Holy Land, of them. They were living under the protection of various sub-tribes of Aus and Khazraj. They did not possess any right other than what the Haleef-protecting tribe-cared to allow them.

This Document had completely altered their social and political status. They were being raised to the status of citizens of Yathrib like any other person from amongst the tribes of Aus and Khazraj. This was a great elevation in their status. They were no more aliens or emancipated slaves. They would, henceforth be able to speak up to the Arabs as equals and the word Jew would soon loose the sense of inferiority which it had, hitherto, carried all the world over.

The Prophet (PBUH) was allowing them a further concession, which would soon make them a political force to be reckoned with. He was, on certain conditions, inviting them to become a part of the Ummah of Believers. This invitation happened to be under Divine Guidance and was, therefore, all the more attractive. Although this invitation was also given to the Christians but they were so few in Arabia that the Jews would have been certain to overshadow them always. This invitation, however, had one point which in the end was likely to be unacceptable to them. It was that they had first to accept the Sovereignty of Allah. The invitation being the result of an Ayah of Quran must have made them hesitate but they do not seem to have shown any such hesitation in the beginning. The Words of this Ayah of Quran, are:

> "Say, O People of the Scripture! Come to an agreement between us and you: that we shall worship none but Allah, and we shall ascribe no partner unto Him, and that none of us shall take others for lords besides Allah. And if they turn away, then say, Bear witness that we are those who have surrendered (unto Him)".
>
> 3: 64

The Prophet (PBUH) was trying to create a multi-national Ummah which was to form a coalition of all those who believed in Allah and thus were being asked to form a united front against the godless. He had advocated an idea, which the West have taken up lately but not with the intention of finding a united platform for all religions, but, to find out means of accelerating Christian Missionary activities in Africa and South East Asia. What would have been the shape of a society, in which, all those who believed in Allah, were to form one Ummah, and yet continue calling themselves by their old denominations, would be difficult to imagine.

Hijrah of the Prophet (PBUH) had brought about a fundamental change in the society of Yathrib. There were, in Yathrib, Mushrekeen, who were pagan Arabs and did not follow any set rules, which could fall under the heading of Laws of a Religion. There were, as mentioned earlier, Jews, who, at least in principle, followed the law of Moses (May Allah's Blessings be on him). Because of being the followers of a Revealed religion, they considered themselves as superior to the pagan Arabs, although they lived under their protection. There were some Arabs who had adopted the law of Moses but their position was strangely unidentifiable. They lived among their own families and observed Arab customary law but considered themselves as possessing a higher intellectual creed. If they were asked to choose one of the two camps, in case of a quarrel, they would have joined their particular tribe and not gone to the Jewish camp.

The arrival of the Prophet (PBUH) altered the social structure of Yathrib completely. In fact, it had started undergoing a change since the Bayate Aqba Thani. The Prophet (PBUH) had appointed twelve leaders from among the Medinites who had come to Mecca to embrace Islam. The Prophet (PBUH) had told the gathering, "Bring out to me twelve leaders that they may take charge of their people's affairs.' They produced nine from al-Khazraj and three from al-Aus". This was the beginning of Muslims bringing into existence an organized Islamic Society. "With the appointment of these twelve leaders an organized Islamic Society came into being". On their return to Yathrib, these twelve leaders conducted the affairs of Madinite Muslims, until the arrival of the Prophet (PBUH).

## Almighty's Rule

The Jews had not been able to set up any communal life with the few Arabs who had accepted the Shariah of Prophet Moses. The Prophet of Islam was inviting not only Arabs but Jews, Christians and all others to share with the Believers higher values of the activities of a community organized on the basis of Sovereignty of Allah and equality of man, His most Balanced creation. The result was that, even when the Believers were in a small minority, the social life of Yathrib, due to their presence, had started taking its direction from the Muslims and adopted Islamic values in an imperceptible way.

The Prophet (PBUH) and the small band of his Companions set the pace and texture of social life and thus became the centre of all communal activities. Whenever any issue demanded Allah's commandment for its settlement or the Prophet's own verdict in the matter, the Muslims did make all possible efforts to arrive at the authentic views of Islam on the basis of these two sources. The earlier Revelations of the Quran of Medina period are all relating to laws regarding various aspects of life. Many of them resulted from questions asked at these gatherings where the Prophet (PBUH) invited people to embrace Islam.

He is known to have gone to a Jewish school to preach Islam to them. If there passed a group of people, by the road, he would stop and join them to invite them to Islam, even though they disliked it.

A new social structure based on the Sovereignty of Allah and equality of man was taking shape. A new culture was emerging out of this social structure. Man was being given, for the first time in his cultural life, the proper place in the scheme of things, and man's mind was awakening to his place in this universe. One can find no better key to the internal logic of a society than its conception of man and his place in nature. This high position had been bestowed upon man by Allah Himself, in His Eternal Code of Life. The result was that the social and cultural trends of life in Yathrib, at a time when the Believers were in a small minority, took a turn towards adoption of Islamic values, and life became centralised around the personality of the Prophet (PBUH) and his Companions.

***The Significance :*** As mentioned earlier the Constitutional Charter of Medina has importance for more than one reason. It is the earliest written document of the Government and State of Medina. Later documents like the Peace Treaty of Hudaybiya, the Victory Proclamation of Khayber, and the Overlordship Gazette Notification of Aila granted to the Christian population of that place, were all of the nature of proclamation of cessation of hostilities due to one or the other reason. This Document stands in a different position. It established a state and a government in order to meet aggression. Invasion by Quraysh of Mecca had to be stopped. Defence of a society cannot be assured without first organizing that society. When a society is organized it takes the shape of a state. The state must have law and it must also lay down as to what was the source of law and who in future would be entitled to amend or add to this law. All these steps were being finalised through the Constitutional Charter of Medina. This process has been explained in modern terminology in the following words. "Peace among men and a civilized society, which are one and the same thing, are imaginable only within a legal order equipped with institutions to give effect to principles and norms in the form of law..." The Prophet (PBUH) was laying down that the final authority in Islam would be Allah, through revelations to him. Arabian society was losely governed by custom. There was no written law. Absence of law was a great hindrance to the establishment of a progressive and stable society. The Charter was removing this imbalance. "Whenever men group together and approve of a given standard morality, they must speak finally in terms of a law. Law permits morality to grow and as it grows the standard of law is elevated and morality is further advanced, for the two have reciprocal influence".

In this case, although hostilities had not started, war had been declared and arrangements had to be made to face the enemy. Allah had also Commanded.

> "O ye who believe! Take your precautions, then advance the proven ones, or advance or altogether".
>
> 4: 71

It is beyond doubt that the Document was promulgated to bring into existence the State of Medina so that it could be defended against the impending attack by the Quraysh of Mecca. Discussion leading to the declaration of its contents, if any, are conspicuously absent from both the Seerah and Hadith literature.

***No Flaws :*** Its authenticity is, however, above doubt of any kind. It cannot be a spurious document. Once Islam and the Muslims had emerged as victorious, not only within Arabia, but had also liquidated the two strongest empires of the then civilized world, there was no need for them to concoct a document of the early period when Muslims were very few and not very strong. In actual fact once they stepped out of Arabia, they paid no particular attention to it. It is genuine both from external evidence and from the inner evidence of its contents. The idea that it is the sum total of a number of agreements arrived at on a number of occasions is so illogical that it should be ignored completely. As is well known, the events which took place after the promulgation of the Charter, developed with such after, and in such an unforseen manner that a situation had arisen where there was no need of fresh terms being issued, or new agreements gone into with any party.

The idea that the document in its present shape is the result of numerous agreements is the result of the basic misconception, that it was an agreement. One may ask "agreement between whom, because the Document was being issued with the heading "From Muhammad, The Prophet of Allah." Its contents were Legal Orders and not paragraphs of an agreement. A charter from some one in power can be amended or additions made to it by the authority issuing the original charter. From Badr onwards the Prophet (PBUH) did not have to issue new instructions to any one in Yathrib. The Jews were getting weaker every day and signs of rebellion on their part had developed immediately after Badr. They had not "followed the Believers and not fought along with them." They had not, therefore, qualified for any of the concessions granted to them through the Charter.

If anything, any fresh document, would have curtailed concessions granted to them from the incidence of rebellious behaviour of the Jewish tribe, Banu Qainuqa, immediately after Badr, the Jews were not in a position to request for a reappraisal of their relations with the ruling party.

The arrival of ultimatum from the Quraysh of Mecca was a serious affair. They were a powerful tribe and had the influence which leaders of thought possess in a society. They exercised the sole authority of laying down the religious ceremonies and the Arab way of life. They held the monopoly of carrier trade between southern Arabia and the flourishing market of Middle

East, and were very rich as compared to the rest of Arabia. An attack by them, against Yathrib, would wipe out this small agricultural town of Najd. War in any case "is not a pass time. It is a serious means for a serious object".

The Meccan object was very serious. Muhammad (PBUH) had "mocked their Way of Life," and taken refuge in Yathrib to save their Way of Life they had to destroy him completely. They had awoken to the danger from the time of the second Bayah of Aqba. As already mentioned when some of the Companions started migrating to Yathrib they "assembled in their council chamber, the house of Qussay bin Kilab, where all their important business was conducted, to take counsel what they should do in regard to the Prophet (PBUH), for they were now in fear of him." It was suggested that "they should put him in irons behind bars." This was objected "on the ground that news would leak out that he was imprisoned, and immediately his followers would attack and snatch him away then their numbers would so grow that they would destroy the authority of the Quraysh altogther".

After some further discussion Abu Jehl came out with a new plan. This was "that each clan should provide a young, powerful, well born, aristocratic warrior; that each of these should be provided with a sharp sword; then that each of them should strike at him and kill him. The Banu Abde Manaf could not fight them all and would have to accept blood money which they would all contribute". Having failed to kill him they were not able to liquidate Islam in Mecca. They could not, however, let it prosper in Yathrib. They were afraid, as they said that "Their numbers would so grow that they would destroy the authority of Quraysh altogether". They decided not to permit their numbers to grow and decided to act quickly. They knew of the disappointment of Abdullah bin Ubay. His people had made a sort of jewelled diadem to crown him and make him their king, when Allah sent His Prophet (PBUH) to them; so when his people forsook him in favour of Islam he was filled with enmity realizing that the Prophet (PBUH) had deprived him of his kingship. However, when he realised, that his people were determined to go over to Islam, he went too, but unwillingly, retaining his enmity and dissimulating.

The Quraysh sent a letter to the people of Yathrib, but addressing it to Abdullah bin Ubay. The letter was, in fact, a declaration of war. It said, "you have given protection with you, to our men. You should kill these people or turn them out of Yathrib. We swear by Allah that if you do not do that, we will all attack you and having destroyed you, will capture your womenfolk". This was a very good excuse for him to use force and turn the Prophet (PBUH) and his Muhajir Companions from Yathrib. He was the head of a very powerful tribe, which appears to have been numerically stronger than others.

Its members were alive to the needs of religious revival. Out of twelve leaders chosen to look after the affairs of Muslims of Yathrib, nine belonged to his tribe. He decided to use force if the occasion demanded to kill the Prophet (PBUH) and the few Muhajir Companions.

The Prophet (PBUH) heard of his decision and went to him. Very little of the conversation between them is recorded. Abdullah bin Ubay was confronted with a new reality. Islam, although a religion of peace, denoted complete submission to the Will of Allah. It meant the acceptance of the Sovereignty of Allah which in practical life was demonstrated by obeying the Laws of Allah. This is what is meant by:

> "I created the Jinn and humankind only that they might worship me". 51: 56

And one of the Commands of Allah is that He has Ordained fighting for the Believers.

> "Warfare is ordained for you". 2: 216

The occasion for which this Commandment has been primarily Ordained is when some other group fights against you. It says:-

> "Fight in the Way of Allah against those who fight against you, but begin not hostilities". 2: 190

It has to be remembered that this Ummah is One:-

> "Verily this Ummah of yours is One Ummah".
> 23: 52

The Prophet (PBUH) brought home to Abdullah bin Ubay in these words:-

> Do you realise that if you use force the Muslims from Yathrib will fight alongside the Muhajir Muslims and you will be shedding blood of your tribe on both sides.

He realised the mistake he was making and decided not to use force against the Prophet (PBUH) and his Companions. His change of attitude was the result of his fear of being defeated at the hands of determined fighters. History is replete with instances, where people have had recourse to peace for fear of being hurt, in the end. The philosophy of Ahimsa—non-violence—is also the product of such logic, because the same people believe in Kali Devi, the goddess, who quenches her thurst from blood of gory murders. Peace accepted by him was of this kind. When we could not use force he resorted to mischief and remained a hypocrite and a tool of the Jews until his death.

History books are silent on further details of the conversations, that took place between the Prophet (PBUH) and Abdullah bin Ubay, it would be correct to assume that the latter must have asked the Prophet (PBUH) the way Yathrib was to be defended against the Mekkans. The details of the Charter lead us to the conclusion that the Prophet (PBUH) must have replied that the Muslims would defend Yathrib and if the others would like to share that responsibility the Believers would permit them to join in this great honour. It could also be said that, as a result of the urgent need to defend Yathrib, the Prophet (PBUH) formulated the plan of establishing the state of Yathrib, giving it a Constitution, and laying down the responsibility of defence on Believers. Abdullah bin Ubay could not help accepting this plan. The next event mentioned in history books is the Constitutional Charter itself.

The Charter was dictated under the shadow of an impending war of extreme intensity. Its defence paragraphs must belong to the same period. The concessions granted to the Jews are linked with defence paragraphs and must belong to the same period. The paragraphs covering general administration were also the demand of the time. There are no further events in the history of Yathrib, which could have resulted in the issue of further the documents. The division of the Document of Professor Sergeant in 'A, B, X, Y, etc, amounting to eight different documents can certainly be called a futile effort, made merely to create doubts and with no fruitful object.

The war that was visualised when dictating this Document lasted for nine years and had, before ending, embroiled the largest Empire of that period in it, thus initiaing the longest war of history— The war between the Crescent and Cross—which is raging even today, fourteen centuries after the Charter came into force, and is no-where near its end as yet. Islam until then had laid greater stress on the building of character of individuals. The Charter ushered in the collective life of the Ummah. The principle that Muslims formed a nation by themselves, even when they lived in surroundings, which were not purely Islamic and it was given prominence by the Charter. The contents of the Charter make it clear that even when living as a numerical minority. Believers take over the administration of the society on condition that the principle of the Sovereignty of Allah is being acted upon.

As mentioned earlier, as far as details are concerned, when dictating the Charter, greater emphasis has been paid to matters relating to the defence of the state, than to other matters. The Prophet (PBUH) as a result of the wisdom and insight granted to him by Allah, kept his mind centered on the period after the war when need would arise for rehabilitation of people. In the words of a modern military thinker, "The true national objective in war lies in the 'after war'. If the civilized world is to be saved from collapse, there is urgent need to produce true grand strategists to replace the blind exponents of mass destruction". He argues that "If you concentrate exclusively on victory, with no thought for the after effect, you may be too exhausted to be profited by the peace, while it is about certain that the peace will be a bad one, containing the germs of another war". The author is speaking from experience of two World Wars. Britain won both of them but lost the peace that followed.

The experience of modern world over the last two centuries has shown that the war to end war has yet to be fought, unless laws of war laid down by Allah are observed in total. The war that was initiated by the Quraysh of Mecca and won by the Prophet (PBUH) ended, as far Arabia was concerned, because the Prophet (PBUH) keeping the after-war period in view had done nothing, during and at the end of war, which could keep alive the hatred generated by war. Modern wars have tended to increase hatred to a point, when, a rapprochement becomes impossible. We need, therefore, to study his life, his teachings, his foreign policy and the manner in which he fought his war and then magnanimously pardoned his enemies. It will show a pattern of human behaviour unparalleled in the annals of human history.

The Prophet (PBUH) had accepted the responsibility of defending Yathrib against the threatened attack, when Yathrib had yet no state, no government and no army. He and his Companions were the total force available for this onerous task. There were no armaments, no provisions, no transport animals and no finances to provide all these instruments of war. He had, however, men, who were prepared to lay down their lives on the Path of Allah. He had trained them to such unchartered heights of Belief in Allah, that no weapon could force them to abandon their positions.

He also knew his enemies. They were resourceful. They were rich merchants and could furnish their army with the most sophisticated weapons. They also had the means to last them during a long drawn war. They had friends among Arab tribes.

They could, as a result widen the zone of war and have him surrounded and they had the means and facilities to make the blockade permanent, but his Belief in Allah outweighed those considerations. It is true that "once war begins, no one can tell how it will go. There are some who urge that we should abolish all armaments, and refuse to fight on any pretext. If this view is put forward on religious grounds, I will not deal with it beyond saying that it does not seem to me in accordance with the Bible... If on the other hand, its advocates believe that it would make for peace, it is inconsistent with recent events. China offered little or no resistance to Japan, yet that did not save her from the loss of territories as large as Europe, and the slaughter of some thousands other citizens".

The position of Believers, at the time of declaration of war by Mecca, was far more precarious than any community of peaceful and peace-loving people, who are threatened by a neighbour, who does not approve of their Ideology and their Way of Life. The enemy was the same, who had persecuted them in Mecca, ignoring relation of blood and friendship. A small number, a little over seventy had migrated to Habsha, and now less than fifty males had reached Yathrib and found a place, where they hoped to live according to Allah's given Way of Life, and they were being threatened with war and possible extermination. They had no alternative but to accept war. If they decided to avoid war, where could they go. They would have become stateless. The result would have been that the Islamic Society, which was visualised by the Prophet (PBUH) as a result of Revelations to him, from Allah, would not have been possible to be established. Allah's Promise was that they would be uppermost if they were Believers, was enough for them:-

> "It is a promise from Allah in truth; and who can be more truthful than Allah in utterance"? 4: 122

And:-

> "(It is) a Promise of Allah. Allah faileth not His Promise". 39: 20

And Allah has promised that:-

> "Faint not nor grieve, for ye will overcome them if ye are (indeed) believers". 3: 139

> "And verily Our word went forth of old unto Our bondmen sent (to warn) that they verily would be helped. And that Our host, they verily would be the victors". 37: 171-173

They were indeed Believers in its fullest meaning. No group of any Ummah of days gone by had reached heights of Belief in Allah which they had proved to have reached, and were yet to prove on many an occasion.

***Most Required :*** Documents of this nature are not issued in a vacuum. There is always a background and a pressing need for them. In fact, pressing necessity, for the execution and enforcement of such documents alone made them acceptable to people. Such documents, whether they are named as agreements, treaties, charters or constitutions, are promulgated because the very existence of those societies depends on bringing into existence means of laying down the pattern of communal life, and such documents provide and guarantee a disciplined life of the community. Apart from rights and duties of individuals and groups such documents lay down restrictions and penalties for the breach of rules of conduct, expected of those for whose guidance they are issued.

Preparations to meet the threat of war are taken in hand, when the danger is real and the entire society recognises it. War cannot be taken lightly because it "is a social phenomenon too complex to be governed by any simple formula". Except the Prophet (PBUH) himself no one was either qualified nor was there anybody who had the moral strength to accept the responsibility of making the decision to defend .Yathrib or when the decision had been taken to take defensive preparations in hand and then conduct the war.

To accept the duty of defending a state and its people is a decision of great moral character. An ill prepared nation is in serious danger of losing its war. To lose a war means to surrender the "right of freedom of thought" and to lose freedom of thought means to lose the right to live according to one's chosen Way of Life, which includes one's mode of worship. The Muslims could not afford to lose the war. They had chosen the Islamic Way of Life of their free will.

It was being challenged by the people, who had persecuted them for nearly thirteen years. They were determined that if they could not win the war they would fight to the last man. The battles fought by the Believers for the defence of Yathrib were all fought with the determination that they would fight until each one of them had achieved Shahadah. The Prophet (PBUH) had trained his Companions to wish for Shahadah and he was certain that they will come up to his expectations. His historic words, just before the attack of Meccan Army started at the battlefield of Badr are a testimony of the Believers having absorbed this philosophy. He had said:-

O Lord!
If this little band of Believers
Is wiped out today
There shall be none left
To obey your Commandments
Until the Day of Judgement.

There had been wars before and there were to be wars in future as well, but this war was different both in conception and the manner in which it was expected to terminate. Both sides were fighting to defend their respective Way of Life. It could end in not only the defeat of one army or the nation it belonged to but it was to end with the end of the Way of Life to which the loser belonged. It was a war aimed at the extermination of the Muslim's Ideology and Way of Life. The idea, that all wars are fought for differences, which can be solved peacefully, does not appear to be applicable to this war. Normally it can be said that, "Just how senseless and futile an expedient it really is, can usually best be judged by those who lose rather than by those who have won". In this case it was not applicable because the losers were to forego the freedom of living in accordance with their chosen Way of Life.

This Document had been dictated keeping in mind this Philosophy of War that to remain a Believer in Allah was only possible when Sovereignty of Allah could be proclaimed and life was led in accordance with His Commandments. To achieve that it was essential, that land occupied by Believers had to be defended to the last. It was, therefore, necessary, that Yathrib had its Basic Law – its Constitution – promulgated in a manner that its defence preparations could be taken in hand legally and constitutionally. Hence the correct heading of the Document can be "The Constitutional Charter of Yathrib... Medina".

It was not an agreement with the Jews as Allama Shibli Noamani calls it. He says "The Prophet (PBUH) sent for Ansars and Jews and dictated an agreement....which was accepted by both parties". Another eminent writer Jalal-ud-Din Jaffery writes, "When the Prophet (PBUH) arrived in Medina, he had an agreement written between the Ansars and the Jews". Naeem Siddiqui, the only one out of all Urdu writers has shown a different approach to the problem. He writes, "The Prophet (PBUH) created an organisation for the arming of the State of Medina, through which he integrated the Muslims, the Jews and the unbelievers, into a new society. He had a written document of the nature of an agreement, prepared. The nature of this document was of a proper constitution and it can be correctly called as the first written constitution".

Nearly all writers of Seerah in Urdu have called the "Charter" as an "Agreement," between either the Prophet (PBUH) and the Jews, or between the Believers and the Jews. An eminent learned man like Syed Abul Hassan Ali Nadvi has termed it as an agreement of peace with the Jews. Having correctly said that, "The Prophet (PBUH) on this occasion gave a writing to the Muhajirs and Ansars, "he adds "which contained an agreement of peace with the Jews". Another eminent historian writes, "On arrival at Medina, the Prophet (PBUH) during the very first year of Hijrah considered it appropriate to execute an agreement with all nationalities on the principle of internationalism so that a national solidarity should continue in spite of the ethnic and religious differences". Khalid Alvi, referring to the Jews writes, "He (the Prophet PBUH) made an agreement with them".

It could be that the word agreement has crept in because of absence of a proper equivalent of the term "Charter," in Urdu. The mistake dates back to Ibne Hisham, due to absence of a technical term for "Charter" in that age. He has used the word Aahadahum which has been translated as "covenant." The sentence as a result reads " the covenant between the Muslims and the Medinans and with the Jews".

Muslim and non-Muslim writers of Seerah in English, who belong to the present age, have also relied on Ibne-Ishaq, in more or less the same manner as Urdu writers. Abu Bakr Sirajuddin (Martin Ling) who has written with great devotion says, "and the Prophet (PBUH) now made a covenant of mutual obligations between his followers and the Jews of the Oasis". A non-Muslim writer of Pakistan origin says that before the signing of the agreement a thorough exchange of views had taken place. This may be correct but no work of early period seems to mention a thorough exchange of views. He writes, "After a thorough exchange of views, an agreement was reached and was reduced to writing".

Muir while translating the Document uses the words "Charter of Muhammad the Prophet" instead of "Charter from Muhammad," but in introducing it he writes, "It was natural that Muhammad, holding these sentiments should desire to enter into a close and binding union with the Jews, and this he did in a formal manner shortly after reaching Medina. He associated them with himself by a treaty of mutual obligation drawn up in writing". The difference between an agreement and a Charter is very vast. An agreement is between two equals and a Charter is given from one to others. An agreement can be rescinded by either party. A Charter can be altered, amended or cancelled only by the authority which promulgated it. Apart from the heading given to the document its contents alone can guide later researchers to give their verdict on it, whether it was a treaty, an agreement or a Charter.

Treaties are between states and usually the heading says so For instance, "Security Treaty between Australia, New Zealand and United States of America". Similarly Pacts are between independent sovereign states. For instance, "Pact of Mutual Co-operation (CENTO)" was signed between a number of states including Pakistan, Turkey and Iran. Recently a new name for mutual treaties has appeared. This is called a "Convention." For instance, "Convention regarding the Regime of the Straits"

Let us, once again, look at Meethaq-e-Medina in a little greater detail, particularly its heading. It says:-

"This Document (writing) is from Muhammad, The Prophet of Allah (PBUH.)"

It is clear that it is neither an agreement nor a treaty because it is not between Muhammad (PBUH) and some others. It is from him and he is the Prophet (PBUH) of Allah. Those receiving the Document are being told that the person issuing this Document is doing so in his capacity as the Prophet of Allah. Then it goes on to say that it is being given:

"To"

"Quraysh and Yathribite Believers".

Believers whether from Mecca or from Yathrib were all his followers known as his Companions. No group of people in the history of mankind have shown their devotion to their leader as was shown by his Companions to Muhammad (PBUH) the Prophet of Allah. When marching out to the battlefield of Badr, the leader of Ansars of Yathrib, Saad bin Muadh said, "We believe in you, we declare your truth, and we witness, that what you have brought is truth, and we have given you our word and agreement to hear and to obey; so go forth where you wish, we are with you, and by Allah, if you were to ask us to cross the sea and you plunged into it, we would plunge into it with you, not a man would stay behind. We do not dislike the idea of meeting your enemy tomorrow. We are experienced in war, trustworthy in combat...."

Whatever else description or name may be given to this Document it cannot be called an agreement between the Prophet (PBUH) and his followers. It was being given by him to them and they were all included in it, both the Muhajirs from Mecca and the Ansars of Yathrib.

There were others as well. They were:-

"those who will follow them and fight alongside them."

It would be applicable to others as well, provided these others followed the lead of his followers, the Believers, from Mecca and Yathrib. Apart from following the Believers they had to take part in fighting alongside the Believers to qualify themselves as recipients of this august Document. This heading ends with a brief last remark, "They will form ONE UMMAH to the exclusion of others." It means that if the others qualified as recipients of the Document, then they and the Believers, the Companions of the Last Prophet of Allah, will form an Ummah apart from the rest of humanity. It was a great honour, that was being bestowed on them but the price was also very high. They had to accept the Believers as their leaders and continue to follow them by joining in war with them against their enemies.

Thus the Document was primarily issued as the Basic or Fundamental Law The Constitution of Yathrib, so that defence arrangements could be taken in hand, on behalf of the entire population. The Believers, being the group which had sworn allegiance to him as a result of the Bayah formed the manpower of his army. The march to the battlefield of Badr proved this fact. None others were prepared to sacrifice themselves for a cause, in which they did not believe. History has recorded one more Charter given by the head of a state. This was King John of England. This Charter, however, was taken by force by the barons of the realm, because, "King John was very unwilling to grant it.

This was on the 15th of June 1215 A.C., that the Great Charter was sealed with the king's great seal. He agreed that 24 barons shall be appointed to see that he kept the promises which it contained. He agreed only because he was compelled.... He never meant to keep the promises that it contained, and he did not keep them. He sent to France for soldiers and when they came he made war on his own people. He asked his friend the Pope for help and the Pope helped him by ex-communicating all barons, by London under Interdict, and by telling John that he had no need to keep his promises". The surprising part of the whole story is, that, there was not much in the Charter, which an honest ruler of an average society need to have objected to.

It may seem strange that the Pope of all the people, should have advised a Christian ruler to go back on his promises. It was, however, not the first time, nor the last time, that the head of Church had advised a prince to go back on his promises. In one case, "the Pope, who seeing his plans being nullified, by this (peace treaty) initiated the Magyars to break the peace; oaths sworn to infidels not being binding". The Charter given at Yathrib was in the spirit of Islam, the New Way of Life. It had to be in accordance with all ethical, moral and legal principles laid down by Allah, for Believers in Him and His Prophet (PBUH). The time of its issue was the most critical period in the history of Islam—a time when the threat against Islam and Muslims was the greatest. This fact must be kept in mind while studying the Clauses of the Charter.

The position in which the Muslims were placed at this time has been misrepresented by some Western writers. Preparations for defence of Yathrib have been interpreted as aggressive designs against the Mekkans. A well known British historian writes that "Muhammad had now, as it were, thrown down the gauntlet, which the Mekkans could not but pick it up. He had effectively challenged them to a full scale trial of strength". It appears that after writing a few more sentences he remembered that it was the Mekkans who had declared war. He adds; "The Meccan belief thought Muhammad would avoid them rested on a misappraisal of the relative strength and fighting qualities of the two parties". He has avoided to give the source on which he has based the superior strength of the Muslim Army.

# 5

# *Believers' Rights*

The historic chapter deals with the Laws which affect Believers only. For practical purposes the whole Charter concerns the Believers. However, there are some Clauses whose subject matter concerns Believers only, while there are others which affect those people who have not accepted Islam but will be working under the leadership of Believers. The heading of the Document, which also forms Clause I deals primarily with Believers clears all doubts about its nature and also that they are the people forming the Government of the state.

One of the significant points to note is that the Charter is addressed primarily to the people; the common man; the Believer whether a free man, a freed man or not free till then.

"This is a Document from Muhammad the Prophet (PBUH) between the Believers, Muslims of Quraysh and Yathrib and those who followed them and fought with them. They form one Ummah to the exclusion of others."

It includes others with a condition, otherwise the Believers Quraysh from Mecca and from Yathrib form One Ummah to the exclusion of the rest. This formation of Ummah was not to be confined to the Believers of these two places. Whosoever voluntarily Believed in Allah and Muhammad (PBUH) as a

Prophet which in practice meant that he lived in accordance with the Laws of the Quran and Sunnah, became a member of this Ummah.

There may have been similar Charters in other parts of the world. We have already referred to a Charter issued by a king of England in 1215 A.C., which is known as the Great Charter – Magna Carta. There are many differences but the first difference lies in the people to whom the Charter is being given. While the Constitutional Charter of Medina is given to the common man, the Magna Carta is given:

> "To the archbishops, bishops, abbots, earls, barons, justiciars, foresters, sheriffs, stewards, servants, and to all his bailiffs and faithful subjects."

The subjects also formed categories and were at the mercy of the bishops and sheriffs and in practice held no social status unless they happened to be retainers of the categories enumerated above. The common man, the man in the street had no voice or weight until centuries later, when contacts with Islam is Spain and the Holy Land had brought about a certain amount of awakening among the Europeans, returning from Muslim lands.

The promulgation of a Constitution or Fundamental Law by a people or to them by the ruler signifies the commencement of organized life of that Millah. Organized collective life alone is most important characteristic of a human group from a herd of animals. Meccan life was the life of individual Muslims placed amidst unfriendly surroundings. Such a life could not last for ever. It cannot last even in the twentieth century. There are a number of countries today where Muslims find it impossible to live as Muslims. Hijrah of the Prophet (PBUH) was inevitable. Hijrah and the declaration of war by Quraysh created the situation where a Fundamental Law became essential to be promulgated. Islam became a living organization with the Charter controlling the collective communal life of those who had accepted Sovereignty of Allah and His Prophet (PBUH). Allah's Sovereignty was to control and direct the life of these individuals from hearth to the farm or the shop and would include the behaviour and inner feelings from the Mosques to the Battlefield.

It must be remembered that the Charter is being issued and promulgated by Muhammad (PBUH) The Prophet of Allah and not by Allah, although it is primarily for the people who have accepted Allah's Sovereignty. This fact reminds a Believer that he has accepted the Sovereignty of Allah, because, Muhammad (PBUH) has said so and the individual has accepted his Prophethood. It is the character, the conduct and the life of Muhammad (PBUH) although regulated, controlled and directed on the Right Path by Allah, which has made men believe in him, when he said, "Allah is the Creator, the Sustainer and Master of the Day of Resurrection."

It is his statement that Allah the Merciful, the Loving, the Compassionate and Who has appointed him as His Last Prophet. Therefore, be it understood and remembered that when a Believer accepts the Sovereignty of Allah, he does not relegate the Prophet (PBUH) to a position of no consequence. It is the acceptance of his Prophethood which has prompted the Believer to Believe and have Faith (Imaan) in Allah. Therefore, as Law Givers, they both remain side by side. This is the explanation of repeated reminder of Allah regarding the position of Muhammad as a Law Giver and not one who as a result of applying himself to a problem, at hand, does Ijtehad and deduces supplementary law, under certain given conditions. Allah has repeatedly Commanded:-

"Say: Obey Allah and the messenger". 3: 32

The preceding Verse is worth noting:-

"Say: If ye love Allah, follow me".

Whereever the Command to "Obey Allah" occurs it is

followed by "Obey the Messenger." Obedience to Him is given singly only in one Verse, where it is said "Obey My Command" (20: 90) and not the usual Word, "Obey Allah."

**Original Laws**

The position of Muhammad (PBUH) as a Law Giver in accordance with Allah's Own Commands is direct. His Commands take the place of Law directly and independently. Any reported Command of his, which does not fully support the Words of the Quran, can be rejected as Maudhu-Spurious, concocted and coined by some one and not merely as of a secondary nature, which, may or may not be applicable in all cases. He knew the place he held. He could not give an Order which would be contrary to the Dictates of Allah. Allah has said about him:

> "By the Star when it setteth your comrade erreth not,
> nor is deceived, nor doth he speak of (his own desire)".
>
> 53: 1-3

The Quran and the Sunnah are complementary to one another. Neither can be understood except by studying the other. If Allah Himself has, in a dozen places bracketed His Rasul with Obedience to Himself then we must also give to his Commands an equally important position. It is Muhammad (PBUH) who has had to say that the Quran is not the result of his authorship. Who, except Allah and his own Conscience, was there to stop him from crediting himself with the authorship of the Quran Who was there, except Allah, his Creator and his own truthfulness to stop him from declaring himself as God in human garb? After all, there were many in Arabia, who, by the queer theory of Trinity, then prevalent, gave to Jesus Christ the position of the Son of God, and of the God who came to earth to be crucified for the sins of humanity.

The Quran is the Word of Allah because, apart from the Quran itself, Muhammad (PBUH) has said so. Muhammad's command, therefore, must be believed and acted upon as eternal commands, in the same spirit as Commands of Allah.

The Clauses of the Charter dealing with Believers only are very few. As the Charter was addressed to the Believers initially the clauses dealing with Believers only precede all others. We have already dealt with Clauses I including the few words given above.

*Clause 2:* "Quraysh Muhajireen will continue to pay blood-money among themselves in accordance with the existing custom."

This Clause has thus laid down:-

1. The Principle of payment of blood-money will continue.
2. Its amount and manner of payment can be in accordance with the tribal custom.
3. Uniformity in the amount etc. is not demanded.

Quraysh Believers had migrated to a new place, the city of Yathrib, where there must have been local customs regarding the payment of blood-money. It was neither advisable nor in accordance with the Spirit of Islam, which was meant to cover the whole of the Globe, to lay down permanent laws regarding matters which should, preferably, be decided in accordance with local customs, conditions and requirements. Within Arabia itself there were different standards of payment of blood-money, in view of this it was decided and proclaimed that local and tribal practice, in the case of blood-money would continue to be followed in future.

**Law in Force**

Islam is the Last Revealed Way of Life. It has lasted for fourteen centuries and has to remain during the coming one thousand or one million centuries that will take this universe to reach its destination in the immeasurable void. A Way of Life which has to last for ever, and, to be applicable in all places at all times, cannot have eternal laws for situations which must undergo changes with change in time and place. Allah alone possesses the knowledge and the Wisdom and knows what aspects suffer change. He has, as a result, not Laws for problems, situations and matters which are likely to undergo changes. Those matters, which are of lasting nature, have been the subject of Laws given by Allah and His Rasul.

If the problem had been posed to a man, it would have been impossible to bring the permanent and the temporary, to reconcile. The permanence of Islamic Laws has been possible only because Allah and His Prophet (PBUH) have meticulously avoided to give Laws, for aspects of human life, which are of changing nature.

All men are equal. They will always remain equal. Hence Equality of man has been brought under Law. And yet the question of electing, selecting, nominating or appointing a leader of society. Khalifa or Imam has not even been touched because this is a purely social problem, the solution of which is subject to change with time and place. Uniformity is advisable but only where it is possible. Where uniformity is likely to create hardships Allah and His Rasul have left it to the Believers to come to a decision through discussion. The Prophet (PBUH) himself was Commanded to decide problems after consulting his Companions. But once a decision has been taken then all have to see to it, that it is suitably carried out.

***Clause** 3:* "They will redeem their prisoners with kindness and justice common among Believers."

The word "they" cannot refer to anyone else but those to whom the Charter was being issued. It was a state of Muslims in which laws of Islam were to be administered. The Fundamental Law had included "those who followed them," but that was to be seen as to who were prepared to follow them and defend Yathrib along with them. Muslims of Quraysh and Yathrib were being given the Document and as such this Clause referred to them jointly. The subject is the redeeming of prisoners, which could be tackled at the level of the Federal Government of Yathrib and none else.

It must be noted that the, "redeeming of prisoners of war is being made a collective responsibility," of the Ummah. It is also worthnoting that the standard of sentiments involved in redeeming prisoners of war is "the kindness and justice common among Believers." The kindness and justice of Believers cannot be of any other kind than that of Allah Who is Most Merciful, and His Prophet (PBUH) who has come as "Mercy to Mankind."

## Centre of Power

This Command of Allah's Messenger was not confined to the Believers of Yathrib only. It was the first Muslim state, which expanded within a century to cover two continents and had started influencing the third as well. This order did not merely apply to the subjects of the state of Yathrib. Although the Charter was given to the then existing Ummah, this order was and is applicable to the Ummah of Islam for ever. The present writer has no knowledge of this Order being amended, deleted, cancelled or replaced by any Quranic Injunction or an order by the Prophet (PBUH).

The question arises as to what has the world of Islam done to redeem the Muslim prisoners of war in the hands of various victorious nations, who during the last three centuries have availed themselves of the weakness of Muslim peoples and while occupying Muslim lands have taken millions of Muslims as prisoners of war. These Muslims are kept as prisoners jointly and singally in these territories known as European colonies. Generation after generation has grown up and lived as slaves and the Muslim World elsewhere has not moved a finger even to redeem them. We have to admit that a greater part of Muslim World was, until few years ago, under the domination of one or the other Christian power, but nothing has been said regarding the redeeming of millions who, though in majority, in their homelands, are living as slaves and leading a life worse than the life of ethnic minorities. This Clause of The Constitutional Charter of Medina is still operative and I, as, an humble individual, and a student of Muslim history, would submit, that, it needs further thought by the intellectuals of Muslim World.

Until the issue of this Charter there was no question of redeeming prisoners of war. The armies in those days did not belong to the nation. There was no notion of an Ummah.

They used to belong to the kings and when a king was killed in war and was defeated the personnel of that Army had no one else to look to. If they were taken prisoners they were made slaves. If they escaped they became robbers and highwaymen. Very few managed to reach their homes. Yathrib was not a country or a state in the normal sense of the word. It was a place, a piece of land, where the Muslim Ummah, the Believers in Allah and His Rasul (PBUH) had commenced a communal life and were beginning to demonstrate the New Way of Life granted by Allah. Ummah which was then coming into existence was completely new. Those who were to fight the battles of this Ummah were the Army of the Ummah and not of the land comprising the territories of Yathrib. Hence he Ordered that the Ummah will redeem their prisoners of war, and not only that, but they will do so with love and justice which is a hall-mark of Believers in Allah and His Prophet (PBUH) and Mercy to Mankind.

This order was so new and unique, that, the moment the Prophet (PBUH) had dictated it and the scribe had written it, there must have been a demand from "The others", who were present, that this Law should be applied to all. Hence Clause 5. There were some who were not even satisfied with the words "all parties will redeem their prisoners with kindness and justice common among Believers." Their names had to be inserted that such and such tribe and so and so group, "will be governed on the above lines." The demand was placed a second time and names of four more tribes had to be included for the fulfilment of this humane responsibility which was to take ten centuries for other parts of the world like Europe to emulate.

*Clause 8:* "Believers will not fail to redeem their prisoners or fail to pay blood-money on behalf of one of them."

This Clause is to emphasize Clauses 2 and 3. It has been brought in particularly because Clause 2 had mentioned Quraysh only. This Clause emphasizes the contents of both Clauses mentioned earlier and reminds the Believers of today that contrary to the expectations of the Prophet of Allah, they have failed to redeem their prisoners for centuries.

*Clause 9:* " A Believer will not make the freedman of another Believer as his ally against the wishes of the other Believer."

The relations between the master and slave are of personal nature. When a master frees a slave new relations are formed. The trust or lack of trust a person places on his freedman is known only to him. His good points, his weaknesses and his idiosyncrasies are also known to a freedman. Relations of allies are on a different level. A Believer giving protection to a freedman is under-taking certain responsibilities in respect of a person not really intimately known to him while Believers are like brothers to one another. Therefore, when a Believer takes a freedman of another Believer as ally, and gives him protection, it is in their common interest to have the blessings of the other Believer. This order was being given to maintain internal peace of the community.

*Clause 10:* "The Believers who fear Allah, will oppose the rebellious elements and those that encourage injustice or sin or enmity or lack of cooperation among Believers."

It has to be kept in mind that the Believers were to defend Yathrib. It was, therefore, essential that the best of relations existed among them. There were people within Yathrib who were likely to create mischief and create situations detrimental to internal security. The factor which had to be kept in mind was that every Believer had, until then, persons closely related to him, who had not yet embraced Islam. It was possible that some such person was found guilty of injustice, sin, or enmity to Islam or of creating trouble between Believers. On such occasions. Believers were being told that their duty lay with law and order and their loyalty lay with High Command's policy and decision and not with the kindred, however dear they may have been.

It was a very delicate situation and the Ansars deserve all the credit for having come out of this very severe test successfully. The leadership provided by the Prophet (PBUH) and the minor circle of his Companions deserve equal praise for steering the Millah with patience, love and tact, through this most difficult period. "Believers who fear Allah", is the key factor in the shaping of an Islamic society. Love of family ties can over-ride all other situations, except that of men and women, who fear Allah, and as a result of fear of Allah are prepared to sacrifice family interests and affiliations. When the object is to create a flawless Muslim society in which no Believer can be thought of committing a sin, rebellion, injustice or create dissension, then every Muslim is expected to oppose such sinful elements even though they may be his close relations. A country or a state can be defended only if there is peace and harmony within the boundaries of that state.

Such a society can only come about if individuals fear Allah and have firm belief that they will have to answer for their actions on the Day of Judgement.

***Clause 11:*** "If anyone is guilty of any such act all Believers will oppose him, even, if he be the son of any one of them."

This Clause is more or less a corollary to the foregoing Clause. It was being laid down firmly and without any ambiguity that injustice, sin and rebellious acts would not be permitted in that society, which was being created in accordance with the Code of Law Revealed by Allah. This was after centuries that a society was taking shape on the principle of Sovereignty of Allah. This society was to prove to humanity, for all times, that a people, a nation, an Ummah, observing in their day to day life, the Sovereignty of Allah prove in actual practice that their objective was to achieve three things:

(a) A happy and contented individual who has patience, for-bearance and steadfastness and these individuals show love for each other in their normal day to day dealings.

(b) These happy and contented individuals bring into existence a happy and loving society.

(c) They do not fall prey to the temptation of committing aggression or transgression against other nations even though as a result of being a happy, contented and united people they have gained strength and have the capacity of over-running their neighbours. In addition such an Ummah does not engage in any war unless they are attacked first. But whenever they are attacked they punish the aggressor to an extent, that he does not repeat it again.

Such a happy and strong society can come into existence only if its individuals observe law for themselves and for all who may be near and dear to them. This Clause draws the attention of Believers to the injunction of the Quran:-

> "O ye who believe! Be ye staunch injustice, witnesses for Allah, even though it be against yourselves or (your) parents or (your) kindred, whether (the case be of) a rich man or a poor man, for Allah is nearer unto both, (than ye are). So follow not passion".

***Clause 12:*** "A Believer will not kill another Believer for the sake of an un-Believer."

This Clause was a further explanation and an illustration of Clause 11.

Family ties held strong loyalties in Arabia as in all tribal societies. If a member of a family was killed, his kith and kin were expected to avenge that death or be satisfied with the usual blood-money. These prejudices were very deep rooted. The Prophet (PBUH), however, was creating an Ummah, the members of which were to be above all such ties, prejudices and loyalties. He was stressing on Believers and un-Believers alike that the only loyalty in Islam is loyalty to Allah and this is exhibited by obedience to His Laws. The Law of Allah is clear on the subject that a Believer cannot kill another Believer unless by mistake. He ceases to be a Believer if he kills another Believer wilfully.

> "Whose slayeth a believer of set purpose, his reward is Hell for ever". 4: 93

The society was, as yet, a mixed society but laws had to be promulgated, which would gradually develop the society into a society of love, peace and justice all round. This could only be achieved by having strict laws and meticulous observance of those laws. Believers and their un-Believers relations were being told categorically, that no Believer, should be expected to avenge the death of a relative killed accidentally or otherwise by another Believer.

Islam had to step out of Arabia and spread to far off lands. It was to declare, from the beginning, as to where did the loyalties of new-Muslims lie immediately after becoming Muslims. The Code was strict, unusually difficult to observe but the choice of observance of loyalty was between the Sovereignty of Allah and worldly ties. Allah had to be given preference by those who claimed to have accepted Him as their Lord and Master.

*Clause 13:* "No Believer will help an un-Believer against a Believer."

This Clause in conjunction the foregoing sets a standard of behaviour for Believers in a mixed society where Believers are placed in a non-Believer majority, even though general relation may be on the best of terms. Believers must remain united among themselves, if they desire to possess weight, as an Ummah, however small their number may be.

This Clause could be used as precedent and for relations between Muslim states, so that inter-state relations between Muslim states are kept at friendly level and instances of acute differences between them do not arise. It would then coincide with the directions given in the Verse quoted below:

> "Let not the believers take disbelievers for their friends in preference to believers." 3: 28

Disobedience of Clause 13 and the Verse quoted above have brought about the situation, that vast areas populated entirely by Believers have fallen prey to un-Believers and millions of Muslims are forced to live as atheists. It is punishment for having rebelled against both the letter and spirit of the Quran and the Charter.

6

# Non-believers' Rights

The Jewish tribes of Yathrib were rich and had fairly large number of members prominent in business. They, however, had no political or social status among the Arab population. They appear to have migrated from Syria during one of their exodus resulting from Assyrian invasion. Some writers are of the opinion that they were settled in Yathrib even before the Arabs. This does not appear likely. The theory, that they were Arabs who had been converted to Judaism also does not appear plausible. They were, at the time of Prophet's Hijrah, adherents of one or the other of these Arab tribes (Aus and Khazraj). They had, however, preserved a sort of intellectual ascendency, owing to their being in possession of the Scriptures and their fame for the occult sciences, the pagan Arabs consulting their rabbies on occasions and paying heed to what they said."

**All Protections**

The Prophet (PBUH) gave them a privileged position in the Constitutional Charter, provided they followed the Believers loyally and fought alongside with them. They possessed strong forts just outside the main city of Yathrib and each tribe was independent in every respect, each having a separate fort. They had all the weapons of the period and boasted of their prowess as fighters. When the Quraysh were defeated at Badr, one of their tribes, Banu Qainaqa, in reply to the Prophet's advice of good behaviour, they boasted of their strength and rebelled. They are a people of the Book. The way in which the Prophet (PBUH) was laying the foundations of bringing humanity on one platform would have benefited the Jews in the long run, but they were short sighted and did not avail of the special position, they could have enjoyed under the terms of the Charter. In spite of the behaviour of leading Jews of Yathrib the Prophet (PBUH) continued treating them with kindness and until a Jewish tribe did not commit an act of treason or outright rebellion he did not take any action against them. He pardoned two of the rebellious tribes, when they surrendered.

Those terms of the Charter, which were of general nature and those in connection with defence of the state, were applicable to Jews as well. There were, however, some Clauses which referred to the Jews only. The Clauses of general nature included the heading (Clause 1) in which it was laid down that those who followed the Believers and fought alongside with them will form one Ummah with them. This was a great attraction for the Jews. They were being elevated to the status of equality with Arabs and in some respects they were becoming superior to them, because, they were becoming equals of the ruling party of Yathrib, the Believers. Clauses like Clause 5, which laid down that "All parties will redeem their prisoners with kindness and justice according to practice among Believers," are being studied elsewhere. In this Chapter only those Clauses will be brought under discussion, which pertain to Jews exclusively.

*Clause 16:* "Those Jews who follow us, will be helped and will be treated with equality."

We have touched on this Clause very briefly, under Laws pertaining to defence. As the Clause mentions Jews particularly, we feel that it must be due to some special reason, that the question cropped up again, although it had been touched upon in Clause 1, where it referred to "those who," followed them. The only reason, for the mention of Jews specifically, could be that they had, during the dictation of the Charter, asked a direct question about the subject.

Clause 15 had spoken of "Believers are all friends to each other to the exclusion of all others." The Jews and 'the others' were being denied the friendship and equality with Muslims, which had been promised in Clause 1. The Jews must have felt that their position, in respect of equality with Muslims, needed to be clarified. They must have asked a specific question, "What about us." The answer came in the form of Clause 16 that "Those Jews who follow us will be helped and will be treated with equality."

This Clause shows their keenness to gain an equal socio-political status with the Believers. As yet they knew very little about Islam. They may have been still under the impression that the Prophet (PBUH) will announce himself as a sect of Judaism, and not as final shape of Islam, the Way of Life, preached by Ibrahim and Musa (Alaihi-ssalam). The Prophet having sensed the worries of Jews dictated the next Clause.

*Clause 17:* "No Jew will be wronged."

Jews had been persecuted all the world over to such an extent that it was rare to find a place where they could live an honourable life. It may have been, that the Jews themselves have followed a policy of persecution in respect of communities which happened to be weaker than them. It could also be that whereever they happened to be in a minority, they took recourse to mischief and intrigue, which invited persecution against them. Centuries of such mischievous and selfish behaviour gave them a reputation that they attracted hatred merely by the mention of the word Jew, where-ever they went. The only person in authority, throughout history, who has shown compassion and kindness to them through the enactment of a

Law is Muhammad (PBUH) the Prophet of Allah. This historical Clause placed the Jews on a pedestal of honour, respect and safety which they had not enjoyed under their own kings. This assurance of safe and respectful life was independent of the Clause giving them equality with Believers if they fought alongside them on the Path of Allah.

It is clear that the Clause governing their status of equality must have been the result of their volunteering to take part in the defence of Yathrib against an attack by the Quraysh of Mecca. It could be because according to Yaqubi, the famous geographist, they were from an Arab stock. He says that "Jews of Medina were basically local Arabs and were Judaised by immigrants who fled from Palestine after the Roman invasion. It could also be through Jews who migrated earlier. In any case, they had not only adopted the Law brought by Moses but had also imbibed the universally adopted national character of Jews based on miserliness, cheating and mischief mongering, and had, as a result lost their status as honest citizens, as in other parts of the world."

The history of the scattered tribes of Jews has been a history of fraud, criminality and cunning; sabotage and destruction", but he being "Mercy to Mankind," could not refuse a request of a down-trodden people even though they may have deserved such a behaviour in the past. The Jews, however take their roaming around the world as a boon from above. They call it, "A beneficent protection, which God has instituted in the life of the Jews is, that He has dispersed them all over the world".

The Prophet (PBUH) was giving them equality because they were a part of mankind, created and fashioned by Allah. To a Muslim, equality has become a second nature, as a result. "A barefooted Beduin, in a ragged cloak, would walk upto a king, shake him by the hand and wish him good morning, completely disregarding horror of the whispering courtiers".

It may appear strange that the Jews were accepting to live under Laws of the Quran and the Commands of the Last Prophet of Allah as loyal citizens and fight for the safety of the New Deen in a chance, for receiving the status of free citizens of Yathrib. It may be because in this way they were becoming co-rulers along with Arabs, as their equals. It speaks of their urge for living an honourable life of equality with the high born in Arabia and be subject to Laws, which gave equal status to men, irrespective of their ethnic or geographical origin. They were proving the dictum that, "The most obvious and recognized characteristic of just laws is that they are equal", for all concerned. Justice has been recognized as the central theme of Islam.

It is based on the principle of equality of men in the eyes of Allah. When human beings, irrespective of the colour of their skins, the language that they speak and the creed they prefer to follow, are treated as equals before law, there is no possibility of injustice prevailing. "Injustice arises when equals are treated unequally and also when unequals are treated equally". This was the first time, that Jews were being treated as equals, and were to enjoy complete freedom. "Closely related to the value of equality is that of freedom. These two values are often defined in terms of the other. Freedom is most often defined, in terms of absence of restrictions, which we see as one way of defining equality.

Freedom as a value calling for absence of restrictions or restraints is laden with contradictions. Society can exist only if human behaviour is predictable and controllable to some extent Unconditional freedom could result only in chaos in all areas of activity".

It appears that Jewish mind has always wanted uncontrolled freedom. Movements like Socialism and Communism have been supported by Jewish intellectuals with greater zeal than thinkers of other schools of thought. The treacherous behaviour of Jews in different parts of the world, at various periods of history is the result of unbridled thought of their thinkers and intellectuals. They have a history which abounds in rebellious conduct even under their own rulers. The number of occasions, when anti-Jewish communal disturbances have taken place are too numerous to be mentioned in an essay of this nature. A few instances may, however, be mentioned.

Jews massacred in Alexandria (216 B.C.).

Antiochus killed 40,000 Jews in Jerusalem(170 B.C.).

Titus killed 11,00,000 Jews and destroys the Temple (70 A.C.).

Desolation of Judea (135 A.C.). Rebellion of Jews. Romans killed 580,000 (136 A.C.).

Rebellion of Jews at Alexandria. Jews massacred (415 A.C.).

Umar took over Jerusalem not a single person was killed (655 A.C.).

No more Jews killed in the Middle East. Jews banished from England (1020 A.C.). Jews returned to England (1060 A.C.). Jews massacred in London on Coronation day of Richard I.

Christian priests joined in the massacre. (1189 A.C.).

Jews besieged in the castle of York. (1190 A.C.).

They cut each others throats. Hunderds killed.

Jews of both sexes imprisoned in England.

Their eyes and teeth pulled out.

A large number butchered by king John. (1204 A.C.).

700 Jews slain in London (1262 A.C.).

Statute that no Jew should enjoy a freehold (1269 A.C.).

Jew moneylenders forced to hang a plate on their breast or quit England. (1274 A.C.).

267 Jews hanged, accused of clipping coins. (1278 A.C.).

All Jews 16511 banished from England.(1290 A.C.).

Jewish fate in France and other countries of Europe during 14th and 15th centuries is a grim story.

Several hundred thousand banished from Spain. (1492-1494 A.C.).

Addicts against Jews rescinded by Pope Sixtus V Cromwell permitted them to return to England. (1650 A.C.).

These instances of persecution of Jews speak of the manner they have been hunted from place to place. Their own laws of war and peace are primarily responsible for introducing cruelty during and after war.

According to their own history books, the behaviour of Jewish personalities of note has not been praise-worthy either. "Edom and Jeshurun were rivals and great were the cruelty of the Hebrew arms in their countries. When David was king, his sister's son Jacob went down and killed Adonites in the Ghrov twelve thousand men and Jacob's brother Abishai killed eighteen thousand of them... Other ten thousand taken captives, he brought to the top of the rock, and there he made them the king's tumblers, casting them headlong down together, by the sharp rocks, that they were all broken in pieces".

There have been numerous occasions during 20th century in Europe and particularly in Germany when great atrocities have been committed against Jews because they had captured the economic life of these countries. Efforts have been made to get rid of them. Israel has been created for this purpose, but the Jews have not left either Europe or America. Christianity appears poised to start a fresh campaign to annihilate them during the 21 st century of the Christian Era, while Muhammad (PBUH), gave Yathrib a Charter in 7th century, which said:- "No Jew will be wronged."

Professor Sergeant has tried to prove, that the Charter is not one Document but a collection of eight different documents. He, however, admits the authenticity of the Document, and does not deny the existence of the Clause "No Jew will be wronged." This guarantee of safety was being given to a people, who did not hold the status of nationals of that city and were living at the mercy of the tribes, which had given them protection.

Muslims have always shown magnanimity to the Jews. When they were banished from Spain between the years 1492 and 1494 A.C., "it was to Turkey that the persecuted Spanish Jews fled for refuge in enormous numbers." The persecution of Jews by Christians appears to he natural justice, after a lapse of centuries. They persecuted, in their time, those who fell into their hands. "The Jews used to bum their prisoners alive and most barbarously mutilate the slain".

Yathrib was witnessing a change. A new order was being established by Muhammad (PBUH) who has been sent by Allah, as "Mercy to mankind." All barbarities, all prosecutions, all wrongs to humanity were being made as illegal. All men were being declared as equal. Even the Jews, the downtrodden of East and West were being promised, that no harm will come to them as long as they committed no sin or crime. They were being given a place in the Charter, which was being offered without any pressure. Centuries later king John of England gave a Charter, at a time when "The capital was in rebel hands, the whole administration was at a stand still. Without his exchequer, John had no revenues. He had to yield. The king agreed to meet the barons on the meadows of Runnymede, between Staines and Windsor, and there signed the Great Charter". It would be interesting to read the Great Charter and compare it the Charter of Medina and see which Charter gives more freedom, equality, justice and human rights. Jews have had a chequered career throughout history. They have invited this fate because of their internecine warfare. They butchered one another, whenever and whoever had the upper hand. Their final self-inflicted blow came when, "After the defeat of Bar Cochba, in A.C. 135, much of Judea was left a desert and some towns of Galilee were also ravaged".

They seem to have a rebellious nature. If they were not quarre-lling among themselves, they would rebel against authority, how-ever benign it may have been. They rebelled against Nebuchad-nessar and "resolving to settle the Jewish problem once for all, as he thought, he recaptured Jerusalem, burned it to the ground, destroyed the temple of Solomon, drew Zedekia's sons before his face, gauged out their eyes, and carried practically all the popu-lation of the city into captivity in Babylonia."

During one of their marches in captivity and when their women were ordered by their guards to sing for them, they are supposed to have composed a song, bemoaning of their separation from Jerusalem. The words are:-

> "By the river of Babylon, there we sat down,
>
> Yes, we wept, when we remembered Zion,
>
> We hanged our harps upon the willows in the midst thereof.
>
> For there, they that carried us away captives, required of us a song.
>
> And they that worked us required of us mirth.
>
> Saying, sing us a song of Zion.
>
> How shall we sing the Lord's song in a strange land"

In later days, Jews have suffered only at the hands of Christians because of their having had a hand in the supposed Crucification of Jesus Christ. We have given a list of well known instances of persecution of Jews but did not include the migration of Jews to Babylon during the sixth century when Justinian with-drew citizenship from all those who were not members of Orthodox Church. Jews, as a result, chose the kindlier atmosphere of Babylon, which, at that time was under the Iranians. When the Iranians reconquered Syria, at the beginning of the 7th century, the Jews, who had been left behind, sided with the invaders. They paid heavily for this when Emperor Heraclius reconquered the country.

During the "early period of Arab rule they prospered. The Jewish towns and villages remained Jewish, paying taxes to Muslims, instead of Christian rulers, but otherwise continuing their normal life".This kind of treatment by Muslim rulers was in the spirit of the Constitutional Charter of Medina, which had categorically made it highly illegal to do any wrong to the Jews. The only other people who have been kind to the Jews are the Iranians. Yazdgard I was most kind to them. His "married to a Jewess, was so well disposed to them, that they called him "The Christian King".

The Prophet (PBUH) was so kind to the Jews that, he, made it illegal for everybody to harm the Jews, unless they were guilty of a crime. Also he laid down that :

***Clause 18:*** "The enemies of Jews will not be helped."

Both these Clauses were independent of the Jews following the leadership of Believers otherwise. These concessions were given to them as ordinary citizens of Yathrib. This was a great step forward towards freedom, equality and basic human rights of man considering that this legal Document was being dictated verbatum in the year 622 A.C.

In the normal course of events, this is not much of a concession to a group accepted as free citizens of a state. It becomes a great concession when no civic duties are imposed on that group. It gives the impression that although their Arab Haleefs were giving them protection yet they were on friendly terms with the enemies of the Jews previously. They were now being told that their enemies will not be befriended.

**No Discrimination**

These two Clauses give a clue to the consistently good treatment of minorities by Muslim rulers. These two Clauses have served as a Sunnah of the Prophet (PBUH) indicating the manner in which, minorities living under Muslim rule should be treated, Muslim rulers have never persecuted people on whom they may have had to rule. Persecution of the weak appears to be a part of the European race and Muslim, in their earlier period, were fortunate to have escaped European influence. Even during the present civilised century Europeans have prided themselves on their superior strength to dominate other people. A German writer of early twentieth century, Ludwig Welliman, "affirmed as early as 1903, that, the race is called upon to dominate the earth, to exploit nations' treasures, and the physical strength of man, to make the passive races simple subaltern organizations for the evolution of its nation".

When Germany overran France, during the Second World War, it set about to depopulate France, so that France was not able to provide itself with adequate manpower during any future war. "The annual total of French births which did not exceed six hundred thousand in 1939, would be halted or worse, since there would also be economic difficulties and privations skilfully organized and maintained by the victor".

Jews, though a mislead people, have been unfortunate throughout history. They have been persecuted in all lands except where Islam reigned. We know how they suffered in the Middle East and England. Their fate in Germany during twentieth century has been worse. To persecute them for having particular religious views has been highly unjust. It appears, that Europeans are too narrow minded, to permit others to hold views, which differ with their own views, and yet nearly all European nations pretend to be secular. One of those who have suffered at the altar of their Secular Christianity writes, "Christian Missionaries, who came from secular states of Europe, with public funds, introduced education on the Western pattern, which spread all over the country. Admission to these Christian schools was conditional on accepting Christianity".

In some cases and particularly after independence "they were baptised forcefully, at the Victory College Chapel". The writer goes on to say, "What is most essential for the dignity of man and social progress is freedom of thought, the very freedom, which the Churches have striven for, through centuries of religious wars and persecution to destroy". The Last Way of Life, sent to mankind, through Muhammad (PBUH), happens to be the only Way of Life, with the school of thought that there will be complete freedom of thought and has forbidden use of force in "Deen."

"There is no compulsion in religion." 2: 256

*Clause 29:* "The Jews will contribute towards the war when fighting alongside the Believers."

The last Clause dealing with the subject of Jews was in relation to their enemies not being helped. Immediately after that Clause matters of defence were taken up. As a result the Jews must have asked about contribution towards the war, in case they also took part in it. It was logical for them to come forward and share the expenses of the war. This, however, was a general statement and Jews under the protection of Arab tribes must have wanted, that their names be specifically mentioned in the Charter. It had been dictated earlier that those Jews who fought alongside the Believers will be considered as part of the Ummah. When they had accepted to share at the cost of war at the time of joining in Jihad on the Path of Allah, they were entitled to become a part of the Ummah on by the Jews would have gradually brought humanity on to the same platform.

Mankind is destined to become one Ummah eventually, when they will be following the same Law. Clause 28 already dictated says, "When you differ on anything the matter will be referred to Allah and Muhammad (PBUH)." Reference to Allah means the Dictates of the Quran and reference to Muhammad (PBUH) signifies his Sunnah. It meant that the mode of worship was to remain separate but the Law governing the society was to be that of Islam. Orientalists have failed to comprehend the significance of Prophet's approach to forge an Ummah in which all People of the Book, should live as One Ummah. Muir accepts that "No expression regarding either the Jewish or Christian Scriptures ever escaped the lips of Muhammad (PBUH) other than of implicit reverence".

And yet on the same page he writes: "In his later years Islam diverged rapidly from all sympathy with the Bible". He has given no proof of this divergence. He, however, has realised that, "It was the opposition of the Jews, and the martial superiority of Islam that imperceptibly led to the exclusive authority of Muhammad (PBUH) and the Quran".

If Muir had read the Charter carefully, he would have realised that exclusive authority of Muhammad (PBUH) and the Quran had been established from the beginning of Islam in Medina. The Jews failed to perceive, and so has Muir missed the point that unity of human race was the object of the Final Way of Life being Revealed to Muhammad (PBUH). It was the Jews who sabotaged it and it is Christian Missionaries and the Zionists who are still on the path of war with Islam the Deen of Peace. Allah has said:

"Mankind were one community". 2: 213

Differences arose and people forgot the true Faith. Messengers were sent to guide them back to the right path. Some listened and some did not. Although many Messengers were sent the main theme remained, as the Sovereignty of Allah. When the Last Messenger came, he tried to bring people on to the same platform. A beginning was made, but when people of the Book laid stress on their own separate identity and ignored the Sovereignty of Allah, the experiment failed. The present writer feels that, the result was that for the future the order came, that, who ever accepts Islam must submit completely.

> "O ye who believe Come, all of you, into submission (unto Him)". 2: 208

***Clause 31:*** "The same applies to Jews of Bani Al-Najjar, Bani Al- Harith, Bani Saeeda, Bani Jasham, Bani Al-Aus, Thaliba and the Jaffra and the Bani Al-Shuraiha".

***Clause 34:*** "Those in alliance with the Jews will be given the same treatment as the Jews."

The Jews were accepting the responsibility of joining in the defence of the state. They had allies abroad. As the Jews had promi-sed to become a part of the Ummah, it was only fair to consider and treat their allies in the same manner as the Jews.

***Clause 37:*** "The Jews bear their own expenses and the Believers bear their expenses."

The subject matter of defence continues. The question of pay-ment has arisen again. This refers to expenses connected with each ethnic contingent of the Army. Each was to pay for its own contingent.

***Clause 43:*** "The Jews must pay with the Believers."

This was to refer to expenses of general nature like blood money or other damages, in which both parties had to share the expenses.

***Clause 47:*** "The Jews of al-Aus, including their freedom have the same standing as other parties to the Charter."

This Clause speaks for itself. Late-comers were being accommodated.

These were Clauses in respect of Laws binding and giving rights to Jews. Irrespective of what status they had possessed prior to the Hijrah of the Prophet (PBUH), they were to be governed and treated in accordance with the dictates of this Document. It is incumbent on all students of Seerah and early history of Islam to bear in their minds the contents of the Charter. Without reference to this important Document no opinion can he formed on the behavior of one or the other party.

# 7

# *Seat of Power*

After the social boycott of Banu Hashim came to a happy end, particularly on account of the Divine revelation concerning the boycott document, the holy Prophet (PBUH) had heaved a sigh of relief. But, unfortunately, soon thereafter Hadrat Abu Talib fell seriously ill with little hope of survival. He had fallen ill before also, and it is related that on one such occasion he had called his illustrious nephew by his bed-side and asked him to pray to Allah, whose Messenger he was, to remove his illness. The holy Prophet (PBUH) had prayed and Hadrat Abu Talib had recovered, whereupon he had told his nephew:

"God listens to your prayers".

"Allah will answer your prayers also if you obey Him."

It is narrated by Allama Qastalani in "Marvehebud Dunya" that when the notables of Quraish came to visit Hadrat Abu Talib during his illness, he addressed them thus:

"God will remain pleased with you, if you all respect Kaaba above everything else, do not deprive any one of his rights, do not oppress each other, do not give up looking after the needs of your kinsmen and keep the tradition of truth and trustworthiness.

"I also desire, as my last will, that you should deal with Muhammad (PBUH) in a befitting manner as he is the most trustworthy person among the Quraishites and the most truthful throughout Arabia. He is presenting a religion which appeals to the heart but some how it becomes difficult to proclaim its acceptance by mouth, because of the fear of violent opposition from other people. But, I believe, he will have an upper hand in future and the Quraishites will be deprived of sharing honours with him."

It is related in 'Tabaqat' that, shortly before he breathed his last, he called his relatives and expressed his will:

"You will always flourish if you follow Muhammad (PBUH) and obey him."

He also called his illustrious nephew close to him and said:

"My nephew! when I pass away, it would be better for you to go to your grandfather's maternal tribe Bani Najaar in Medina, as those people are known for providing protection to their kinsmen at all cost."

Hadrat Abu Talib died at the age of eighty, six months after the withdrawal of the boycott. His death gave a grievous shock to the holy Prophet (PBUH), as was quite natural, because it was this uncle of his who had left no stone unturned to extend protection and support to him and who suffered trials and tribulations and even the three-year boycott of his entire relatives only for his sake.

No sooner had the holy Prophet (PBUH) recovered from this shock that his loving wife, who cared for him more than for any one else and who was the first to 'believe' Hadrat Khadija passed away at the age of sixty five in the 10th year of Prophethood. The holy Prophet (PBUH) laid her dead body in the grave with his own hands at a place called *Hajoon*. This year was termed by the holy Prophet (PBUH) as the 'year of grief.'

After the demise of Hadrat Abu Talib, the idolaters of Mecca, realising that he was deprived of his protector, started hurting the holy Prophet (PBUH) in many ways. One day, while he was passing through a crowded market place, a ruffian from among the Quraishites threw dust on his head and face and the holy Prophet (PBUH) entered his house in that condition whereupon his daughters started weeping and comforting him. It has been narrated, on the authority of Hadrat Aishah, that the holy Prophet (PBUH) used to say that "as long as Abu Talib was alive, the Quraishites lay low". The same tradition has been reported by Baihaqa, on the authority of Urwa bin Zubayr.

It has been recorded in Tabaqat that when excesses against the holy Prophet's (PBUH) person became too common, after the death of Hadrat Abu Talib, it was of all persons, Abu Lahab who stood up to protect the holy Prophet (PBUH) and asked him to carry on his missionary work in the same manner as he did before. Support from Abu Lahb who inspite of being the holy Prophet's (PBUH) uncle, was his greatest enemy astounded every one. When Abu Lahb chanced to see how Harith bin Qais was misbehaving with the holy Prophet (PBUH) once while the latter had come out of his house, he threatened Harith bin Qais of dire consequences. This fellow was so perplexed at this change in Abu Lahb's stance that he ran to the precincts of Kaaba and announced that Abu Lahb had renounced his ancestral faith.

The notables of Quraish rushed to Abu Lahb's house to verify this, but the latter told them that he had not renounced his faith, but that he would provide the holy Prophet (PBUH) the same kind of protection as his deceased uncle, Hadrat Abu Talib had done. But, since fate had arrayed him on the other side of the fence, Abu Lahb gave up the patronage which he had extended, when pressed by Abu Jahl and Uqba bin Abi Moeet.

After the death of Hadrat Khadija, there was no one in the holy Prophet's (PBUH) house to look after his two daughters, Hadrat Umme Kulthoom and Hadrat Fatima. After giving it a serious consideration for quite some period, the holy Prophet (PBUH) sent his proposal of marriage with Hadrat Sauda bint Zamaa, who was of almost the same age as he himself and was considered quite capable of looking after his two daughters.

Hadrat Sauda had embraced Islam alongwith her first husband Sakran bin Umroo, and the couple had migrated to Abyssinia where her husband had died. Hadrat Sauda could not get a better offer of re-marriage and she immediately gave her consent and Hadrat Hatib bin Umroo, representing Hadrat Sauda, solemnised the marriage and she moved to the holy Prophet's (PBUH) house. In fact, it was Hadrat Khula, the same noble lady who had arranged the holy Prophet's (PBUH) marriage with Hadrat Khadija, who played the role of an intermediary in the marriage with Hadrat Sauda.

The same lady, later, had arranged the holy Prophet's (PBUH) marriage with Hadrat Aishah. When she approached Hadrat Abu Bakr's wife, Hadrat Umme Rumaan, with the proposal, she responded positively but asked for time to consult her husband, Hadrat Abu Bakr. The latter had already given his consent to give Hadrat Aishah in marriage to Mutam bin Adi's son. He, therefore, went to the latter's house to ascertain whether the proposed marriage of Hadrat Aishah with his son was firm and final or not. But, as God had willed, Hadrat Abu Bakr came back without going back on his commitment to give his daughter in marriage to Mutam's son. It was Mutam's wife herself who, on the plea that her son will also renounce their ancestral faith after his marriage with Hadrat Aishah, broke off the marriage proposal.

Hadrat Abu Bakr, being thus free to marry Hadrat Aishah, elsewhere, immediately called the holy Prophet (PBUH) to his house and solemnised the marriage, though Hadrat Aishah went to her husband's house after his migration to Medina.

Since the holy Prophet (PBUH) had given up hope of gaining more converts in Mecca because of the continued ill-treatment meted out to him by the idolaters of this city, he thought of contacting the powerful and influential tribe of Banu Saqif at Taif, which lies 50 kilometers east of Mecca. It was at the close of the 10th year of Prophethood that the holy Prophet (PBUH) set out for Taif on foot. He met there Abd-ul-waleed, Masood and Habib, the three sons of Umroo bin Umair, who wielded all the power and authority in that city. But their reaction to the holy Prophet's (PBUH) preaching smacked of arrogance, misconception and conceit.

They turned away and gave an insolent reply. One of them said:

> "I will tear the curtains of Kaaba to shreds if God has sent you as His Messenger."

The other said:

> "Did God have no other choice before deciding to appoint you as His Messenger?"

The third one said:

> "I will not talk to you; because, if you are actually God's Messenger, it would be improper on my part to speak on this subject, and if you are not His Messenger then any discussion with you is purposeless."

Apart from this rude behavior, they incited the rogues and scoundrels of the city to stand in two rows along the path and pelt stones on the holy Prophet (PBUH) when he was departing from Taif.

So, they not only shouted scornfully at him and indulged in booing and hooting but also threw pellets of stone on him with such ferocity that his feet got wounded badly and blood collected in his shoes and Hadrat Zaid bin Harith, while trying to protect the holy Prophet (PBUH) from the rain of stones, received grievous injuries on his head. Whenever the holy Prophet (PBUH) tried to sit and take rest, the rowdies made him stand and walk through the barrage of stones being pelted on him. With great effort, he came out of the limits of Taif and sat resting against the walls of an orchard of grapes belonging to two chieftains of Quraish, Sheeba and Uqba, sons of Ah Rabeea. Both of them were there and saw the holy Prophet (PBUH). They sent a bunch of grapes in a plate to him through their slave Addas. Before eating the grapes, the holy Prophet (PBUH) uttered:" In the name of Allah the Most Merciful". Addas was taken aback and said:

> "By God! No one in this country is conversant with these sacred words."

The holy Prophet (PBUH) enquired:

> "Where do you come from and what is your religion?"
>
> "I am a Christian of Ninevah;" he replied.

The holy Prophet (PBUH) then said:

> "You belong to the city of Jonas, son of Mathew, one of God's pious servants".

The slave could not restrain his inquisitiveness:

> "How do you know him?"
>
> "He was my brother; he was an Apostle and I am also an Apostle," the holy Prophet (PBUH) explained.

Hearing this, the slave, in extreme ecstasy of reverence and regard, began to kiss the hands, the head and the feet of the holy Prophet (PBUH) and exclaimed:

> "I bear witness that you are God's Servant and His Messenger. By God! when I had left Ninevah there

were not even ten persons there who knew the name of Mathew."

Seeing this, the Sons of Rabeea said:

"This man has spoiled even our slave."

When Addas came back to them, they enquired:

"Why were you kissing the hands and feet of that man?"

"My master! There is none better than this man on the earth. He informed me of a thing which only an Apostle can know", the slave replied.

They advised him:

"Addas! Do not renounce your faith, it is better than his."

But Addas had turned a Muslim inwardly and nothing could shake his newly acquired faith.

Sitting under the shade of the boundary wall of the orchard, the holy Prophet (PBUH) cleaned his wounds and blood-soaked shoes. He looked ahead on the path leading to Mecca, where also people were equally unkind to him and treated his preaching with indifference. He turned to the Almighty and prayed with a voice choked with emotion:

"My Lord! I complain to you against my own helplessness and lack of resources as also against the disrespect and disregard with which I am being treated by these people.

"You are the Most Merciful, the Ray of hope for hapless and helpless persons. You Alone are my Master, my Allah".

"In whose hands are You leaving me—in the hands of those strangers who treated me cruelly or in the hands of those whom You have enabled to attain success in their conspiracies against me? If You are

> not displeased with me, then I do not care how any one treats me, as You alone are my best Supporter. I seek refuge under your Benevolent shadow. I seek refuge in the Light of Thy Being which drives away all darkness and brightens up everything. I surrender before Your Will; Your Holy Being is the Fountain-head of all power, the source of all strength."

The holy Prophet (PBUH) was suffering untold persecution only for telling the people that "he had received the revelation from Allah that He alone is to be worshipped and obeyed, that no one should oppress any one else, that there was no compulsion in religion, that Allah is One, has no partners, He rules over the entire universe and that he (the holy Prophet (PBUH)) was His Messenger sent to dissuade people from the worship of other than Allah and that he was just a man from among themselves deputed by Allah to guide them to the correct path, teach them to use their latent wisdom and thereby distinguish between good and evil and ponder over Divine portents in order to understand the role of Prophets whose obedience would lead to the obedience of the Almighty". The holy Prophet (PBUH) also told them that the Quran was God's own words and that every one would be resurrected after death for reward and punishment in the Hereafter which will be the eternal life."

While the holy Prophet (PBUH), accompanied by his faithful servant, Zaid bin Harith (who had refused to leave him and go with his parents) was returning from Taif to Mecca, Zaid spoke to his master:

> "How will you enter Mecca, as the Quraishites had already turned you out of that city"?

The holy Prophet (PBUH) responded:

> "Whatever you see is known to Allah. He will certainly create conditions conducive to my mission as He

> Himself is the Protector of His religion and He will provide me the necessary support for my ascendancy over the non-believers".

The holy Prophet (PBUH) stopped, on way, at Nakhia and then went to Hera from where he sent message to Matam bin Adi enquiring whether he would extend his protection to him if he entered Mecca to which he responded in the affirmative and asked his sons to go to the Kaaba fully armed. Thereafter, the holy Prophet (PBUH) entered Mecca under Matam's protection, the latter escorting him on camel-back. Matam shouted aloud, on reaching the precincts of Kaaba:

> "I have taken Muhammad (PBUH) in my protection."

The holy Prophet (PBUH) then circumambulated the Kaaba while Matam bin Adi and his armed sons stood guard. Abu Jahl enquired from Matam if he had adopted the holy Prophet's (PBUH) religion or merely provided him protection. On being told that he had only offered to protect the holy Prophet (PBUH), Abu Jahl said:

> "No one can dare oppose you. If you have provided him protection then each one of us will also protect him."

The holy Prophet (PBUH) had sent the aforesaid message to Matam bin Adi through Abdullah bin Uraiqat who was respected by the people of Mecca. The holy Prophet (PBUH) and Hadrat Abu Bakr used to repose full confidence in this man as he never betrayed the secrets and, despite being a polytheist had great regard for the holy Prophet (PBUH). In fact, it was Allah, Who, in order to provide succour to His Prophet (PBUH) after his suffering at the hands of the people of Taif, created a soft corner for the Prophet (PBUH) in Matam bin Adi's heart and he signified his consent to provide full and unconditional protection to him, with complete liberty to preach his faith. But there was no change of heart in Abu Jahl and Abu

Lahb who kept on vilifying the holy Prophet (PBUH) and poisoning the ears of those among whom he preached Islam.

Since the Hajj season was approaching and people from various tribes and regions of Arabia had started coming to Mecca, the holy Prophet (PBUH) visited the resting place of each tribe and contacted their respective chiefs and preached the tenets of Islam. Some of them were receptive to the preaching and some reacted adversely, but the holy Prophet (PBUH) kept up his proselytising efforts.

One day, the holy Prophet (PBUH) arrived at the resting place of the tribe of Banu Bakr bin Wael who had come from the central and eastern regions of Arabia and were famous for warfare, as they had repulsed a number of invasions made by the Persian army to annex their tribal belt bordering the eastern coast of Arabian peninsula. During his preaching among them, the holy Prophet (PBUH) had enquired from them regarding their capability to resist the armed might of Persia and being told in reply that they could not match their strength with that of the Persians, he said aloud:

> "O, Bakr bin Wael! A day will come when you will have victory over them, marry their women and take their boys as slaves."

Abu Lahb, who was closely following the holy Prophet's (PBUH) movements reached the resting place of Bakr bin Wael, after the latter's departure from there, and spoke about the holy Prophet (PBUH) thus:

> "This man once occupied a very honourable position among us but now he has come at his wits' end."

They also believed Abu Lahb's words, as they thought that what the holy Prophet (PBUH) had prophesied about the fall of the Persian empire was but mere idle talk and a figment of imagination, although, much later, they saw with their own eyes that the prophecy came true.

Accompanied by Hadrat Abu Bakr and Hadrat Ali, the holy Prophet (PBUH) visited a large camp at Mina where a number of chieftains were assembled. On enquiry by Hadrat Abu Bakr, it transpired that they belonged to the tribe of Bani Shaiban bin Saleba. Encouraged by Hadrat Abu Bakr, the holy Prophet (PBUH) started his preaching thus:

> "I call you towards Islam. You have to bear witness that there is no worshipful being save Allah, Who has no partners and that I am His Messenger. So, I ask for your support and assistance to spread this faith, a duty that has been assigned to me by the Almighty, because the Quraishites have become united in opposing this Divine mission and are refusing to believe in my Prophethood."

One of them, named Mafrooq asked the holy Prophet (PBUH) to elaborate his mission, whereupon the latter recited the following verses from Sura Al-Anam:

> "Say: Come, bring your witnesses who can bear witness that Allah forbade all this. And, if they bear witness, do not bear witness with them. Follow not the whims of those who deny Our revelations, those who do not believe in the Hereafter and deem others equal with their Lord.

Say: Come, I will recite to you that which your Lord has made a sacred duty for you: that you do not ascribe anything as His partner and that you do good to your parents and that you do not slay your children because of penury - We provide for you and for them—and that you do not go near lewd things whether open or concealed. And that you slay not life which Allah has made sacred, except in the course of Justice. This He has commanded you in order that you may discern."

Mafrooq and other chieftains, when they heard the recitation exclaimed:

"By God! these are not the words of human beings. Had it been the composition of soothsayers, poets and sorcerers, who could have discerned the difference better than us. Please tell us more about your faith."

In response, the holy Prophet (PBUH) recited verse 90 of Sura Al-Nahl:

"Allah enjoins justice and kindness, and giving to kinsmen, and forbids lewdness and abomination and wickedness. He exhorts you in order that you may take heed."

Hearing this, the chieftains were so deeply affected by the marvel of the holy Quran that they remained mute for a while, and then Mafrooq broke the silence:

"O, Qurashite brother! you have called us towards best conduct and virtuous and good deeds. Your own people are an ignorant folk that they reject you and have unitedly adopted the path of flasehood."

Another Chieftain, an elderly person, Hani bin Qabisa said:

"I heard every word that you recited. By God! Whatever you have said is absolutely true. But we can not renounce our old faith and become your followers, as a result of our present session, without consulting others of our tribe. It will not be appreciated generally. We will go back to our people and reflect on your teachings. So, you may have to wait till our decision is conveyed."

Another chieftain, Musanna, referred to two other obstacles in the way of their conversion, which arose from the geographical location of their tribal area. When asked by the holy Prophet (PBUH) to elaborate, he said:

"One is the mountaineous terrain of Arabia and the other is the Persian mainland and Khosro's canals therein. The Persian overlords have obtained a promise from us that we will neither start doing something new nor introduce any change in our status quo. Your call might conflict with the wishes of the Persian rulers. We can support you in your effort against the Arabs but not against the wishes of Persians."

Then, the holy Prophet (PBUH) addressed them:

"You did well that you spoke the fact, as you perceive it. But the position is that any one who calls people towards Allah, does not pick and choose. He has to accept the call whole-heartedly and with complete surrender before Allah."

The tribesmen kept on looking at the appearance and bearing of the holy Prophet (PBUH) – so captivating and appealing that it kept them spell-bound. Then, the holy Prophet (PBUH) surveyed the gathering and said:

"You will see that the day is not far off when Allah will bestow upon you the lands and all the belongings of the Persians. You will have authority over their daughters. Will you then remember Allah with praise that is due to Him?"

Their faces brightened up and one of their chieftains, Noman bin Shank said:

"O, Quraishite brother! We accept your words".

Thus, came to end the long session with them and the holy Prophet (PBUH), accompanied by Hadrat Abu Bakr and Hadrat Ali, took leave uttering these holy words of verses 8 to 9 of Sura Al-Fath:

"We have sent you as a witness and a bearer of good tidings and a warner, so that you (mankind) may believe in Allah and His Messenger and may honour Him and revere Him and glorify Him at early dawn and at the close of day."

Tabaqat' contains the details regarding the holy Prophet's (PBUH) meetings with various tribes and what has been given above, in this book, is based on this source. During Hajj season in the 11th year of Prophethood, the holy Prophet (PBUH) visited Aqaba where he saw the tents of Khazraj tribe. According to Ibne Ishaque, after their formal introduction with the holy Prophet (PBUH), they consented to listen to him and sat in a circle. They were extremely impressed by his preachings and recitations from the holy Quran and then said to each other:

> "He appears to be that very Prophet, of whom the Jews have been warning us. We should take the lead before the Jews themselves accept his teachings."

Thus, they all embraced Islam on the spot and spoke:

> "When we had set out from our homes, the condition of our people was deplorable. There was disunity in their ranks and they were enemies of one another. No wonder, your teaching might make them united again. The faith that we have accepted will be preached by us among them. And if Allah causes them to rally round you, then no single person in the whole of Arabia would be your equal in power and authority. God willing, we will meet again next year in Hajj season."

The six persons of Bani Khazraj of Medina, who had embraced Islam, have been named in 'Tabaqat' as under:

> Abu Yamama, Asad bin Zorarah, Jabir bin Abdullah bin Rubab, Aqba bin Aamir, Rafay bin Malik, Qutba bin Aamir and Auf bin Al Harith.

Medina is an ancient city of Arabia blessed with fertile soil, invigorating climate and peaceful environment. The Jews inhabited this place since ages. The cataclysmic deluge that inundated Yemen in olden days, whose traces are still to be seen there, had rendered thousands of Arab families homeless who migrated to various places in peninsular Arabia. Aus and Khazraj, the two brothers, who were also affected by the devastating flood in Yemen had migrated to Medina, and are the fore-runners of the two influential tribes of this place known after their names. Previously, these two tribes were settled on the barren tracts of Yathrib, while the Jews held sway over the fertile area. It was after a war fought by Aus and Khazraj tribes with the Jews that the latter were displaced from the fertile lands. After the advent of the holy Prophet (PBUH), the place came to be known as Medina tun Nabi (the Prophet's (PBUH) city) and the tribes of Aus and Khazraj as Ansar (Helpers).

In any case, the Jews of Medina enjoyed undisputed superiority over the tribes of Aus and Khazraj. The former were better off financially, were more cultured and better educated. It was from these Jews that the six tribesmen of Aus and Khazraj who had embraced Islam at the hands of the holy Prophet (PBUH), had learnt that a Prophet was expected to be sent by God.

After the conversion of these six Medinites, twelve more of them, including those five who had already met the holy Prophet (PBUH) earlier, visited Mecca during the Hajj season next year. Of the other seven, who had not met the holy Prophet (PBUH) earlier, five belonged to the tribe of Khazraj and two to that of Aus. On this occasion, the holy Prophet (PBUH) obtained from them the oath of fealty which meant:

> "That we shall not associate any partners with Allah; that we shall not commit theft, or adultery or kill our own progeny, level no false accusations against others; and that we shall not withold our support to the holy Prophet (PBUH) in implementing good deeds and obey him, whether we are rich or poor and whether the holy Prophet's (PBUH) commandments appear agreeable or disagreeable to us and even if some one else is accorded preference over us; and that we will

> not dispute any decision concerning administrative matters (except when they are manifestly heathenish); and that we shall speak the truth, wherever and in whatever circumstances we are; and that we shall not be cowed down by the calumny of those who will taunt us."

The oath ended with the promise of paradise for those who abided by it and a warning for those who violated any clause thereof, their fate to be decided by Allah, Who might punish or forgive.

## Prophet in Town

When these twelve new converts of Medina returned to their city, accompanied by Musab bin Umair whom the holy Prophet (PBUH) had deputed with them to preach Islam, they worked very hard to propagate the faith and very soon Islam claimed a very large number of adherents and, barring a few families in Medina, the entire city embraced Islam, the credit for which goes entirely to the untiring efforts of the Ansar. But certain thought-provoking incidents, which are also of general interest, took place in Medina during the proselytising campaign launched by the Ansar.

One such incident relates to the conversion of the elders and other persons of Bani Abdul Ashal. It so happened that Hadrat Asab bin Umair, who had already embraced Islam sometime ago, entered an orchard in the company of Asaad bin Zarrah, and started preaching and reciting the holy Quran to a group of the tribe of Bani Abdul Ashhal. In the meanwhile, the two elders of that tribe Saad bin Maaz and Usaid bin Huzair who had seen the Muslims reciting the holy verses earlier in the orchard of Bani Zafar, chanced to see Asab bin Umair and Asaad bin Zarrah preaching among the tribesmen. Saad bin Maaz asked Usaid bin Huzair to go and stop both of them from weaning the ignorant tribesmen from their ancestral faith. Saad would have gone there himself but did not do so because of the presence of Asaad bin Zarrah who was his maternal cousin. Usaid picked up his spear and approached the group in a threatening posture and asked the two Muslims preachers to disperse and never attempt to preach again.

But, unruffled by this provocation, Musab bin Umair received Usaid with due courtesy and requested him, very politely, to give him a patient hearing and in case his words offend him, no further preaching would be done among the people of his tribe. Usaid agreed to this fair and reasonable request and sat down among the group. Hadrat Musab bin Umair started talking to him, in a very appealing manner, about Islam's notion of mono-theism, the holy Prophet's (PBUH) apostleship and his enviable character and conduct, about resurrection after death and the Divine plan of reward and punishment in the Hereafter and ended his speech with recitation of holy verses.

The marvel of Quran had worked on Usaid's body and soul, affecting him so profoundly that his face flushed and he completely softened up. When Hadrat Musab bin Umair finished the recitation, Usaid could not help remarking:

"Indeed, what an elegant composition!"

"What is one required to do if he embraces this religion?" This was Usaid's query.

"He has to wash himself, wear clean clothes and then profess that Allah is One and Muhammad is His Messenger. Thereafter he has to offer prayer." This was the detailed reply of Asaad bin Zarrah and Hadrat Musab.

Usaid lost no time in washing and wearing clean clothes. Thereafter, Hadrat Musab formally converted him to Islam. Hadrat Usaid then, indulging in loud thinking, said that if only one man, Saad bin Maaz, could enter the fold of Islam, the entire tribe would be converted to this faith. So, he persuaded Saad bin Maaz to meet the group of Muslims, on whose hands he had embraced Islam. The latter did so and he too got converted, whereafter he addressed his tribesmen:

"O, Bani Abdul Ashhal! What do you think of me?"

"You are our chieftain and an extremely kind person, always giving good counsel." This was their unanimous opinion.

Thereupon, Hadrat bin Maaz told the gathering:

> "I will not speak to the men as well as women of the tribe until you profess belief in Allah and His Messenger."

The sun had hardly set that day, when the entire tribe embraced Islam save one man, Sahibul Aseeram Umroo bin Thabit, who also became a Muslim just on the eve of the War of Uhud wherein he was martyred. According to the holy Prophet (PBUH), he will enter paradise in the hereafter.

While Islam was gaining a foothold quite rapidly in Medina, the heathens of Mecca continued opposing Islam and the holy Prophet (PBUH), despite the latter's kind treatment to their destitutes, orphans and the needy and spending whatever money he had on the general welfare of the poor and the hungry. The holy Prophet (PBUH) once said:

> "I will not like to keep with me a heap of gold as large as the mountain of Uhud for a duration longer than three nights, except what I have to re-pay to my creditors."

He is reported to have also stated that "large heartedness and generosity are the real hallmarks of wealth and not the mere accumulation of money and material." These were not empty sermons. The holy Prophet (PBUH) acted upon these words. He used to spend in Allah's way whatever he earned. No one ever returned empty handed from his door. His 'companions' also acted similarly. They preferred to starve themselves than to see others starving. Hadrat Aishah relates:

> "The holy Prophet's (PBUH) bed was of leather stuffed with barks of datepalm and his family members never ate bread of wheat to their full satisfaction for even three consecutive nights since his arrival in Medina till his passing away."

Contrasted with this, the well-to-do persons of Quraish loved money and its ostentatious display, as is the weakness of all men of wealth. Even their philanthropic acts were meant to show off their riches. They were prey to all kinds of vices that arise from accumulation of wealth—obscenity, lewdness, usurping the properties of relatives, amassing money in all manners right or wrong, looking down upon the less fortunate, indulging in drinking and gambling and so on.

All the Prophets who are sent to reform the society come across similar situations, as the forces of evil combine to oppose the truth. Even, a great Prophet like Moses, realising that he would have to face such adversities in preaching the true religion, prayed to the Almighty:

> "My Lord! I fear that they will deny me. On this account, I shall be embarrassed and my tongue will not speak eloquently. Therefore send for Aaron"
>
> (Al-Shuara, verses 12-13).

Moses called for Aaron's help in accomplishing the extremely onerous responsibility of preaching a new faith among a wrong-doing folk. He wanted a helping hand so that he could devote his entire attention towards calling people to the right path. The Quran also mentions how Moses also prayed to God:

> "My Lord! Relieve my mind
>
> And ease my task for me:
>
> And loosen a knot from my tongue
>
> So that they may understand what I say"
>
> (Ta-HA-Verses-25.28).

The holy Prophet (PB.UH) did not have to pray to the Almighty for opening up his heart and mind as Prophet Moses had to do. The former had already been sent by God as "mercy for the worlds." When the holy Prophet (PBUH) went to Taif to preach the faith, after giving up hope of converting the people of Mecca, he was ill-treated, stoned and injured, as already described at length earlier. It has been narrated that while he was stopping at, a place called Qaruns Saahib, while returning from Taif, the holy Prophet (PBUH) saw a detached lump of cloud overshadowing him wherein Gabriel was clearly visible, who addressed him thus:

> "Allah has taken note of all that which your people have told you in response to your call and that the angel who has authority over mountains is available to carry out your order, whatever it may be."

Thereafter, the Angel of the Mountains informed the holy Prophet (PBUH) that, as commanded by the Almighty, he could turn the mountains that surrounded Mecca up-side down and thereby crush that city, only if he so desired. But the holy Prophet (PBUH) replied that he hoped that the coming generations of the people of Mecca will receive the guidance and believe in mono-theism. Had he willed, he would have, in retaliation of the brutalities which he had suffered at the hands of the people of Mecca, caused complete devastation of Mecca and its inhabitants. But, since he was sent as the last and the noblest Apostle of God he decided to forgive the sinners and not to wreak vengeance.

When the revelation regarding congregational prayer in the afternoon of Friday was received, the holy Prophet (PBUH) sent written instructions accordingly to Hadrat Musab bin Umair to arrange for the weekly congregational prayer in Medina, as it was not possible to hold such prayers in Mecca because of the continued opposition of the polytheists.

Now that the majority of the people of Medina had embraced

Islam and the time was ripe for setting up an Islamic polity in that city, the incident of Meraj, ('Ascension') took place at Mecca while the holy Prophet (PBUH) was extremely unhappy and despondent on account of the behaviour of the people of Mecca. He was consoled through Divine revelation in these words:

> "Endure patiently. Thine endurance is only by the help of Allah. Grieve not for them, and be not in distress because of that which they devise. Indeed Allah is with those who keep their duty towards Him and those who do good deeds."
>
> (Al Nahl-Verses 127-128).

Again, the Almighty provided the much-needed solace to the holy Prophet (PBUH) in these words:

> "Have We not caused thy bosom to dilate, (And eased thee of the burden.)
>
> Which weighed down thy back:
>
> And exalted thy fame?
>
> But lo! with hardship goes ease"
>
> (Nashrah, verses 1-5)

***Grand Entry :*** The holy Prophet (PBUH) was fifty three years of age and had completed twelve long years of Apostleship that the momentous event of Meraj took place. Although the date and year of this event are disputed, yet it is generally recognised that it happened in the night of 27th Rajab, long before the emigration to Medina. It is related that on that night, which the holy Prophet (PBUH), weary of preaching during the day, rested in the house of his paternal cousin sister, Hadrat Umme Hani in Shob Abi Talib, he lay down on bed after Isha prayers and had hardly gone to sleep that Gabriel aroused him, took him to the holy Precincts of Kaaba, opened his chest, washed it with Zam Zam water and enlightened it with Divine Light. Then Gabriel asked him to mount 'burraq', a heavenly steed, larger than a donkey and smaller than a mule, commanding it to behave as the rider was the most Illustrious person ever born. Gabriel also rode with him.

The opening verses of Sura Bani Israel describe this event thus:

> "Glorified be He who carried His servant by night from the Mosque of Kaaba to the Mosque of Al-Aqsa (in Jerusalam) the neighbourhood whereof We have blessed, so that We might show him of our tokens. He, only He, is the Hearer the Seer."

This is all that the Quran mentions about the Ascension. The details appear in the 'traditions' of the holy Prophet (PBUH), there being 25 such 'traditions' concerning Meraj alone. According to these traditions, the holy Prophet (PBUH) stopped at Medina where he offered prayers and was informed by Gabriel that he would migrate to that place. Then Gabriel took him to Mount Sinai, then to Bethelhem where Prophet Jesus was born. The land journey ended at AI-Aqsa Mosque and Gabriel took him to Solomon's Temple where all those Prophets who had preceded him were present and they all offered prayer led by the holy Prophet (PBUH).

Thereafter, he was presented drinks in three different cups - one containing milk, the other alcohol and the third water. He picked up the one that contained water. Gabriel was pleased at the holy Prophet's (PBUH) choice of drinks and said that this was exactly according to the Divine Will.

Then appeared a ladder, by Divine order, spanning the earth and the heavens and the holy Prophet (PBUH) was led to the skies through this ladder. On the first sky, the man and the angel, i.e. the holy Prophet (PBUH) and Gabriel, stopped and the guarding angels enquired from Gabriel about the identity of the man accompanying him and when told that he was Prophet Muhammad (PBUH), who was summoned for an audience with the Almighty he was admitted in. No body saw how he was received in the presence of the Creator, the Omnipotent, Omniscient, Omnipresent Being, but, at least, the angels came to know that the 'light' in the form of Adam before whom they had prostrated themselves in Primordium ('azal') had been granted the great honour of visiting the Creator Himself.

It is narrated, allegorically, in the Traditions that, on the first heaven, the holy Prophet (PBUH) was introduced by Gabriel to Adam, the precursor of mankind. Here the holy Prophet (PBUH) was shown an image of reward and punishment in the hereafter. The details of those observations are given in Hadith literature. The holy Prophet (PBUH) was conducted to various heavens where he met John the Baptist, Prophets Jesus, Joseph, Enoch, Aaron and Moses. On the Seventh heaven, where angels keep-on moving in and out of 'Bait-e-Mamour', "he met Prophet Abraham. Thereafter, the holy Prophet (PBUH) reached the 'last limit' beyond which even Gabriel could not proceed. The holy Prophet (PBUH) went ahead all by himself where he was granted the honour of audience with the Almighty. What transpired no one knows, but, according to hints available in the 'Traditions', prayers (originally, fifty times a day) were made obligatory and the verses 285 and 286 of Sura Baqra were revealed:

> "The Prophet (PBUH) believes in that which has been revealed to him from his Lord and so do the 'believers'. Each one believes in Allah and His angels and His scriptures and His messengers—We make no distinction between any of His messengers—and they say:

We hear and we obey. Grant us Thy forgiveness, our Lord! To You is the journeying.

> "Allah does not take to task a soul beyond its scope. For it is only that which it has earned and against it only that which it has deserved. Our Lord! condemn

us not if we forget or miss the mark! Our Lord! Lay not on us such a burden as you laid on those before us! Our Lord! Impose not on us that which we have not the strength to bear! Pardon us, absolve us and have mercy on us! Thou, our Protector! give us victory over the disbelieving folk."

Also, it was indicated to the holy Prophet (PBUH) that, barring polytheism, all other sins can be hoped to be forgiven, reward for ten good deeds can be expected if only one good deed is intended and that an evil deed becomes punishable only when it is actually committed.

On way back, when Prophet Moses was informed by the holy Prophet (PBUH) about fifty times daily prayers, he advised that he should seek some remission from the Lord as based on his personal experience of the Jews, he could say that the followers of the holy Prophet (PBUH) would hardly be able to comply with such a heavy obligation. The holy Prophet (PBUH), therefore, represented to the Lord for remission and, ultimately, five-time daily prayers were fixed. On the return journey, as in the outward journey, he stopped at Jerusalem, where all the Prophets had assembled, and led the morning prayer. Therefore, he returned to Mecca riding the 'buraq'.

He spoke to Umme Hani about his heavenly journey and the observations. Although his cousin sister persuaded him not to talk publicly about this mysterious event, as it might provide the opponents yet another opportunity to falsify and vilify, the holy Prophet (PBUH) decided otherwise.

It was day-break and the Quraishites were coming to the precincts of the Kaaba. The holy Prophet (PBUH) arrived there and met Abu Jahl face to face. Tauntingly he enquired from the holy Prophet (PBUH) if there was something new or fresh to talk about. The holy Prophet (PBUH) merely said:

"Last night, I had been to the holy Land."

This startled Abu Jahl and he started shouting aloud to attract others' attention, and he told them about the holy Prophet's (PBUH) nocturnal visit to the holy Land at Jerusalem. When they all assembled, the holy Prophet (PBUH) narrated to them the entire incident of Ascension. But they all derided him. Abu Jahl, a cunning person that he was, went near Hadrat Abu Bakr and told him about the holy Prophet's (PBUH) Ascension. But the latter, instead of showing any surprise or hesitation, asserted that he believed in what the holy Prophet (PBUH) had narrated, as he knew that the latter received messages from the Lord in heavens. Hadrat Abu Bakr then rushed towards the holy Prophet (PBUH) who was surrounded by a jesting crowd of Quraishites.

When, on his enquiry, the holy Prophet (PBUH) affirmed that he had narrated the incident of Ascension himself, Hadrat Abu Bakr expressed his belief in what he had said. Since, Hadrat Abu Bakr had visited the holy Land, he enquired about its prominent features which the holy Prophet (PBUH) described correctly, because the Almighty had enabled him at that time, to see Jerusalem again. Among those who were present at that time, there were a few others also who had visited the holy land. They were almost stunned to hear from the holy Prophet's (PBUH) mouth such a clear and correct description of the Land and in their heart of hearts, they believed that the holy Prophet (PBUH) had actually gone to Jerusalem overnight, but their intransigence stood in the way and they did not openly declare their belief in the holy Prophet (PBUH).

It was only Hadrat Abu Bakr who kept on saying loudly, on hearing the detailed description of Jerusalem that the holy Prophet (PBUH) had spoken the truth. This earned him the title of 'Siddique' or one who acknowledged truth of the holy Prophet's (PBUH) version of Ascension although it, did not appeal to the sceptics. When the people of Mecca demanded further proof from the holy Prophet (PBUH), he told them that, on way to Jerusalem, he had seen a caravan carrying such and such goods and that one of their camels got frightened at the sight of the speeding 'burraq'. He further said that he had stopped beside a caravan, whose people were resting and fast asleep, at night and that he drank some water from their vessel and had left a tell-tale to remind them that some one had drunk water while they were asleep. When those caravans arrived, they confirmed the holy Prophet's (PBUH) words. But their mind still refused to believe the holy Prophet (PBUH).

It is a fact, beyond doubt, that the Ascension was physical as the very opening verse of Sura Bani Israel indicates, and that the Divine intention was to show to the holy Prophet (PBUH) some of His tokens, the greatest token being the nocturnal journey itself, during which the distance that could be covered in weeks from Mecca to Jerusalem was covered only in a few hours. Further, the journey in space from Jerusalem to the 'last limit' of the heavens, or galaxies, in a matter of hours and minutes, which was unthinkable then and is unthinkable even now when man has landed on the moon and is trying to travel after Mars and other planets, was the most astounding sign of Divine omnipotence. If God could create the entire universe just by saying 'let it be', He could, undoubtedly, make it possible for the holy Prophet (PBUH) to travel upto Him and return back to his abode on earth within a short span of night. In fact, it should be easier for today's man to believe in the Ascension because now that it is being considered possible to travel in space from planet to planet and galaxy to galaxy through harnessing the forces of nature, the question of the Creator Himself arranging for such a Journey for His Prophet (PBUH) should not be looked upon with doubt and suspicion.

For example, can human comprehension understand how the 'Companions of the cave' slept in a dark hollow place in a rock for well over a century. But this happened, as a few youths remained asleep for a number of years inside a cave while their dog waited outside. The Quran bears testimony to it. This relates to the period when the believers in Christianity were either burnt alive or stoned to death in the Roman empire. These youths had embraced Christianity and had made a public declaration of their faith in the city of Ephesus and had thereby incurred the wrath of the people and officials of the state. They were to be approached and punished. To escape this, they took refuge in a cave and supplicated to God " to bless them with His special care and set matters right for them." Their prayer was granted and conditions were made conducive for them to sleep in the cave for years on end.

When they woke up, they asked themselves about the duration of their sleep. Some one thought that they slept only for a day or even less and then they themselves said that God alone knows how long they slept. Then they fell hungry and one of them went to the market, taking precaution that he would not be spotted by any one. He had a century-old silver coin to buy things which he offered to the shop-keeper in exchange for goods. His out-moded dress and the old silver coin aroused the shop-keeper's suspicion about his identity and a crowd collected around him and he was taken to the city official where he narrated the entire story of his sleep in the cave. During this period the Romans had embraced Christianity and given up idolatry. Therefore, no Christian was persecuted any longer in that city. According to the local legend about this incident, about two centuries had elapsed. When people went to the cave, the 'sleepers' saluted their Christian brethren and lay down whereafter they all expired. The Quran has neither specified the exact number of the 'sleepers' nor the period of their sleep. The following excerpt from the holy Quran throws light on the matter:

> "Some say: They were three, their dog the fourth, and some say:
>
> Five and their dog the sixth, guessing at random, and some say:
>
> Seven, and their dog the eight. Say (O, Muhammad):

> My Lord is best aware of their number. None knows except a few. So, do not contend concerning them except outwardly and do not ask any one of them to say anything about them." (Sura Kahf - Verses 22).
>
> Thus, the Quran clarifies that people will contend concerning their number but God alone knows best and also a few others who have not been specified.

Verse 25 of the same sura says:

> "And they stayed in their cave for three hundred years and add nine."

The verse, immediately following the above one, says:

> "(O, Prophet) Tell that God knows better how long they tarried in the Cave."

According to Hadrat Abdullah bin Abbas, the Quran does not mention that they lived in the cave for 309 years, but that it only refers to people's speculation about the duration of their stay and that the actual period is known only to God, just as people speculate about their correct number, the exact figure being only in God's knowledge.

The holy Quran also relates the incident of a pious man who, by God's command, came back to life after having been dead for a hundred years. This man may be either a saint or a prophet, who thought to himself, while passing by a devastated city whose population had been dead and houses demolished, how would God resuscitate this dead population. His soul was immediately taken by God's command and he remained dead for a century, whereafter he was brought back to life, by God's command, and he was questioned as to the period for which he remained dead. He answered:

> "For a day, or even less, say, a few hours."

The Divine remark was conveyed to him:

> "You remained dead for a hundred years. Now look

> at your food and drink which are still fresh. But, look at your donkey on which you were riding; even its skeleton has been eaten up by worms."

The saintly person must have felt perplexed at this extraordinary incident and when, by God's command, he saw his donkey being restored in its original condition, he exclaimed:

> "Now I realise, God is capable of doing anything:"
>
> Similarly, Prophet Abraham, who is the ancient ancestor of our holy Prophet (PBUH) too, once expressed his wish:
>
> "My Lord! Let me see and observe how you enliven the dead."
>
> "Do you not believe in life after death?" God asked him.

"I do believe my Lord! But my request stems from my earnestness to satisfy my heart and mind". - Prophet Abraham replied, whereupon he was asked to get hold of four birds and to train them like pets and then slaughter them and place a piece of the flesh of each of them on different hills and call them to come which they would do. He complied with the Divine instructions and saw with his own eyes of phenomenon of resurrecton of the dead, an experience which, apparently, defies all reasoning but which is an indisputable fact like the rising of the sun from the eastern horizon every morning.

**Peace for All**

Subsequent to the incident of 'Ascension', the polytheists of Mecca sent words to the holy Prophet (PBUH) that if he could come to them and answer satisfactorily a few questions, they would accept his faith. The holy Prophet (PBUH) went to meet them in the precincts of Kaaba, where the notables of Quraish, including Abu Jahl, Nazar bin Harith and Uqba bin Abu Moit, had assembled and looked over-whelmed with joy that they had, at long last, found a way to check mate the holy

Prophet (PBUH), and were confident that they would have an upper hand, little realising that their fate had already been decided by the Almighty and they were doomed to fail in their nefarious endeavours to humble the holy Prophet (PBUH).

Addressing the holy Prophet (PBUH), they said that they had three questions to be answered by him. The first question related to the youths, who had disappeared a long time ago in history. The second concerned Hadrat Khizr and the third about that great traveller who had visited both the eastern and western fringes of the earth. The holy Prophet (PBUH) had never heard such questions before and he knew that these were prompted by people outside Mecca.

In fact, the polytheists of Mecca had sent their representatives to the 'Rabbis' of the Jews who advised them to ask the aforesaid three questions, and if the holy Prophet (PBUH) answered them correctly then there was no doubt that he was a true Prophet of God. The holy Prophet (PBUH) promised to provide the answer the next day, hoping that Gabriel would tell him the correct answers. But, Gabriel did not turn up and the holy Prophet (PBUH) had no option but to procrastinate and ask for more time, to the utmost glee of the Quraishites. But Gabriel appeared on the third day which the holy Prophet (PBUH) was anxiously awaiting his arrival and counselled him not to promise, in future, that he would certainly do a thing but that he would do it if God willed.

Thus, it was the Divine intention to instruct the followers of the holy Prophet (PBUH) that every work should be undertaken by pronouncing the words "God willing". Sura Kahf was revealed on this occasion which contained detailed answers of all the three questions and the holy Prophet (PBUH) recited this Sura before the notables of Quraish. The answer to the first question, concerning the 'Companions of the Cave,' has already been dealt with and discussed in the foregoing paragraph. The notables of Quraish were dumb founded and stunned when they heard the holy Prophet (PBUH) reciting Sura Kahf in his prophetic and appealing style which was a God given gift to him as to all other holy Prophets.

While reciting the said Sura, the holy Prophet (PBUH) read out the following verse whereupon the polytheists glanced in silence at each other as if they were life-less dummies:

> "And be mindful of the Day (Resurrection) when He will say:

Call those partners of Mina whom you pretended. Then they will cry unto them, but they will not hear their prayer, and We shall set a gulf of doom between them."

The polytheists of Mecca, who were confident that only the Jewish 'Rabbis' knew the answers because only their religious literature contained these questions, were completely flabbergasted, particularly Nazr bin Harith and Uqba bin Moeet, as these were the two persons who had approached the 'Rabbis'. Further the same Sura describes the attitude and entire outlook of the infidels in these words:

> "Those who disbelieve contend with falsehood in order to reflect the Truth thereby, and take Our revelations and warnings as a jest.
>
> "And who does greater wrong than the one who has been reminded of the revelations of his Lord and yet he turns away from them forgetting what his own hands have done for (the Day of Judgement). We have placed coverings so that they do not understand and in their ears is a deafness. And though you call them to the guidance, they can never be led aright.
>
> "And thy Lord is the Forgiver and Merciful. Had He taken them to task for their deeds immediately, He would have hastened on the doom for them; but theirs is an appointed time from which they will find no escape."

Thereafter, in order to make the notables of Quraish take lesson from God's wrath that descended on the settlements of Sheba, Thamud, Madian and the people of Lot, the Divine revelation said:

"And all those townships! We destroyed them when they did wrong, and We appointed a fixed time for their destruction."

**Movement for Education**

About Khizr, the Divine revelation narrated:

"And when Moses said to his servant, I will not give up until I reach the point where the two rivers meet, even if I have to march on for ages. And when they reached the given point, they forgot their fish which, being free, took its way in the waters.

"And when they had gone further, Moses asked his servant to bring their breakfast, because the journey had been quite tiresome.

"The servant said: Did you not see when we took refuge on the rock, I forgot the fish, and none but Satan caused me to forget to mention it, and it plunged into the waters by a marvel.

"Moses said that was the place they had been seeking. So, they retreated their steps again.

"There they found one of Our slaves who had been given mercy from Us, and who had been granted knowledge from us.

"Moses asked him if he could follow him to learn what he had been taught.

"That person said: You can not bear with me, because how can you bear with me when you can not comprehend my knowledge.

"Moses said: God willing you shall find me patient and I will not argue with you.

"He said: If you go with me, you will not ask me concerning anything until I myself mention of it to you."

The person about whom this narration revolves was Hadrat Khizr, as recorded in a Tradition on the authority of Hadrat Abdullah bin Abbas who heard it from Abi bin Kaab. According to this Tradition, once while Prophet Moses was preaching, he claimed that he was the "most knowledgeable person." This assertion on his part displeased the Almighty, Who indicated to him that he should set out in search of a person who will be present at the meeting point of two rivers. On further enquiry by Prophet Moses, regarding any particular sign to locate that person, the Divine instruction was conveyed to him that he should take alongwith him a fish which will disappear in water at the exact location of the person concerned.

When the two (Prophet Moses and Hadrat Khizr) started their journey together, the latter made a hole in the boat wherein they were crossing a river. Thereupon Prophet Moses uttered in surprise:

"You have drilled a hole in the ship so that all the folk and the ship get drowned. Indeed you have done a horrid thing."

Hadrat Khizr remarked:

"Did I not tell you that you can not bear with me?"

Prophet Moses entreated:

"Be not angry with me as I forgot and do not be hard upon me for my fault."

At the next stage of their journey, they came across a boy whom Hadrat Khizr killed. Prophet Moses could not restrain his horror at this act and he spoke out:

> "You killed an innocent lad although he had not shed any one's blood. Indeed you have done something unreasonable."

Hadrat Khizr replied:

> "Had I not told you that you will not be able to bear with me."

Prophet Moses assured:

> "If I ask you after this concerning anything, you can part company with me. You have received an excuse from me."

The two journeyed on till they came to the folk of a certain township, whom they asked for food but they refused to be hospitable. There, the twain found a wall on the point of falling into ruin. Hadrat Khizr repaired it whereupon Prophet Moses said that had the former wanted, he could have taken payment for it.

This exasperated Khizr who told Prophet Moses:

> "This is the parting between you and me. I will tell you the interpretation of that which you could not bear with patience."

As for the ship, Hadrat Khizr explained, it belonged to poor people working on the river and I wished to mar it as there was a king behind them who was taking every ship by force. As for the lad, his parents were 'believers' and I feared that he would be a source of oppression for his parents on account of his disbelief and rebellious nature in future. I thought that the Lord will give them a better substitute for the lad, who would be of good habits and full of kindness. Regarding the wall, it belonged to two orphan boys in the city and there was a treasure hidden underneath the wall. Since their father was a righteous person, the Lord intended that the boys, on coming of age, should bring forth their treasure as a reward from their Lord.

In the end, Hadrat Khizr said:

> "I did nothing according to my own discretion, but on God's command."

Now, the polytheists of Mecca had received answers to their two questions and only one question relating to a globe-trotting traveller remained to be answered. The holy Quran disclosed the name of this traveller:

> "They will ask you about Zul Qarnain; Say, I recite to you something about him."

Hearing this, the heart of the polytheists started sinking and their faces were filled with gloom, as the last weapon in their armoury to defeat the holy Prophet (PBUH) had also proved ineffectual.

***Old Example :*** The holy Quran described Zul Qarnain as a powerful and resourceful person. To start with his campaigns, he took an expedition to the West and reached the setting-place of the sun, setting in a murky sea. There, he saw a people regarding whom the Almighty authorised him to either punish them or treat them with kindness. Thereafter, he set out on another expedition till he reached the rising-place of the sun and found it rising on a people for whom there was no shelter therefrom. In yet another expedition, he came between two mountains where he built a barrier and a wall of molten iron and copper to protect the natives of that land from the raids and pillage at the hands of Gog and Magog.

Although the infidels of Mecca had heard the replies to their questions, yet they did not turn towards the faith and Divine guidance because of the covering that enveloped their hearts, and they dispersed quietly.

How unfortunate were these people who saw the glowing and beaming face of the holy Prophet, (PBUH) heard his angelic voice, knew his demeanour and polite behaviour, were aware of his high and honourable pedigree, had a first-hand experience of his selflessness, sacrifice, noble conduct and kindness towards all and had observed his steadfastness and unflinching faith in his mission, and yet they did not enter the fold of Islam; while others who came to him from far off places, declared allegiance to him at first sight!

Apart from the pressure on Banu Hashim and the persecution of the Companions of the Holy Prophet, a good deal of criticism was levelled against the Prophet's claim that he had received revelations from God—in fact against the very idea of revelation itself. This criticism was directed along four different channels.

Firstly, Muhammad was subjected to mental torture by suggesting other explanations of his religious experience than that it was revelation from God.

Secondly, the opponents could not believe that a human being who did not claim to possess any supernatural power could ever become the messenger of God.

Thirdly, if a human being were to be elevated at all to this exalted position, there were so many other persons who were richer and far more influential than Muhammad. Why was it, the sceptics argued, that God ignored all of them altogether and crowned the helpless Qurayshite orphan with prophethood?

Lastly, Muhammad had nothing extraordinary, nothing dramatic, to parade to substantiate his claim to prophethoood.

We will consider these allegations in the following pages and will note the way in which the Holy Quran repudiates them.

*The Conspiracy :* The commonest allegation against Muhammad was that he was a majnun, that is, possessed by a Jinn. They also suggested that he was a kahin, or soothsayer, a Sahir, that is, magician or sorcerer, and shair, that is a poet.

It is significant to note in this connection that the common allegations which the Meccans levelled against Muhammad are repeated even to this very day. Professor Mcdonald has attempted, though in vain, to explain Muhammad's prophethood in terms of epilepsy and psychopathology. He also believes that Muhammad was a genius. But this aspect is not well defined. The key to Muhammad is that "he was a poet" of the old Arab type without much of poetic skill, with all his being given to the prophetic side of poetry, and that he had a "strange jumble of Jewish and Christian conceptions" as material for his prophetic use.

The view of Macdonald that Muhammad was a poet is slightly different from that of Muir who ventures the suggestion that the supernatural influence, which appears to have acted upon the soul of the Arabian prophet, may have proceeded from the "Evil One" and his emissaries, yet the spirit in which the prophetic consciousness of Muhammad manifests itself is not the same. Macdonald asserts that just as Hassan the poet had his female jinni who overpowered him and pressed verses out of him, so Muhammad had his companion (qarin) who was the source of his inspiration. Muhammad, he continues, is not really a prophet in any exalted sense: "I know nowhere in the Semitic world any appearance like that of the great prophets of the Hebrew. "Rather, this first of all Moslem is in part a combination of 'soothsayer' adviser and admonisher, and a hurler of magical formulae against his enemies, although possessed of ideas which raised him above the common place and suggest that Muhammad a devout soul, if ever there was one and a mystic inspite of his creed—was adrift himself on that sea, and was nearing that shore."

***Attempts of Revolt*** : I have given long excerpts from Macdonald's book in order to give an idea that inspite of the great difference of time there has been no change in the nature of the allegations hurled at the Prophet. The modern critics of

Islam, like the Meccans of the olden days, believe that what the Prophet claims to be a revelation or the word of Allah is nothing else but the frenzied expression of the ecstatic state of his mind.

The Holy Quran has vehemently refuted this charge and has explained that the utterances of the Holy Prophet (peace be upon him) are the revelations of the Lord and their nature and contents provide a bold challenge to those who attribute his prophetic expressions to some base origin, at times to the mental throes of a dreaming reformer, at others to the effusion of a frenzied poet or the incoherent drivellings of an insane man. The Holy Quran categorically repudiates, for instance, the allegation that the Prophet is a poet: We have not taught him poetry nor is it meet for him." At another place the Holy Quran explains the reasons why it is absurd to call Muhammad a poet. A poet is commonly a mental rambler who tries to transform into beautiful verse his wayward whims and fleeting emotions. He is primarily concerned with abstract and remote issues and speculations which have no bearing on the practical problems of human life.

> "As for poets, it is the erring who follow them. Hast thou not seen how they stray in every valley."

Thus, whatever the poet says cannot be consistent and closely knit. Being an expression of the fleeting emotions it is impossible to find coherence and harmony in the views expressed by a poet. Moreover, there is a world of difference between the practical life of a poet and his poetical utterances. His poetry merely expresses his emotional moods and therefore a poet is not required to transform his thoughts into living facts; "And how they (the poets) say that which they do not."

A prophet, on the other hand, is a practical reformer. He says what he means and means what he says. Whatever he professes is also transmuted by him into practical reality. In his great personality, the ultimate values which he preaches take flesh and blood.

Besides, there is complete harmony between the various components of the Prophet's teaching, each message being in entire unison with the whole of his revelation. There is nothing inconsistent, nothing superfluous.

Lastly, unlike poets, the actual impact of the Prophet's activity is the purification and enoblement of human beings. A spiritual Armageddon is fought out by the prophets on the plains of history. Humanity, rent with national antagonism and riven with class-conflicts and threatened by the tyranny of materialism, is freed by the prophets from the servitude of these evil forces and learns to live as the family of God. The Prophets restore peace amongst the different sections of the human race and bring harmony within man. The greed, selfishness, love for material gains, lust for power—all these base urges are purified and in their place human beings learn to live as self-less and God-fearing men whose uppermost desire to serve humanity and weed out corruption and tyranny from human society.

Can a poet achieve all this? Is he capable of expressing something which is consistent and is not in collision with any other aspects of his own preachings? The reply of history to this query seems to be conclusive and the attestation of human experience abundantly clear—and both of them in the negative.

The allegation that the Holy Prophet was under the influence of the evil spirits has also been categorically repudiated by the Holy Quran. How is it that a man who is controlled by a demonic being or a supernatural power of low grade, quite other than the Power that reigns over the universe, can set for himself the sublime purpose of destroying the spell of superstitions which had been interposed between man and his Creator, of restoring the rational and sacred idea of Divinity amidst the chaos of material and disfigured gods of idolatry and of effecting a moral regeneration of a society which had touched a low ebb of degradation, and of giving to humanity a superb code of conduct which does not guide man merely in the sphere of individual righteousness but also in the spheres of politics and economics, law, and morality.

It is impossible for anyone who studies the life and character of Muhammad, who knows what he taught and how he lived, to feel anything but reverence for that noble soul—the greatest of the apostles of Allah. Can a person under the control of an evil spirit develop such deep consciousness of his inner self, and all its different aspects, the consciousness of God Almighty with His numerous attributes, the awareness of the sublimity of his mission, and the stern obstacles that stood in his way, the awareness of the qualities of his friends and the stubbornness of his foes—and yet perfect harmony within himself? Such rare qualities of head and heart are never to be found in those who are under the influence of evil spirits. History shows not a single example of such-like persons whose message created one of the most balanced and noblest civilisations of the world. The Holy Quran says:

> Shall I inform you upon whom the devils descend? They descend on every sinful, false one. They listen eagerly, but most of them are liars.
>
> (xxvi: 221-223)

Similarly, the Quran also vehemently repudiates the allegation that Muhammad speaks under the influence of the jinn. "Have they not thought them that their comrade is in no way under the influence of the jinn. He is but a plain warner." Here "comrade" stands for the Holy Prophet. The Quran exhorts the people to reflect if a man of such great eminence and wisdom, whose whole career was the faithful expression of a fine nature, free of every trace of self-seeking, vanity or affectation, a man of loving personality, of transparent candour and integrity, who successfully guided humanity not only in one aspect of life but in all sectors of life, could achieve such a spectacular success under the influence of the jinn. Never in history has a man, influenced by the spirits, been able to attain such glory as Muhammad did in the short span of twenty-three years of his prophethood.

Coming from a land and a people who had no glorious past of which they could be proud, he elevated them to the heights of eminence, shattered the great empires, undermined the position of long-established religions, remoulded the souls of countless men and women and built up a whole new world—the world of Islam. How can any sane person conceive that this great revolution, which not only changed the map of the world, but also radiated morality and expanded the frontiers of knowledge, could have been brought about by a man who was under the spell of the jinn.

The fact that the opponents who brought forth such allegations were not unanimous in their accusations, is a clear proof of their falsehood. They were thoughtlessly slinging mud at the Prophet (peace be upon him) in the hope that some of it might stick. This is the reason why they could not follow any firm line of criticism. They said all sorts of things. Sometimes they said that he was a poet; at other times they declared his words to be those of a soothsayer or of a magician. It is indeed quite strange that a person who was unlettered, who had no knowledge of the ancient scriptures, should have been the one through whom the world received a book like the Quran which in its sublime composition and its incomparable literary excellence speaks for itself as an irrefutable proof of its Divine origin.

There was also the charge that the Prophet was just an ordinary person who walked in the bazaars, who had his wives and children, that there was nothing unusual or supernatural about him. The Holy Quran has discussed this point at some length and conclusively shown that prophets, who are sent to guide humanity to righteousness, are human beings and thus no Divinity should be attributed to them. Indeed, the Quran itself abounds in statements which stress that Muhammad was essentially a human being:

> Say: I am only a human being like you. My Lord inspires me that your God is only One God.
> (xviii: 110)
>
> Say (unto them O Muhammad): I am only a human being like you. It is inspired in me that your God is One God, therefore take the straight path unto Him. Seek forgiveness of Him. (xli: 6)

The Holy Quran has also mentioned the reason why a prophet should necessarily be raised from among human beings. The Prophet is sent to guide humanity, a function which can be performed only by a human being. He should live as a man, enjoying the pleasures and suffering the ills of human existence, so that those around him could follow in his footsteps. People should be able to see in his personality a living embodiment of virtue and piety. His life should be able to manifest the Attributes of the Creator. His love and concern for humanity should be sublime. He reflects the ideal pattern of human existence. This purpose can be achieved only if a prophet, as human being, exemplifies that pattern in his actual life. It is only as a human being that he could show the right path to the people and could inspire in them the religious devotion and piety.

There is a misconception under which people have been labouring since time immemorial that a person who claims no divine powers for himself cannot be deputed by God to reform and regenerate the human race. The Holy Quran has winnowed out this mistaken notion and has pointed out that the angels, who do not share human feelings and sentiments, cannot prove themselves to be good guides for humanity. Human beings can learn from the actions and practical wisdom of those alone who share human feelings and appreciate the different problems of human life. It is human beings alone, therefore, who have been deputed to deliver to humanity the words of God and to explain their practical implications by leading their lives in perfect accord with the behests of the Creator. Whatever the prophets say or do is ideal in every respect, because they live in constant fellowship with the Great Reality. The Holy Quran says:

> And naught prevented mankind from believing when the guidance came unto them save that they said: Hath Allah sent a mortal as (His) messenger? Say: If there were in the earth angels walking secure, we had sent down for them from heaven an angel as messenger. (xvii: 94–95)

These verses clearly show that a human being alone is competent to guide humanity because his life offers them a practical guidance. Since this world is primarily inhabited by human beings and it is for their regeneration that the prophets are sent, human beings alone can therefore successfully accomplish this great task.

At another place, the Holy Quran states that even if this task was assigned to the angels, they would present themselves before humanity in the garb of mortals, because it is only in the form of human beings that their lives can provide lessons for their guidance:

> They say: Why has not an angel been sent down unto him. If We sent down an angel, then the matter would be judged; no further time would be allowed them (for reflections). Had We appointed an angel (Our messenger). We assuredly would have made him a man. (vi: 8-9)

Another line of propaganda adopted by the opponents of the Prophet to ridicule his revelations was to assert that the revelations were completely human production, the work either of Muhammad himself or that of his human assistants or these were merely the stories of the past. The Holy Quran has repudiated this charge in the following words:

> Those who disbelieve say: This is naught but a lie which he hath invented, and other folk have helped him in it, so that they have produced a slander and a lie. And they say: Fables of the men of old which he had written down so that they are dictated to him morning and evening. Say (unto them, O Muhammad): He Who knoweth the secret of the heavens and those of the earth hath revealed it. Verily, He is Ever-Forgiving, Merciful. (xxv: 4-6)

The charge has been quoted repeatedly in other verses of the Holy Quran in different ways:

And We know well what they say: Only a man teacheth him. The speech of him at whom they falsely hint is outlandish, and this is clear Arabic speech.

Verily, those who disbelieve the revelation of Allah, Allah guideth them not and theirs will be a painful doom.

> (The Prophet invents no lie) only they invent falsehood who believe not Allah's revelations, and (only) they are liars. (xvi: 103-104)

Amongst the various attempts to deride the Quran, it was one of the most powerful charges. It is significant that it has been summarily dismissed by saying that it is nothing but a bare lie . The charge is so foolish and hollow that it hardly deserves any consideration.

The persons who have been referred to in this connection are Jabir, Yasir, Aish, or Yaish, Qais, Addas. They were the helpless slaves of powerful Arab masters. It is indeed strange hat these persons who had been allegedly teaching Muhammad (peace be upon him) the craft of prophethood and had been preparing him for this avocation by narrating to him anecdotes of the past should have been among the first to believe in the divine source of the Quran and should have been willing to suffer persecutions at the hands of their masters for this very belief.

Moreover, none of them was an Arab by descent. They were all aliens who had been sold as slaves in the markets of Arabia. It is indeed surprising that non-Arabs should have been able to produce a book like the Holy Quran which in respect of the elegance of its language, the superb structure of its words and sentences, in the peculiar style of its narration, in the extraordinary beginning and ending of its verses, in its flow of thought, in the introduction of parables and description of events, in the forms of its admonitions and warnings and in the manner of its reasoning and arguments, is unparalleled in the whole range of human history.

The composition of the Quran, in spite of its concern with a variety of subjects, is remarkable. The Arabs were accustomed either to prose or to poetry. Their prose was divided into rhymed and unrhymed. The intellectuals practised in verse. As for prose, its use was for the common people. The Quran did not resemble either the prose or the poetry of the period, for the ending of its verses were different from the rhymes of poetry and the saj' of prose. The Holy Quran, in fact, introduced a new style of expression which was not within the reach of the common man.

Thus, every sensible man must acknowledge Muhammad's unalloyed sincerity in his claim that what he called revelation was not the secret learning from the Christian slaves, but that it came to him from God alone. "The Quran," observes Harry Gaylord Dorman, "is a literal revelation of God, dictated to Muhammad by Gabriel, perfect in every letter. It is an everpresent miracle witnessing to itself and to Muhammad, the Prophet of God. Its miraculous quality resides partly in its style, so perfect and lofty that neither men nor jinn could produce a single chapter to compare with its briefest chapter, and partly in its content of teachings, prophesies about the future and amazingly accurate information such as the unlettered Muhammad could never have gathered of his own accord."

Another line of attack was that Muhammad (peace be upon him) was not the sort of person to whom revelations should have come. He was not sufficiently competent for that. The Arabs in general could not imagine that a man who was a posthumous child and had been deprived even of the love of the mother in early childhood, who had lost the support of the important men of his tribe, who had no riches to display, could be elevated to the position of a prophet. They thought that prophethood should have been bestowed upon one of the wealthy chiefs of the tribes:

> And they say: If only this Quran had been revealed to some great man of the two towns (Mecca and Taif). (xiii: 31)

In refutation of this criticism, the Holy Quran points out that prophethood is a special favour of God and He knows well on whom it should be bestowed. No human being, therefore, has any right to question the choice of Allah and no one is entitled to dictate to Him whom to choose and whom to ignore.

> Is it they who apportion their Lord's mercy? (xiii: 32)

The unbelievers said that they would not believe in the prophethood of Muhammad unless they were also enabled to enjoy the prophetic experiences themselves:

> And when a token cometh unto them, they say: We will not believe until we are given that which Allah's messengers are given. (vi: 125)

The Quran spurns it as a fantastic demand and says that Allah is the best to decide correctly on whom His favour should be showered. Allah knoweth best whom to endow with His Message?

The Quran stresses this by pointing out:

> And thus have We inspired in thee (O Muhammad) a spirit of our Command. Thou knewest not what the Scripture was, nor what the Faith. But We have made it a light whereby We guide whom We will of our bondmen. And thou verily dost guide unto a right path. (xiii: 52)

Then in the chapter entitled Jumuah (Congregation) this point has been further elucidated:

He it is Who hath sent among the unlettered ones a messenger of their own, to recite unto them His revolutions and to purify them and to teach them the Scripture and Wisdom, though heretofore they were indeed in error manifest.

> Along with others of them who have not yet joined them, He is the Mighty, the Wise. That is the bounty of Allah, which He giveth unto whom He willeth. (xii: 2-4)

The last group of opponents comprised those persons who expected revelation to have supernatural accompaniments observable by all. When they saw that Muhammad (peace and blessings of Allah be upon him) was no more than a person walking in the bazaars like all other human beings, procuring articles for his daily use, protecting himself against the cold blasts of the winter and the scorching heat of the summer, they were attempting to establish that a man who shared the life of other mortals and had nothing unusual about him, could not be a messenger of God. For them, a prophet was necessarily superhuman who had hardly anything in common with ordinary human beings. The disbelievers, therefore, expressed their doubts about the prophethood of Muhammad and said:

What a strange messenger is he, that he eateth food and walketh in the streets, why is not an angel sent down unto him to be a warner with him?

> Or (why is not) a treasure thrown down unto him, or why hath he not a garden from whence to eat? And the evil-doers say: You are but following a man bewitched. (xxv: 7-8)

In the chapter entitled Banu Israil the demand for the supernatural signs in Muhammad (peace be upon him) are even more pressing:

> They say: We shall not give thee credence till thou causest for us to bubble up from the earth a spring;
> Or until thou hast a garden of palm and vine, and thou causest in the midst of it rivers to gush forth;
> Or until thou causest the heaven to fall upon us as frag-ments as thou hast said, or thou producest God and angels ascending;
> Or until thou hast a house adorned with gold, or thou ascendest into the heaven;
> Nor shall We give credence to thy ascent until thou bringest down to us a writing which we may read. (xvii: 90-93)

There is some variation in the precise nature of what is expected or demanded of Muhammad (peace and blessings of Allah be upon him), but underlying assumption is that a prophet should possess some supernatural powers by virtue of which he should be able to suspend or disrupt the working of the natural order whenever he desires. In answer to these demands, God commanded Muhammad to announce:

> Say: Glory be to my Lord! I am nothing but a human being (sent) as a messenger. (xvii: 93)

This verse beautifully explains the reason why the demand

that the Divine can be manifested in time only through a serious disturbance of the natural order is foolish. Muhammad is only a warner and as such does not command the supernatural powers of the universe. The sudden bubbling up of springs from the earth, the gushing forth of rivers, the falling down of the sky and the abrupt appearance of a magnificent building made of pure gold, are not the essential accompaniments of a true prophet. On the contrary, the qualifications of a true prophet are his extremely pious and virtuous life, his perfect integrity, his shining and spotless character, his selflessness, his love for humanity and his unfailing and sustained devotion to the cause of Allah and His noble teachings.

The Holy Quran has explained this point at numerous places. In the first instance, it emphasises that the performance of miracles does not lie in the hand of the Prophet:

> And it was not given to any messenger that he should bring a portent save by Allah's leave but when Allah's commandment cometh (the cause) is judged aright, and the followers of vanity will then be lost.
>
> (1: 78)

The Prophet himself confesses his inability to perform miracles at his own sweet will, because it rests with the Almighty God. He says in very clear terms that the Prophet is only a messenger of God who honestly carries out the behests of his Master:

> Say (O Muhammad to the unbelievers): I say not unto you (that) I possess the treasure of Allah, not that I have knowledge of the unseen, and I say not unto you: verily, I am an angel. I follow only that which is inspired in me. (vi: 50)
>
> Say: For myself I have no power to benefit, nor power to hurt, save that which Allah willeth. Had I knowledge of the unseen I should have gathered abundance of wealth, and adversity would not touch

> me. I am but a warner, and a bearer of good tidings unto folk who believe. (vii: 188)

"It must be said," observes Ameer 'Ali "to the credit of the disciples of the Arabian Teacher that they never called for a miracle from their Master. They—scholars, merchants, and soldiers— looked to the moral evidences of his mission. They ranged themselves round the friendless preacher at the sacrifice of all their worldly interests and worldly hopes, and adhered to him through life and death with a devotion to human personality to which there is scarcely a parallel in the history of the world."

He further elucidates this point by adding:

> In an age when miracles were supposed to be ordinary occurrences at the back of the commonest saint, when the whole atmosphere was surcharged with super naturalism, not only in Arabia, but in the neighbouring countries where civilization had made a far greater progress, the great Pioneer of rationalism unhesitatingly replies to the miracle-seeking heathens—"God has not sent me to work wonders; He has sent me to preach to you. My Lord be praised! Am I more than a man sent as an apostle?"...No extraordinary pretensions, no indulgence in hyperbolical language, no endeavour to cast a glamour around his character or personality. "I am only a preacher of God's words, the bringer of God's message to mankind," repeats he always. From first to last no expression escapes him "which could be construed into a request for human worship" [The Quran, Ixii: 1-10]; from first to last there is unvarying soberness of exprelssion, which, considering the age and surroundings, is more marvellous; from first to last the tone is one of simple, deep humility before the Creator.

The Prophet disclaims every power of working wonders and bases the claim for the truth of his divine mission entirely upon his teachings. He never resorts to the miraculous to assert his influence or to reinforce his warnings. It is recorded in Hadith that some of the Prophet's companions took the eclipse of the sun as a disturbance of the natural order on the death of his son Ibrahim. He plainly told his followers that the sun and the moon observed the commands of Allah and they had nothing to do with the death of his son. He emphatically remarked: "Indeed the sun and the moon are two out of the numerous signs of Allah. They do no eclipse due to birth or death of anyone. When you find them in this state, pray to Allah and celebrate His glory.

Instead of creating a halo of awe and mystery around himself, the Prophet appeals to the inner consciousness and credulity.

> "Look around yourself (the Quran says in effect), this wonderful world, the sun, the moon and the stars, holding their swift silent courses in the blue vault of heaven, the law and the system prevailing in the universe; the rain-drops falling to revive the parched earth into life; the ships moving across the ocean, beladen with what is profitable to mankind; the beautiful palm covered with its golden fruit—are these the handiwork of your wooden or stone gods?"

> "Fools! do you want a sign when the whole creation is full of the signs of God? The structure of your body, how wonderfully complex, how beautifully regulated; the alternations of night and day, and of life and death; your sleeping and awakening; your desire to accumulate from the abundance of God; the winds driving abroad the pregnant clouds as the forerunners of the Creator's mercy; the variety of the human race, and yet their close affinity; fruits, flowers, animals,

human brings themselves—are these not signs enough of the presence of a Master Mind?"

The proofs of Muhammad's truth are not philosophically recondite. They do not require any great or profound speculative power to apprehend them. If they did, it would be extremely unfortunate for the masses of mankind—the common people who must of necessity be hewers of wood and drawers of water. To see and feel the force and cogency of some of these proofs demands to an extent the cessation of a strictly philosophic struggle with problems, and the exercise instead of what one calls "wise passiveness" along with the possession of sundry moral virtues such as reverence, candour, and openness of mind to evidence when it is presented ab intra, as well as ab extra. To the Prophet Muhammad, as to the seers of the past, it was not only through intellectual scrutiny that they could find "the secret of the universe" but through honest thinking and making use of a heart that watches and receives. The Holy Quran has beautifully expressed this state of mind in the following words:

> Say (unto them, O Muhammad): I exhort you unto one thing only: that ye awake, for Allah's sake, by twos and singly, and then reflect, (xxiv: 46)

But to all the exhortations of the Quran, the Quraysh turned a deaf ear. They were blind to the signs of God, deaf to the call of the Prophet towards righteousness and towards shunning corruption and abominations. In the language of the Quran they....

> "have hearts wherewith they understand not, and have eyes wherewith they see not, and have ears wherewith they hear not. They are as cattle—nay they are worse! These are the neglectful!" (vii: 179)

Then the Holy Quran also points out the fact that the demand of the unbelievers for miracles was not based on sincerity. The noble life of the Holy Prophet and the sublimity of his Divine message are sufficient to convince any sincere man that Muhammad is a true prophet of God. It is the vanity of the infidels, their grudge against his teachings and their inherited bias that prompted them to make such fantastic demands. Had they been sincere in their quest for truth they would have found ample proofs to believe in the prophethood of Muhammad:

> And those who have no knowledge say: Why doth not Allah speak unto us, or some sign come unto us? Even thus, as they now speak, speake those (who were) before them. Their hearts are all alike. We have made clear the revelations for people who are sure. Verily We have sent thee (Muhammad) with the truth, a bringer of glad tidings and a warner.
>
> (ii: 118-119)

In reply to the pressing demand for miracles, the Quran says that the extraordinary pious life of Muhammad and the wonderful Book revealed to him are themselves the two great miracles which testify to the truth of his claim. Is it short of a miracle that a helpless man, having no material resources, braves for many years the hatred of his people, without any selfish motive whatsoever, and when people rally round him, instead of making them his own bondsmen, he persuades them to bow down before Allah, the sole Master of the universe? Then this very person, who had no schooling whatsoever, presents to the people a Book, which is all wisdom, which contains a code of laws, a manual of prayer and ethics, and is reverenced to this day by a great portion of the human race, as a miracle of elegance of style, of sublimity of message and of truth. These are the great miracles; and miracles indeed these are. The Holy Quran stresses this point:

And they say: Why are not portents sent down upon him from his Lord? Say, portents are with Allah only and I am but a plain warner.

> Is it not enough for them that we have sent down unto thee the Scripture which is read unto them? Verily, herein is mercy, and a reminder for the folk who believe. (xxix: 50-51)

In these verses, the Holy Quran is claimed to be the greatest miracle of Muhammad which pours forth in an inspired tongue "all the revelations of nature, conscience and prophecy. Ask you a greater miracle than this. O unbelieving people! then to have your own tongue closed as the language of that incomparable Book, one piece of which puts to shame all your golden poesy and suspended songs to covey the tidings of universal mercy, the warnings to pride and tyranny."

The Holy Quran further reveals that the advent of Muhammad is not unexpected. All the prophets and the revealed Books that preceded him proclaimed his glorious coming, sang his praise, exhorted their followers to obey him, prophesied extraordinary and unparalleled reforms and wonders to be worked by him, announced the sublimity and perfection of his teachings and declared themselves to be the simple harbingers of the final dispensation, destined for Muhammad:

> Is it not a token for them that the doctors of the children of Israel know it? (xxvi: 197)

> And they say: If only he would bring us a miracle from his Lord! Hath not there come unto them the proof of what is in the former Scriptures? (xx: 133)

The Quran also reveals the fact that the disbelievers were pressing for miracles, not because they were sincere in their demand, but because they wanted to subject Muhammad and his followers to mental torture by talking all sorts of foolish things. Amidst all kinds of doubts and misgivings, when they found themselves drifting to Reality, their obstinacy and self-interests stood in their way.

They were unwilling to abandon their religion, because they knew that it would deprive them of so many sources of expolitation and self-aggrandisement. They realised that with the acceptance of Islam as their code of life they would be required to exercise so many restraints on their untamed lusts and surrender so many material benefits which they had been enjoying since long by unjust and immoral methods. They had been avoiding Islam purposely and had been trying to check its tidal wave and in this they actually had ulterior motives. Even if miracles were performed before them, they would attribute some low motive to them in order to belittle their value as a sign of Allah's power.

The Holy Quran is replete with examples showing that when miracles were shown by the Prophets, the stubborn amongst the unbelievers brushed them aside by telling people that they were nothing but feats of magic. For instance, when the prophet Moses performed miracles the unbelievers tauntingly remarked that they were merely magical tricks with the help of which he wanted to dupe them:

But When our tokens came unto them, plain to see, they said: This is mere magic.

> And they denied them, though their souls acknowledged them, for spite and arrogance. Then see the nature of the consequence for the wrong-doers. (xxvii: 13-14)

In the same way, when miracles were shown at the hand of the Holy Prophet, unbelievers rejected them outright and said it was just a magic:

> Then turned he away in pride and said: This is naught else than magic fram the old. (xxiv: 23-24)

In this verse, Allah has also given the reason why unbelievers did not come to the fold of Islam. It was their arrogance and spite which kept them away from adopting the path of righteousness.

Such was the obstinacy of unbelievers that when the moon was split in twain by Allah at the gesture of Muhammad, they paid no heed to it and overlooked it altogether by saying that it was just an illusion:

> The hour drew nigh and the moon was rent it twain. And if they behold a portent they turn away and say: Prolonged illusion. They denied everything the Truth and followed their own lusts; and every affair is settled. (iv: 1-3)

The Quran further explains that since the unbelievers were fanatics and their vision were cramped and narrow, they could not, therefore, judge wisely between right and wrong. The portents and signs of God, however manifest, had no appeal for them, since their reasoning faculties had become almost dead due to arrogance which they had been constantly showing in their attitude towards the Messenger of Allah:

> Never came unto them a sign of the signs of Allah, but they did not turn away from it. (vi: 4)

The Holy Quran again points out their stubbornness in clearer words:

> Had We sent down unto thee (O Muhammad) a Writing upon parchment so that they could feel it with their hands, those who disbelieve would have said: This is naught else than magic. (vi: 7)

Apart from some of the above assertions, aspersions were cast on Muhammad's motives. The unbelievers tried to convince people, though vainly, that the religious mission of Muhammad, in respect of which he claimed to be actuated by the Command of Allah, had some material interests. He, with the help of these religious tactics, wanted to usurp power and prestige and gain pre-eminence over them. The Quran emphatically refute all such motives which were attributed to Muhammad and insisted again and again that he was only a warner that his function is simply to warn people and that he had no axe of his own to grind in this sacred cause:

> Say (O Muhammad unto mankind); I ask of you no reward for this, and I am no imposter. Lo! it is naught else than a reminder for all peoples. And ye will come in time to know the truth thereof. (xxviii: 86)
>
> Say (unto them, O Muhammad): whatever reward I might have asked of you is yours. My reward is with Allah only. He is the witness over all things. (xxxiv: 47)

The authentic records of the biography of the Holy Prophet show that it had occurred to the Meccan leaders to credit Muhammad with ambition. They, therefore, time and again plied him with temptation. One day some of the important men of Mecca gathered in the enclosure of Kaaba, sent for Muhammad and addressed him in the following words:

> "We have seen no other man of Arabia, who has brought so great a calamity to a nation, as you have done. You have outraged our gods and religion and taxed our forefathers and wise men with impiety and error and created strife amongst us. You have left no stone unturned to estrange the relations with us. If you are doing all this with a view to getting wealth, we will join together to give you greater riches than any Quraishi has ever possessed. If ambition moves you, we will make you our chief. If you desire kingship we readily offer you that. If you are under the power of an evil spirit which seems to haunt and dominate you so that you cannot shake off its yoke, then we shall call in skilful physicians to cure you."

"Have you said all?" asked Muhammad; and then hearing that all had been said, he spoke forth:

> I require none of the things that you offer me. I demand

> nothing, neither riches nor high status, nor kingship, in return for what I have brought for you. I have been sent to you as a messenger of God, a herald of glad tidings and a warning. I have performed my duty by delivering His message to you which has nothing but goodness for you. If you accept then I assure you the good of this world and the world to come. If you reject, I shall remain patient and watch for the verdict of Allah."

We do not find any trace of wavering or despair in the life of the Holy Prophet. A calm and lofty attitude was constantly maintained by him during all the years. The whole tenor of the revelation at this period was marked by a calm confidence, and therein lay the Prophet's strength.

This conversation between the unbelievers and Muhammad clearly brings out the reasons for the opposition of the Quraysh. "The grounds of opposition to Islam," remarks Montgomery Watt, "were thus, besides self-interest, fear of its political and economic implications and sheer conservatism. The situation which confronted Muhammad was a malaise which had social, economic, political, and intellectual symptoms. His message was essentially religious, in that it attempted to remedy the underlying religious causes of the malaise, but it affected the other aspects, and consequently the opposition had many facets".

8

# *No War Pact*

The Prophet (PBUH) once in Medina in the very first year of Hijrah considered in the fitness of things to enter a contract with all the ethnic and religious parties around him so that despite differences racial and cultural unity may be maintained and in civilization and culture there may be spirit of cooperation.

Some select terms of this contract are as under:

1. This is a document from Muhammad (PBUH) the apostle of Allah among the Muslims, Quraysh or citizens of Yathrib, with those who are associated with them (Muslim) and their partners in day-to-day affairs of the administration and maintenance of peace.
2. In spite of the differences in their identities, they will be regarded one nation (people of a country).
3. The Judaic people of Bani 'Auf are one nation with the Muslims.
4. And whoever starts hostilities with these entrants of contract, one and all will oppose him en masse. The Muslims shall come to their aid.
5. The relations of the contracting units shall be based on mutual well-wishing and benefiting and not harming and sinning against.

6. During the wars, the Jews will be contributors in expenditure of war.
7. The rights of the nations friendly to the Jews shall be on a par with the Jews.
8. No one will start any move hostile to his ally of contract.
9. The oppressed shall be supported and helped.
10. Bloodshed on the soil of Medina shall be strictly prohibited to all the partners of the contract.
11. The neighbours too will be deemed on a par with the partners of contract.
12. If something happens among the partners threatening violence, the decision will rest with Allah and His apostle Muhammad (PBUH).

When signatures of all the Madinite communities were taken on this charter of rights, the Prophet (PBUH) wanted to include the tribals of the neighbouring areas also in this agreement, having in view two advantages:

1. To put an end to the tribal mutual clashes and unnecessary bloodshed (of the guilty and innocent alike).
2. The Quraysh of Mecca shall not be able to instigate the tribes that have entered the contract against the Muslims.
   (a) With this intention, the Prophet, in the first year after migration from Mecca travelled upto Waddan (between Mecca and Medina) and included Bani Hamzah, bin Bakr bin Abd-e-Munaf of tribe in the agreement mentioned above. It was signed by 'Amr bin Fehshi Al-Sakhri.
   (b) And for the same purpose, the Apostle of Allah went to Razwi in the month of Rabi I, 2 A.H and brought into the agreement the people of bawat mountain.

(c) And in the same year (2 A.H.) in the month of Jawadi II the Prophet went to Zil 'Ashirah, situated somewhere between Medina and Yanbu,' and after signature of Banu Mudlaj on the contract he returned to Medina.

If he had sufficient time for extending this agreement further, the world would have become conscious of the fact that the Apostle of Allah, Mercy for mankind had come not to draw sword but to bring peace to humanity.

***The Background :*** The Quraysh of Mecca in their aminosity to the Prophet and the Muslims had gone so far that even after their migration to Medina 300 miles from their town they were not at ease and did not let them live in peace. Earlier on the migration to Abyssinia, they had tried to detain them and on the second occasion went in pursuit of them to Abyssinia in an attempt for their extradition. And as we have seen earlier they miserably failed in these attempts. And now when they had come to Madmah, they followed them there too and intended to attack them.

As a preliminary, they had written to Abd-Allah bin Ubai that they had given protection to their man (the Prophet). So they were duty bound to fight against him or compel him to leave their town. Or else they have resolved under an oath to attack Medina, murdering your young men and taking your women as slave girls.

On receiving this letter Abd-Allah bin Ubay decided in favour of giving the Prophet and his Muslim followers a fight. The Prophet (PBUH) got scent of this conspiracy and personally going to the hostile group talked to them directly.

The Prophet said to them: "The Quraish have played this trick upon you so that if you are taken in by them you will come to much greater harm than in violation of their terms. For, if you were to fight against the Muslims you will be slaughtering your own sons. In case you are confronted by Quraysh, it will be waging war against aliens."

This brief talk of the Prophet had such an affect on their minds that the entire gathering got immediately dispersed.

After failure in the first attempt, the Quraysh secretly started their conspiratorial moves with the Judaic community of Medina. And when they were perfectly in league with them, with full confidence in their success they sent the following message to the Muslims of Medina:

> "Do not be proud of your safe arrival from Mecca, and do not gloat over your success against us. We are capable of your ruin even there—your safe refuge, your asylum. After this challenging message they started vexing them.

**The Attacks**

In Rabi I, 2 A.H. one of the tribal chiefs from Quraish, Kurz bin Jabir, Al fahri came to Medina and drove away the cattle of Medinites grazing out of the town and made his escape good, as if to impress upon them that they could strike at them from a distance of 300 miles whenever they pleased.

Then in the month of Ramadan 2 A.H., Abu Jahl gave it out falsely that the Muslims are going to waylay our caravan laden with rich goods. This baseless propaganda against the Muslims was aimed at instigating all those who had a share in trade or their men formed the trade caravan or all those nursing hatred against the Muslims, may come together ready to fight against Muslims en masse. And they succeeded in this mischievous plan of theirs.

With a vast army of one thousand venturesome, valiant, fierce fighters with seven hundred camels and those hundred horses as mounts, Abu Jahl came out of Mecca. The caravan (had not been engaged in attach on its way by the Muslim army and it had reached Mecca safely, but Abu Jahl continued his movement towards Medina and the Muslims were now dead sure of his evil design to attack them.

The Prophet (PBUH) had consulted the companions in this behalf. The muhajirs (migrants) came out with a satisfactory answer (to lay down their lives against the invading army). He repeated his query and they firmly assured him of their faithful obedience. When he put the same question a third time, the Ansar (old residents of Medina) took it that he was waiting for their response. Saad bin Mu'az said, "Perhaps you have taken it on principle that Ansars do not regard it their duty to stand by you and their Muslim brethren if it comes to an encounter outside Medina. On behalf of Ansars I assure you that we are with you under all conditions whether you enter an agreement or reject another. You can take as much from our goods as you please and leave for us as much as you please. That taken by you would be preferable to us than that left with us. We shall obey you, order us what you are pleased. We shall gladly follow you if you take us to the 'Imran spring, we will follow you. And if you order us to enter an ocean, we will enter with you." Miqdad said: "O apostle of Allah! we are not like the people of Moses to say "Go thou, and thy Lord, and fight ye two, while we sit here (Q. V: 24), for we are with you everywhere, right, left, in front and behind, ready to fight."

The Muslims were not in a state of perfect readiness (most of them had come out to intercept a caravan of a few highly armed guards of Quraysh and not fierce fighting forces). There were 313 persons in all, muhajirs and Ansars combined.

Muslims had not been so far permitted to enter wars even in the face of strong opposition and persecution, for Islam is the religion of peace avoiding armed struggle if peace can be maintained without it. That is why, they put up with oppression quietly and moved out of Medina, leaving behind their birth place, houses and wherewithal to abstain from contention. And they overlooked vexation even after getting out of the way of their opponents. But now things had come to such a pass that clash was inevitable, for even survival of Islam dearer to Muslims than even their lives.

After annihilation of this handful of devotees engaged in Allah's clarification and propagation of Divine Faith, none would have been left to take it up. 'Isa (PBUH) had also, at the end of his brief mission of less than three years, compelled by necessity, had ordered his disciples to purchase arms even if they had to part with their clothes, cash and other belongings: Then set he unto them, but now he that hath a purse, let him take it, and likewise his scrip: and he that hath no sword, let him sell his garments, and buy one. Luke 22: 36.

So it was this pressing need of self defence and protection of their Faith that Allah in His Infinite Mercy, permitted them to take to arms in emergencies like the present, after they had very patiently preserved with oppression and tyranny, excesses, loss of life and property, insults and difficulties in living up to the dictates of Faith.

Below is given the first permission as revealed in the Quran:

> To those against whom war is made permission is given (to fight) because they are wronged and verily Allah is most Powerful for their aid. (They are) those who have been expelled from their homes in defiance of rights, (for no cause) except that they say, "Our Lord is Allah." Did not Allah check one set of people by means of another, they would surely have been pulled down monasteries, churches, synagogues and mosques, in which the name of Allah is commemorated in abundant measure. Allah will certainly aid those who aid His (cause) for verily Allah is full of strength, Exalted in Might, (able to enforce His will). —Q. XXII: 39-40.

The Quran, as every body can see for himself, points out the reasons behind this permission, which also brings out clearly the nature of this war— defensive and not aggressive as the wars of the ungodly."

1. The first reason given here is oppressed condition of those fighting in defence of self and their Faith, which the people of our age have termed right of self-determination; justifying even armed struggle in its defence.
2. The second reason is their expulsion from their homes and hearths, deprivation from their wherewithal and that too on the basis of difference of creed.

The so-called peace-loving King Edward VII, in his message to his Indian subjects on the occasion of 50th anniversary of the British rule in India in a tone of great pride among other things, that "during these fifty years no one has ever been harmed on grounds of the difference of creed, when it is no secret that all these Muslims were those who had been tortured, deprived of rights, jailed, exiled, hanged and shot for their only crime that they asserted strongly. "Our Lord is Allah."

3. The third reason pointed out by the Quran is not of exclusive advantage to the Muslims but very wide in its scope, almost universal, covering the two major faiths of the world, Judaism and Christianity, whose protection has also been thus ensured, Mosques of Islam and Muslims finding the last place on this list, probably out of courtesy shown to even these enemies of Allah. Moreover, Muslims had entered an agreement with these two religious communities in Medina and this was out of regard for maintaining friendly relations with them. However, the Muslim community was of the greatest importance, since it were they who pledged and actually laid down their lives in defence of the right of self-deter-mination for humanity at large.

> Without their waging wars through the ages, there would have been no party of selfless, righteous justice-loving party in the world for the defence of the charter of human rights and the world would have never heard of them.

All these factors made it imperative for the Muslims to check them on the way to Medina, in spite of their extreme paucity of arms, mounts and rations they had decided upon total confrontation.

During the month of Ramadan 2 A.H. the Apostle of Allah as the head of the Muslims started from Medina. An idea of their military equipment can be had from the fact that they had only two horses and sixty camels.

Shall we call it a matter of chance that the participants in the battle of Badr were just the same in number as those of the army of Taloot (Saul) against Jaloot (Goliath).

On arriving at the battle field of Badr, the Muslim witnessed the enemy's fighting force three times their own number and in the matter of equipment they stood no comparison with the enemy.

A day ahead of the battle, the Prophet inspected the battle field, pointing out with precision that Allah-Willing such and such men of the opposing force will fall dead at such and such places on the battle ground.

On Friday, the 17th Ramadan the two fighting forces confronted each other. The Prophet (PBUH) entreated Allah for success in the battle against the enemy, saying that if these handful of Muslims get killed, there will be no one left to proclaim the message of Thy Unity. The Muslims also prayed earnestly.

With the aid of Allah, the enemy was defeated at the hands of the Muslims. Seventy of their fighters were killed and another seventy taken prisoners. Abu Jahl was killed exactly at the site pointed out by the Prophet (PBUH) to his companions the previous day. It was he who had brought the hosts (to wipe out the Muslims). Out of the fourteen tribal chiefs who had come together at Darul-Nadwa for deliberations on the theme of the Prophet's (PBUH) murder, eleven lay dead on the battle field. The three survivors had at last embraced Islam.

In keeping with (a) the accepted law of war (b) the passion of the oppressed Muslims for revenge (c) the need of over awing the other tribes of Arabia with horror of war, the situation demanded the killing of the prisoners of war, but the Prophet of Mercy freed them all on payment of ransom. The ransom for the freedom of the literate prisoners was literacy of the children of Ansar.

The trial of strength of the two parties of the battle of Badr proved true to the prophecy of the Quran while permitting the Muslims to fight against the invader:

> "Allah will certainly aid those who aid His (cause),
> for verily Allah is full of Strength, Exalted In Might
> (Able To Enforce His Will)." —Al Quran XXII: 40.

That is why, this battle has been termed Yaum-ul-Furqan (the day of evidence or proof), since the Muslims and the people of the Book had been provided with evidence on the true nature of the Islamic Faith. Allah has elsewhere mentioned this incident, the Battle of Badr, in the following words:

> Allah had helped you at Badr when ye were helpless:
> then fear Allah: thus may ye show your gratitude.
> — Al Quran III:123.

A few days after the battle of Badr, Safwan bin Umayyah, whose father was killed in Badr and 'Umair bin Wahab whose son was a prisoner in the hands of Muslims, came together in a desolate spot outside Mecca and talked about the Prophet (PBUH).

Umair said to his associate: "If I was not indebted

irredeemably, and I had not been worried about the helplessness of my family in my absence (death) I would have myself gone to Medina and would have made short shrift of Muhammad (killed him)."

Safwan blurted out: "I shall clear thy debts and support thy family during my own life-time."

'Umair, assenting, said to him: Settled. But this secret of ours should not be allowed to leak out." Then he got his sword sharpened and poisoned and started off on his mission.

On arrival in Medina, he was making his camel sit in front of the Prophet's mosque when the camel started gurgling. 'Umar Faruq (R) saw and recognizing him, it occurred to him that this devil has come with an evil intent. And so he approached the Prophet (PBUH) informing him that 'Umair bin Wahab was coming and was fully armed. The Prophet said: "Let him come to me." 'Umar (R) got hold of the hilt of his sword and holding his neck took him to the Prophet who asked 'Umar (R) to free him, and asked 'Umair to come to him. 'Umair coming before him greeted him formally. The Prophet asked him: "What brings you here? He said in reply: "I have come to see my son a prisoner here."

The Prophet further enquired: "And how about this sword of yours." He tauntingly remarked: "Of what use is this sword? And what have our swords achieved when pitted against you?" The Prophet (PBUH) said to him: "Be honest and come out with the truth 'Umair repeated his reply. The apostle of Allah said: "Look here, you and Safwan had gone to a desolate spot in the hills outside Mecca. Safwan has taken upon himself relieving thee of my debts and support of thy family, and thou hath promised him my head with which intent thou art here. 'Umair, thou did not care to think that Allah Himself is my Protector."

On hearing this much from the Prophet, he was confounded. He submitted: "Now I am satisfied that you are certainly the

Prophet and a Messenger of Allah." It was easy for us to falsify you about heavenly realities and revelations and were engaged in it with impunity. But I have no explanation for this secret that was strictly between Safwan and me. No third person could have got wind of it. I must be grateful to Allah Who made it (the disclosure to you of our well-guarded secret through super natural means) the cause of my embracing Islam.

The Prophet said to the companions: "Teach your brother his Faith, make him memorize the Quran and free his son." Umair said: "O Apostle of Allah! Kindly be so good as to permit me to go to Mecca and call people to Islam. And now I intend to vex and torment the idolaters in the same way as I did to the Muslims before this."

After 'Umair had left for Medina, Safwan used to say to the elite among the Quraysh: "Just wait. Shortly there is going to be good news from Medina which will relieve you of the shock of Badr."

But when Safwan learnt that 'Umair had embraced Islam, he was shocked and he viewed not to speak to him for the rest of his life, nor allow any benefit to go to him if it can be helped.

'Umair came to Mecca. He used to proclaim the message of Islam and many people embraced Islam through his efforts.

After the disgraceful defeat at Badr, Abu Sufyan, now the outstanding leader of Quraysh, had under an oath denied himself a change of clean clothes and bathing his body, until he had avenged himself and the community of Muslims. So he came out of Mecca with two hundred mounted men and on approaching Medina he detached himself from them and in the darkness of the night entered the town all alone (by stealth) and met his friend Salam bin Mashkam a Jew and spent the night with him in a drinking orgy of sorts. Probably in their mutual consultation, it was decided that the time was not appropriate for an attack. So during the last part of the night he came out and setting fire to fruit laden trees of Muslims and murdering a Muslim and his ally, returned home.

On receiving information, he and his retinue of too hundred men were given a hot pursuit upto Qarqarah-al-kadar. So this pursuit of the invaders has come to be called 'Ghazwah' (Expedition) of Qarqarah-al-Kadar. On the return journey, the contingent of the Abu Sufyan dropped their tiny bags of parched, ground barley and therefore this is also known as Ghazwah-al-Saweeq.

Next year, the Quraysh of Mecca attacked Medina once again. This time, they had collected funds from the citizens in general. The poet Abu 'Uzzah in his campaign in Tahawah had reconciled Banu Kananah to come to the aid of Meccans in their strife against Madinite Muslims. Fifty thousand Mithqal of gold (about 225 kilogram) and a thousand camels from Syria, the collective property of Meccan traders, was also donated by common consent generously to war fund. In short, an army of five thousand blood thirsty fighters of various tribes, comprising three thousand camelry and two hundred strong cavalry and seven hundred armoured infantry men, came to attack Medina.

The Prophet was in favour of the defence of Medina from inside. But the young zealots (who had remained deprived of participation at Badr insisted on confrontation with the enemy outside in the open. And the issue was decided in favour of the majority. With true democratic spirit, the Prophet did not insist on his own and that of older men's nature and wiser opinion nor the decision once taken was changed (when on second though the younger lot repented and requested revision). So the Muslims came out to the mount Uhud, about three miles from Medina and confronted the enemy from Mecca.

The Muslim fighting force comprised one thousand men. But at the nick of the moment and most critical juncture, the arch-hypocrite, Abd-Allah bin Ubay bin Salul played foul and betraying the Muslims left with his three hundred misguided and hypocritic companions. The burden of facing the enemy hordes, five thousand strong (furious with passion of revenge) came to the shoulders of the remaining seven hundred. The Muslims had inflicted defeat on such a powerful enemy with numerical superiority and much more and better equipment, and twelve of their standard bearers were killed (eight of them at the hands of 'Ali Murtaza alone).

But the Muslim contingent of archers stationed by the Prophet (PBUH) to guard a mountain pass, the only vulnerable position for the Muslim ranks, was deserted by them (under the erroneous nation that the battle was over and they too were free to collect booty from the defeated, fleeing army). They misunderstood and disobeyed the Prophet (PBUH). The clever enemy took advantage of this error on the part of Muslims and taking a round surrounded the Muslim from both sides. (Khalid bin Waleed, yet in the opposite camp, with his cavalry attacked the Muslim, through the vulnerable and now unguarded pass and created havoc. Causing great loss and dispersing the greater part of the rest).

Among the companions of the Prophet (PBUH) the following 12 were with him: Abu Bakr, 'Umar, 'Ali, Abd-al-Rahman bin 'Auf, Saad bin waqqas, Talha bin Abdullah, Zubayr bin-al-'Awam, Abu'Ubaidah bin Jarah, and four others, Allah be pleased with all of them, never left him alone (to fend for himself). The enemies threw stones at him. That thrown by Ibn Qumayyah wounded his forehead and that by Ibn Hisham his arm. Utbah's stone broke four of his teeth. Again, he had fallen into a deep pit and it was erroneously given out that he has been killed. Honourable woman from Medina rushed to Uhud. Once in the battle field, Fatimah (R) washed her father's wounds, and stopped haemorrhage with burnt mat (ash). 'Ali Murtaza (R) brought water in his shield and 'Ayeshah Siddiqah (R) and Umm-e-Sulaim (R) took up small leather water bags and brought water to the wounded lying on the battle field. Seventy companions of the Prophet (PBUH) were war casualties.

The heaviest loss in this battle field was the fall of Mus'ab bin 'Umair who had come to Medina as an ambassador of Islam, a connecting link between Mecca and Medina and whose sermons converted the tribes of Aus and Khazraj to Islam, was martyred here. His wife, Hanmah bint Jahash had received news of the martyrdom of her brother and maternal uncle and had quietly recited the Quranic words of resignation to the Will of Almighty Allah. "Verily to Allah do we belong and it is to Him that we are destined to return" and prayed for their forgiveness. After that, she was told of her husband's martyrdom, on hearing which still gave out a loud cry of anguish and grief. The Prophet remarked: "See, how much she loved her husband."

In this battle, the prophet's uncle, Hamzah (R) (lion of Allah and His Apostle) also got martyred. His dead body was desecrated by the unbelieving lady Hindah. After the war was over, Safiyah, mother of Zubayr (R) came to see the dead body of Hamzah, her brother. Zubayr tried to stop her but that brave lady insisting on seeing it, saying: "I know that my brother's dead body has been mutilated and desecrated. But this is something to be proud of for us. My dear son, I am neither going to cry over it nor scream but only to pray for him."

***Great Warriors of Islam :*** Anas bin Nadhar too had been martyred in this battle. This valiant soul noticed certain brave and courageous Muslims who, throwing away their arms were sitting crest fallen and in great grief. He asked them: "What is wrong with you?" They said to him "The Apostle of Allah has passed away." Anas said to them passionately: "When the Apostle of Allah laid down his life, we too should sacrifice ourselves for the same noble cause. What use is living after him." And entering the thick of the battle he fell on the enemy in a rage, received seventy wounds of deadly weapons and entered heaven.

Saad bin Rabi' was another martyr in this battle of Uhud.

After the battle was over, the Prophet sent out his men to search his deadbody. One of them saw him in pangs of death lying among the wounded and dying. When asked about his condition, he replied: "Take me for dead now. But have the goodness to convey my respects to the Prophet of Allah. And also say to him pray to Allah that He may reward him with a reward greater than any given to any prophet for his guidance to his people. And convey from me this message to the Muslim community that so long as there is a single eye among them that winks if the enemy is allowed to get to him, they will have no excuse to offer to their Lord for that negligence."

A companion of the Prophet (PBUH) has stated that he went to see Abu Bakr (R). Sitting on his chest I found a small girl whom he was kissing and fondling. I asked him about that child and was told that she was the daughter of Saad bin Rabi'. He was superior to me and on the Day of Reckoning, he will be among the heralds of the Apostle of Allah.

'Amarah bin Ziyad too was one of the martyrs of this battle. When in the pangs of death he had dragged himself somehow to bring his cheeks in contact with the feet of the Prophet, dying the most peaceful death.

All these valiant supporters of Islam had performed deeds of extra-ordinary temerity and valour in this battle. 'Ali (R) had single handedly killed eight opponents as mentioned earlier. Talhah had used his hand as the shield to protect the Prophet from the enemy's arrows. This hand of his had become palsied and crippled for ever.

***Exemplary Conviction :*** A lady of Banu Dinar tribe had lost her father, a brother and husband (having probably heard the false rumour about the Prophet (PBUH) Medina) came to the scene of action and enquired about him. People told her that by the Grace of Allah he was all right. But she wanted to make sure and he was pointed out to her at a distance. Thus assured she exclaimed showing her satisfaction:" Now that the Apostle of Allah is among us, any grief, however tormenting has become bearable."

Overlooking Faults and Forgiveness by the Prophet (PBUH) and his Prayer for the Pagan Oppressors.

Some companions of his suggested to him to curse the pagans (when he himself was badly wounded by them). The Prophet, however, said to them in his usual mild tone: "I have not been sent to curse but to call (mankind to Allah and His Faith) and as Mercy to them. 'O my Lord, guide them (to the right path) for they know me not."

After the battle of Uhud, the enemies of Islam and Muslims, adopted various methods of harming Muslims. So in the 4th year after Hijrah:

> Seven persons of Adal and Qarah communities were instructed by the Quraysh and sent to the Prophet (PBUH) with the request that since their tribes were ready to embrace Islam some preachers should be sent with them to teach Islam to them. The Apostle of Allah sent with them ten companions of his as preachers of Faith with 'Asim bin Thakit leading this party. When these companions (on a mission of preaching) with their treacherous guides had come in their range to become easy targets, two hundred armed men came out and wanted to arrest them alive. But the companions confronted them and eight of them fell fighting. Two of the party Khubaib bin 'Adi and Zaid bin Wathnah (Allah be pleased with all the ten of them), were however arrested by these barbarian, and sold out to the Quraysh of Mecca.

The Quraysh kept them confined without food and water for a few days in the house of Harith bin 'Amir. One day, a child of Harith playing with a household knife approached

Khubaib. Out of love with little children Khubaib lifting him up placed him on his thigh and taking the knife from his hand put it aside. The child's mother noticing that her child with a knife was with the prisoner who had been starved by them. So out of fear of safety to the child a loud scream left her lips. Khubaib, however assuringly remarked: "She mistakenly is under the impression that I can kill her child, not knowing that a Muslim is not guilty of perfidy. And they are very kind to every one, particularly children.

The tyrants of Quraysh took him to the cross offering him his freedom on condition of rejecting Islam. Both the prisoners said in reply: "What is life worth after rejection of Islam?" They then asked him: "If you have any desire, let us know." Khubaib as their spokesman said to them: "Permit us time for two raka'ats (units) of prayer if you can." They were permitted. They said the desired prayer, not taking much time and saying: "We could have spent longer time in our prayer but we did not like to be misunderstood that it was out of fear of death." They hard-hearted tyrants, put them on the cross and asked the lance bearers to keep piercing every part of their body constantly.

How firm was their belief in Islam and Pleasure of Allah and eternal bliss in life to come can be inquired by the fact that they patiently persevered with all sorts of calamities without complaint!

### Holy Prophet, Best in the World

One of the spear-bearing tyrants asked him after giving Khubaib a painful prick: "At this stage you too must be wishing all this for Muhammad and your own redemption." Khubaib replied in a passionate tone: "By Allah, I would not like that even a thorn may prick him for my deliverance."

He also recited some lyrics of his depicting the position of a true Muslim. Last of all, he prayed to Allah that he had conveyed the Message of His Faith to these people and entreat Thee that Thy Apostle may be informed of our plight and the beastly treatment of the pagan opponents.

Abu Bara' 'Amir also played the same trick, the same dirty game. He came to the Prophet (PBUH) and requested him for the services of some preachers of Islam for the education and guidance of Najd. He wanted to take them with him. 'Amir's nephew was the ruler of Najd. 'Amir had given assurance of protection to them. The Prophet assigned this duty to Munzir bin 'Amr Ansari at the head of seventy others, all well-versed, select in religious knowledge. When they reached Birr-e-Mannah, the homeland of bani 'Amir, Haram bin Malham was deputed to see Tufail the ruler with the letter of the Prophet. This herald was killed by the ruler. He was pierced with a spear going from the back through the chest. Falling on the ground, he had proclaimed his view of life and wealth, uttering: "By the Lord of Kaaba, I have achieved felicity."

These words of the dying person had such a magical effect on the murderer that he went to the Prophet and embraced Islam. The ruler got the rest also killed. Kaab bin Zaid saved his life getting behind those being killed and getting back he informed the Prophet of what had happened.

In the 8th year after Hijrah, the Muslims had to besiege Mecca during the month of Ramadan under an emergency. The reason behind it was that one of the terms of Hudaibiyah Treaty was that:

For ten years, there will be no war. The communities wishing to ally with the Prophet's community may do so and others who prefer to join Quraysh are free to do so. So Banu Khuzaah allied with the Prophet and Banu Kananah went with the Quraysh. Hardly two years, had elapsed when Banu Kananah attached Banu Khuzaah and the Quraysh too came to their aid with arms. 'Akrama bin Abu Jahl, Suhail bin 'Amr (he had signed the treaty), Safwan bin Umayyah (the well-known elite of the Quraysh with their followers, all under cover fought against Banu Khuzaah).

These people (Khuzaah) requested for clemency, took refuge in Kaaba as the safest asylum, but they were mercilessly put to the sword. When these oppressed people appealed to them for mercy in the name of Allah (For Allah's sake) they, (the Meccan pagans) most blasphemously turned on them with loud proclamations of "Allah is nobody today (—is mere nothing)."

Forty of them that had somehow escaped the blood thirsty swords of Banu Kananah and Quraysh came to the Prophet (PBUH) with their tale of woes.

For reasons of 1. Abiding by the terms of treaty 2. Redressal of grievance with full justice 3. Future protection of allies and tribes bound by treaty. The Prophet was forced by the demands of justice and fair play, to take immediate strongest action against the offenders, he, like the previous emergency of Badr (in the month of Ramadan) started with a ten thousand strong force for Mecca also in the month of fasting. They had hardly covered two days journey when Abu Sufyan Al-Harith bin Abd-al-Muttalib and Abd-Allah bin Abu Umayyah met him on the way. They were men who had tormented the Prophet very much and had left no stone unturned in wiping out Islam. The Prophet sighting them turned his face in the other direction. Umm-e-Salma submitted that Abu Sufyan was his first cousin and Abd-Allah is also the first cousin, the son of 'Atikah, his real paternal aunt. Such close relations should not remain deprived of merciful affection.

At the instance of 'Ali (R) they came to the Prophet and asked for his forgiveness in the words of the erring brothers of Yusuf (PBUH).

By Allah! Indeed has Allah preferred thee above us, and we certainly been guilty of sin —Q. XII: 91 The Apostle of Allah said in reply:

This day, let no reproach be (cast) on you Allah will forgive you. And He is the Most Merciful of those who show mercy! — Al Quran XII: 92.

The Apostle of Allah wished to take the Meccans by surprise. (They should not get wind of his arrival. And so it did come to pass that when he with his companions had camped outside Mecca and to strike terror in their hearts he had ordered lighting of fires not only for cooking their food but also big fires to make the mountain side ablaze. The thousands of these fires gave the Meccans an idea of their helplessness and not to even think of disturbing peace by taking to arms. The Apostle of Allah, Mercy for mankind, had aimed at a bloodless victory, an entirely peaceful revolution.

**Peace Proclaimed**

The next morning, the Apostle of Allah ordered the army to enter the town by different routes and observe strictly the following rules:

1. Whoever throws away his arms should not be killed.
2. One entering Kaaba should also be spared.
3. One confining himself to his house should not be pursued.
4. Whoever chooses Abu Sufyan's house for safety should be left alone.
5. And so also those entering the house of Hakeem bin Hizam.
6. Those absconding should not be followed to be brought back.
7. The wounded and the disabled shall not be killed either, nor
8. The captives should be treated as free person for reckoning.

The only contingent that entered the town under the command of Khalid bin Waleed experienced some resistance but the Meccans to their heels. The others entered without the least resistance. In the confrontation two Muslims and 28 opponents lost their lives. When on 20th Ramadan, the chosen Apostle of Allah entered Mecca, his head was bowed and he was reciting Surah Al Fatiah (Q. XLVIII) and mounted on a camel was going to the House of Allah, when riding this camel along with him was Othaman (R) son of Zaid (R) his freed slave. Once there he cleansed the house of Allah of the pollution of all sorts of idols 360 in number. He was bringing down each one of them with the end of his bow or his stick and was reciting the Quranic verses:

1. Truth has (now) arrived and falsehood perished: for falsehood is (by its nature) bound to perish.

   —Q. XVII: 81.
2. The truth has arrived, and falsehood showeth not its face and will not return. —Al Quran XXXIV: 49

After this iconoclastic activity was over, he called 'Uthman bin Abi Talha. His family had been the bearer of the keys of Kaaba since long. During the early days of his prophethood, the Prophet (PBUH) had asked him ('Uthman) to open the Kaaba and he had refused to oblige. And the Apostle of Allah had prophesied: "All right, you will see on some future day that these keys will be in my hand and I shall entrust them to whomsoever I like." And 'Uthman had asked him whether all the males of the Quraysh would have been brought low and annihilated. And the Prophet (PBUH) had replied: "No, they would be much more honoured and dignified.

The Prophet taking the keys from him opened the door of Kaaba and entering made every corner of it resound with loud cries of Allah-o-Akbar (Allah is the Greatest), and then in prayers of thanks laid his forehead on the ground as the most devout and grateful servant of Allah the Greatest and the Exalted in Might.

During this period, all those elite of Mecca had come together who:

1. Had slain many Muslims or got them killed in other ways.
2. Had expelled hundreds of Muslims from their homes and hearths.
3. To destroy the Islamic Faith and wipe out Muslims had undertaken journeys to Abyssinia. Syria, Najd and Yemen.
4. Who had not let the Muslims live in peace after they had left for (Medina) three hundred miles off.

All those who had done all in their power to annihilate their Muslim adversaries with the power of money, might, strategy and deceit, and for twenty one years had made it their only concern.

The Apostle of Allah, mercy for Mankind, when he came out after thanks giving for Allah's Graciousness, 'Abbas (R), his uncle, submitted that the key be now entrusted to Bani Hashim. But the Prophet did not agree with his suggestion saying: "This is the day of generosity and one of gifts and donations. And calling 'Uthman he handed over the keys to him, saying: "Whoever tries to snatch them from you will be a Usurping tyrant."

*Historic Address :* After this act of great generosity to one who, in the light of his past conduct, hardly deserved it, he turned to the crowd of those tyrants, murderers and barabrious bereft of civility and sense of justice, who could go to any length in opposition. He addressed them thus:

> "O ye the community of Quraysh! This day Allah has brought you down for your haughtyness based on Jahiliyah and pride of ancestry when the truth is: All

of us are the progeny of Adam and Adam was fashioned out of clay. Then he recited the Quranic verse:

> O mankind! We created you from a single (pair of a male and a female, and made you into nations and tribes that ye may know each other (not that you may despise each other). Verily the most honoured of you in the sight of Allah is (he who is) the most righteous of you. (Q. XLIX: 13)

Then he said:

> This day let no reproach be (cast) on you. Allah will forgive you and He is the Most Merciful of all those who show mercy. —Al Quran XII: 92

Then the Apostle of Allah taking his seat at the Safa hill, took Baiah (oath of allegiance and fealty) from those coming to embrace Islam. On this occasion, Umar Farooq (R) was presenting them one by one before the Prophet (PBUH). Those entering this contract (Baiah) had to affirm the following terms:

1. I shall not associate any one with Allah in His Person, Attributes, His worthiness of being worshipped and wor-thiness of being invoked for aid.
2. I shall not steal, fornicate (commit adultery), commit un-authorized murder, neither be guilty of female infanticide, nor slander any one.
3. I shall to the best of my ability obey the Apostle of Allah in all matters relating to Truth and Justice.

The women had, in addition to the above, were to affirm:

> In mourning for the dead they will not slap their faces nor pinch them (with the nails of their fingers). Neither tear the hair of their heads nor tear their garments to pieces, nor wrap themselves in black clothes (as a sign of mourning even to the extent of a black band on the arm), nor yet sit over the graves in mourning.

The procedure adopted here was that the Prophet (PBUH) used to immerse his hand in a basin full of water and each pledging female individual would come and immerse her hand in the water after the Prophet had taken out his own hand. On other occasion in pledging loyalty to Islam (obedience to Allah and His Apostle (PBUH)) it was deemed sufficient to a verbal affirmation (without any symbolic formality).

The next day after the conquest of Mecca, the Prophet was circumambulating Kaaba when Fudalah bin 'Umair intended to murder the Prophet. With this evil intent when he approached him, he said: "Is Fudalah coming?" Fudalah said: "Yes it is Fudalah." The Prophet asked him: "What were you intending to do a little earlier?" Fudalah said: "Nothing was remembering Allah." On hearing this (falsehood), the Prophet (PBUH) laughed and said to him: Make your peace with Allah (entreat Him to forgive you for your evil intent of a heinous crime and falsehood). And saying this he placed his hand on his (Fudalah's) chest.

Fudalah later stated: "With his hand on my chest I had a strange experience of mind. After that no one was so dear to me as Muhammad (PBUH)"

"From there, I started for home. On the way I met my beloved girl, with whom I associated and passed my time. So she requested for a brief chat. She had an important thing to say to him.

I replied to her offer saying: "Allah and His Apostle prohibit such things." (This immediate change of heart on conversion is amazing indeed! And this is not an isolated example. The early Islamic history is replete with them).

Let us here mention briefly the incidents of forgiveness of certain specific heinous crimes of the outstanding enemies of Islam in Mecca on this occasion as an important part of Seerah.

As we have seen, the fighting men had been ordered to

desist from attacking and killing people (general Amnesty), except four men and two women who, due to the nature of their crimes were liable to Qisas or punishment like for like under the Divine Law.

It was proclaimed that they should be killed.

Out of the four men only Ibn Khalal was killed. He had embraced Islam but he had killed his slave for delay in preparing food for him. After this, he had escaped, fleeing to Mecca. The other three, Ikrama bin Abu Jahl, Hiba bin-al-Aswad and Abdullah ibn Abi Sarah were left off.

1. Ikrama not only because of his alliance with his father Abu Jahl in atrocities against Islam, even armed struggles, he had recently against the allies of Muslims, banu Khuzaah, he being the main culprit in the tribes annihilation.
2. Hibar had wounded Zainab, the daughter of the Prophet, with his spear causing abortion and consequent death.
3. Abdullah ibn Sarah had given out that revelation (in fact) came to him and Muhammad (PBUH) on hearing from him get it set down in writing.

Could these culprits expect mercy from any save the Mercy for Mankind?

Among the two women, the one guilty of intentional murder was killed under the Islamic law of 'Qisas', equal for equal.

Among those forgiven was Hindah, wife of Abu Sufyan. Mad with wild rage, she had arranged murder by artifice of Hamzah the uncle of the Prophet, in a secret arrangement with Wahshi, and after his death, she came to the battle field, took out Hamza's liver, tried to chew it and mutilated his body cutting his nose and ears had made a wreath for herself to put it round her neck.

Wahshi too was forgiven who had killed Hamzah by deception and then had desecrated his dead body by mutilation together with Hindah.

So it is evident like broad day light that the army of Muhammad had not conquered Mecca but conquered the hearts of the Meccans, through the civility and unlimited mercy and forgiveness of Muhammad (PBUH).

After the bloodless conquests of Mecca and most of them embracing Islam, there was no question of taking possession of their goods as booty as customary in battles, the Muslims who had been robbed of every thing they had there in Mecca had been taken by the pagans both forcibly and voluntarily (to remove the hitch in migration). It was all over now, some of them, however, claiming the houses they had left behind and now in possession of Meccans.

The Prophet (PBUH), however did not agree, meaning that whatever they had left in the way of Allah, they should not even think of getting back.

***The Consequences of the Meccan Conquest:*** The Reasons of Entry to Allah's Religion in Crowds. According to the revelation a little later, people entered Allah's religion in crowds after victory with the Help of Allah. (Q. CX: 1-2). There were several reasons for it:

1. Many tribes had alliances and pacts with the Quraysh and their entry to the fold of Islam would have meant violation of trust.
2. Many tribes were too weak to act independently but were related to or allied with the Quraish. They feared severance of these relations and wrath and revenge of Quraysh which was too much for them.
3. There were some others who were waiting for the Muslims to dominate Quraysh which alone would be proof of their belonging to Allah's party, since through

> the centuries many attempts of powerful invaders had failed, bereft as they were of Allah's Help. Abraha Ashram, conqueror of Yemen, coming for mention in the Quran (companions of the Elephant- Q. CV: 1) was annihilated sixty-years before the conquest of Mecca (8 A.H.) by Allah's own forces, the natural agencies, having come with the intent of demolishing Kaaba. There were some persons alive having witnessed it. So to some, the Prophet's getting the better of his own people was the true criterion of his being a true Prophet of Allah and they were waiting for conquest of Mecca.

Therefore, after the easy bloodless, perfectly peaceful take over of Mecca the former pacts disappeared into this aid, the influence and pressure of the Quraysh was no more of any consequence, and Muslim's position as aided by Allah was also made clear to the doubters so far.

And lastly, the resistance to the preaching of Islam had dissi-pated. The preachers could preach freely and the listeners (aud-ience) listened unhindered and without fear, the charm of the True Faith drew crowds automatically.

After the conquest of Mecca, Hawazin and Thaqif tribes having a common border with Meccans thought to themselves that if they were to defeat the Muslims, all the groves and other properties of the Meccans in Taif shall become theirs without any risk. And they shall have avenged for their iconoclasm.

They brought the Bani Madar and Bani Hilal tribes also to their side as allies and with an army of four thousand strong they started for Mecca, coming down in the valley known as Hunain. Under the advice of their chief, Malik bin 'Auf, they had also brought their women, children and cattle and other goods with them. The advantage of this measure pointed out by him had been that nobody could even think of desertion of all those to save his own life.

On receiving this information, the Prophet (PBUH) who did not like to be engaged in a battle adjacent to Kaaba and within the sacred precincts, also advanced towards the invading army.

An addition of two thousand fighting men comprising also the freshly converted to Islam was made aside the idolatrous allies under protection, thus making the Muslim army twelve thousand strong. They were feeling proud of their numerical strength to some extent and hence had become a little mindful of their usual alertness and precaution. It is borne out by the Quran:

> And on the day of Hunain: behold! your great numbers elated you, but they awaited you naught: the land for all that it is wide, did constrain you, and you turned back in retreat. —Al Quran IX: 25

The enemy lay in ambush in a narrow pass with a party of archers. When the advance guard of the Muslim army (comprising those devil-may-care-type of young men who were hardly armed or not, at least, the requisite arms) reached the enemy's range of shooting. They rained down so many arrows on them that they were forced to fly in panic. Only about a hundred on them that they were forced to fly in panic. Only about a hundred companions of the Prophet firmly held their positions in the battle field. The Prophet (PBUH) when he saw the enemy advancing and his own army running away for safety, displayed unique valour and perseverance. He got down his mule and said:

> "I am a Prophet, there is not a shade of doubt about it I am the son of Abd-al-Muttalib."

What he meant to convey was that success or failure in an armed conflict was not the criterion of his position as a true Apostle of Allah. Rather it lay in his own identity and personality.

At this stage of confusion, Abbas (R), the uncle of the Prophet, started calling them by their distinguishing features as Muhajirs (immigrants) and Ansar (the helpers) and they responded to this call like a flight of pigeons without delay. Now the army was arranged in a totally different order, with muhajirs and Ansars in the forefront. With the renewed attack in this order, the enemy took to flight, getting divided into two groups:

1. The leader of this group, Malik bin 'Auf with this fighting men took refuge in the fort at Ta'if.
2. The other group comprising their women and children alongwith their goods went into concealment in the Autas gorge.

The Prophet (PBUH) ordered siege of the Ta'if fort, and to take vigilant care of Autas gorge he appointed Abu 'Amir Ashari, who on getting there took possession of the families and goods of the enemy. When the Prophet learnt about performance of Abu 'Amir at Autas, he ordered lifting siege of the Ta'if Fort, since they were faced with the calamity of losing their most precious assets, wives, children and goods. There were 24,000 camels, 40 thousand goats, four thousand oqiah (about 420 kilogram) silver and six thousand women and children in all.

The Prophet had stayed very close to the battle field, where six chiefs of the Hawazin tribe came to him appealing for mercy. Some of these men were those who had rained stones on him when he was visiting Ta'if on a preaching mission, and Zaid (R) had lifted him unconscious to carry him to safety.

The Prophet (PBUH) said to them: "Welcome! I had myself been waiting for you. Two weeks have elapsed and the booty has not yet been distributed. In consideration of your request I can release prisoners coming to my share and those of my family. And if there were Muhajirs and Ansar alone with me (as fighting men) I could consider their shares also. But as you can see for yourself, I have here with me even those who are yet unbelievers.

So we will have to tackle this problem in this way: come to me tomorrow morning after the early morning prayer (Fajr) to present your request in the presence of the assembly of common people. Let us see if a solution can be found." He concluded saying: "choose for yourself your good or your families since the invading army cannot be reconciled to total deprivation. (They must get something as return for their (taking) pains)."

Next morning the same representatives presented themselves on the scene and in public gathering repeated their request for the release of their prisoners to the Prophet.

***Great Amnesty :*** The Prophet of mercy said to them: I hereby release the prisoners, my own and those of Banu Abd-al-Muttalib free (without demanding any ransom for them). The Ansar and Muhajirin with one voice declared that they too were releasing those coming to their shares.

Now it came to Bani Saleem and Bani Fuzara. It was something strange to them that the invading enemy, luckily vanquished also, should be shown such mercy and generosity. So they did not proclaim their prisoners released. The Prophet called them and after deliberation, 6 camels was settled as the equivalent of one prisoner and the Prophet paid it to them, and the remaining prisoners were also set free. He also donated one changes of clothes to all the prisoners at parting time.

Among these prisoners was also Shima' bint Harith the daughter of the Prophet's wet nurse Halimah. The Prophet recog-nized this foster sister of his and spread out his sheet on the ground to sit on. He said to her: "It would be much better for you to stay here with me. However, you are perfectly free to go back home if you please. She wanted to return home and was sent away to her own people honourably.

The booty was distributed on the spot. The largest shares were awarded to those who had recently embraced Islam. The most sincere, Ansars, received nothing. He consoled the younger lot showing dissatisfaction saying would they not be pleased taking him with them while others take some petty goods. They were very much pleased. Some of them were moved to tears of joy on hearing these words from the Prophet (PBUH). It had afforded them much greater pleasure than those receiving booty.

Some poet has expressed the Prophet's generosity in the following verse:

> To me Khayber and Hunain stand witness (to the fact)
>
> That you most generously give away what you win through conquests.

***Breach of Faith :*** Yahudi, as a matter of fact, should be the name of the offspring of Yehuda, the third son of Yaqub (Jacob) only. But somehow the progeny of all the twelve sons of Jacob came to be called by this name and now the Israelites are usually termed Yahudi or Jews a denomination which due to their transgression and evil traits of character had become the most detestable among the nations of the world. They, in their vain glory and self-conceit, claim to be the chosen of God, worthy of exaltation and rule over the rest of the world, Here and in eternal bliss Hereafter when the rest of humanity is fit only to be the fuel of Fire of Hell, the horrible pit.

Of all that tall talk and braggadocio only this much is true that they are the progeny of a long line of Prophets and so many high ranking prophets were raised from them through the ages and they were really a fine people chosen by Allah in a particular period for a sacred mission borne out by the Quran also and for some time they proved worthy of it too. "But long ages passed over them and their hearts grew hard" (Q. LVII: 16) and through shameful breach solemn covenants, persecuting their prophets, even killing them, calling Allah "close fisted" "Allah is indigent and we are rich", saying to Moses, their great benefactor, "Go you and your Lord and fight, we are sitting here," and many worse blasphemies which brought Allah's wrath and they were deposed from leadership of humanity, cursed and dispersed.

Their own and last of the Israeli line of prophets, 'Isa (PBUH), kind-hearted as he was, but witnessing their despicable conduct, had called them (venomous) vipers and their progeny and had also prophesied that the kingdom of God (leadership and guidance of mankind) shall be taken away from them and entrusted to another community that may make it blossom, coming into full bloom.

When the appointed time for this prophecy came true (materialized) and Muhammad the Apostle of Allah, Muhammad (PBUH) (called Ahmad in another prophecy by 'Isa the son of Mary):

> 'O children of Israel! I am the messenger of Allah (sent) to you confirming the Turat (which came) before me and giving gladtidings of a messenger to come after me, whose name shall be Ahmad.
>
> —Al Quran LXI: 6),

The Jews finding them conflicting with their self-devised independent views about 'Isa whom they almost handed over to the Roman governor to be crucified, they were very much annoyed and in their rage finally decided to vex, tyrannize and get him out of their way if possible as they had earlier done with his predecessor 'Isa ibn-Maryam.

Although the Jews in the very first year of migration had entered an agreement of peace for all the communities of Medina yet their inherent evil nature and diseased mentality could not remain hidden for long and eighteen months after signing the contract they had entered with the Prophet and the Muslim community mischiefs one after the other were witnessed.

When the Muslims with the Prophet (PBUH) had gone to Badr, a Muslim woman went one day to the locality of Banu Qainuqa' to sell milk. Some Jews played a mischief and stripped her in the market place. Hearing the screams of the woman, a Muslim rushed to the scene and in a rage murdered the mischief mongering culprit, Jew. The Jews gathered together on the spot of murder and they killed the Muslim creating a tumult. On his return from Badr, the Prophet called the Jews to enquire about this riot. They returned the signed copy of agreement with the Prophet to him and the Muslims and appeared bent on a war against the Muslims.

Things had now come to an insurrection and the Jews were punished in as much as forcing them to leave Medina and go to Khaybar to settle down.

***Chain of Misdeeds :*** As stated earlier, the Quraysh had written to the unbelievers of Medina after migration to fight against the Prophet but due to the sagacity and clever handling of the situation it came to naught. After defeat at Badr they again wrote, but this time to the Jews of Medina:

"You are a powerful community, economically well off, in possessions of properties and forts. Fight against Muhammad or else we shall do such and such with you, taking off even the ornaments adorning the ankles of your women." On receipt of this letter, their Banu Nadir tribe was determined on violation of the agreement with the Prophet as well as deceitfully harm him.

It was in 4 A.H. that the Prophet went to the locality of Banu Nadir to collect a national subscription (it was probably to pay the blood money in connection with a murder). They seated him beneath a wall and planned that (the accursed) Ibn Hajash going upon the wall would let fall a heavy stone over him and thus end his life.

After sitting there for some time, he was informed by supernatural means (Allah's own special agencies) of the impending danger and left the place in time.

At last Banu Nadir were punished with banishment from Medina to get settled at Khayber. They loaded all their goods, even the doors and windows of their houses they had themselves razed to the ground, on six hundred camels and settled in Khayber.

The Third Conspiracy of the Jews, The General Insurrection Resulting in the Battle of Ahzab (Confederates) or Battle of Trench

The outstanding feature of the 5th year A.H. is battle of Ahzab. Banu Nadhir did not sit idle even after their banishment to Khayber. They resolved to make a united effort for the total annihilation of the Muslims, involving all the tribes and religions of Arabia. They should participate with their select seasoned swordsmen. They selected twenty chiefs to induce all the tribes of Arabia to come together in a aggressive war against the Muslims. Their efforts were fruitful. In the month of Ziqadah 5 A.H. a formidable army of ten thousand strong including idolaters and Jews with some others, invaded Medina. The Quran calls it the Battle of Ahzab (the confederates).

1. Quraish, Banu Kananah, under the command of Suiyan bin Harb
2. Bani Fuzarah under the command of 'Uqbah bin Hussain
3. Bani Murrah under the command of Harith bin 'Auf
4. Bani Ashja' and Najd is commanded by Masood bin Dakheelah

When the Muslim found themselves incapable of facing them in the open, they acted at the instance of Salman Farsi's (of Persia or Iran), an outstanding companion of the Prophet, they decided to dig a trench (for the first time in Arabia) and started work on it with great enthusiasm. Each team often persons had dugged out forty yards. While at it, the companions recited the following verse:

We are those who have taken an oath of fealty

At the hands of Muhammad to adhere to Islam forever

The Prophet himself helped the companions in the digging operations, breaking hard rock and removal of earth. In this strenuous labour, his chest was covered with dust. He undertook work where others failed.

The battle worthy Muslims were three thousand in all. They came to the battle field in such a manner that the trench was in front of them and Sala' mount at the back. Banu Quraizah the Jewish tribe, resident in Medina and under obligation as signatories of the agreement that we can call Medina charter of Human Rights, the chief of the Banu Nadir, Huya bin Akhtab visited them in the darkness of the night and insisting on them to violate the agreement made them join the invading hordes. The Prophet repeatedly sent his heralds to them to bring them round and desisting from breach of faith, but they flatly refused to listen to them saying: "Who is Muhammad to us that we should listen to him? We are not bound to him by any bond whatsoever."

After that Banu Quraizah started disturbing the peace of the town. The lives, honour and property of Muslim women and children was imperilled. In this helpless situation, a detachment from this non too big a number had to be sent back to Medina to guard it, and maintain peace if breach was wickedly created by the Jews. Banu Quraizah were under the impression that the ferocious attack of ten thousand from outside and we inside the town creating lawlessness, can make life miserable for Muslim, they will be totally wiped out leaving no trace behind.

Since the Prophet was by nature peace-loving and anti-war, he held consultation with the companions on an offer of peace on the term of payment of one third of their produce (of duties). But the Ansar preferred war. Saad bin Mu'az (R) and S'ad bin 'Ubadah (R) speaking on the resolution submitted: When we were polytheists and idolaters, we never gave them anything (under pressure). Now that Allah has honoured us with Islam, how can we give them one third of our produce. For them we have nothing but our swords.

The invading army besieged them (Muslims) for twenty days. A few occasional single handed combats were also witnessed. 'Umar bin Abdan who boasted of equality with thousand men in combat was killed easily by 'Ali Murtuza (R) in one such single combat. And Naufal bin Abdullah bin Mughira too was killed in an encounter. The Meccans offered ten thousand dirhams for the dead body of Naufal. The Prophet (PBUH) told his men to hand over the dead body. Nothing in return was needed.

When they could not confront Muslims during this period of siege, they were dejected and left one night bag and baggage surely grieved.

***Last Act :*** After getting rid of this troublesome affair, the Prophet called Banu Quraizah to explain their position face to face (show cause for their dastardly conduct). Now Banu Quraizah in a state of self imposed siege in their fort woefully prepared for a trial of strength. At this stage, the Muslims came to know that the Banu Nadir chief Huya bin Akhtab was still with them in the fort.

This role of a trouble maker was not the first instance on the part of Banu Quraizah. At the time of Badr, they had strengthened the position of Quraysh with war material and arms. But then the kind hearted Prophet (PBUH) had forgiven them.

Now that they had taken refuge in their fort, the Muslims had no other cause left open to them but to have a go at them. They were factually besieged now by an invading army in zil-Hijjah, which lasted 25 days. The siege now becoming intolerable and sick of it they contacted the Muslims of Aus tribe with whom they were on terms of friendship since long and reconciled the Prophet to agree to the arbitration of Saad bin Mu'az (Aus chief) in their (Banu Quraizah's) affair and his arbitration should be acceptable to him.

Banu Quraizah came out of the fort and their case was entrusted to Saad bin Mu'az. What high hopes Aus and Banu Quraizah might have been nursing after Mu'az was accepted arbiter by both the parties? But this manly arbiter and God fearing Muslim after necessary investigations gave the following verdict:

1. The combat-worthy males of banu Quraizah be put to sword.
2. Women and children be taken as prisoner of war (slave).
3. Their goods be divided as booty.

In the materialization of this arbitration, what we learn from a report in Bukhari by Abu Saeed Khudri, that able-bodied combat-worthy men were killed. But the tradition has nothing to say about the women and children being taken as prisoners (slaves). It must also be kept in mind that the arbiter of their own choice, had pronounced for them the same punishment which they inflicted on their criminals and prescribed by their Shariah.

We have reasons to believe and precedents to show that Banu Quraizah had left their case in the hands of the Prophet (PBUH) the greatest punishment that would have been pronounced could be their banishment from Medina to settle in Khayber. The cases of Banu Qainuqa' and Banu Nadir are two precedents before us. The Prophet (PBUH) had mercifully exempted some of them (Banu Quraizah) also from the pronounced punishment. For example Zuhair (Jew) had received pardon from him with wife, children and his goods. And Rifah (Jew) had also been spared his life.

9

# Possession of Mecca

Medina was agog with stories of mass conversion of the people to Islam. There were converts in Mecca as well but the infidels outnumbered them. While, during the 'Ascension', the holy Prophet (PBUH) was given various guidelines, it was indicated to him that he would have to emigrate for the ultimate victory of the Faith.

Verse 80 of Sura Bani Israil points to this, where the holy Prophet (PBUH) was advised to pray:

> "My Lord! Cause me to enter with a firm incoming and go out with a firm outgoing; and grant me from your Presence a sustaining power."

According to Ibne Abbas, this verse contained the Divine command for the holy Prophet (PBUH) to migrate from Mecca.

**Final Victory**

Twelve years of Prophethood had elapsed in Mecca and, despite his best efforts to convert the polytheists of that city, the holy Prophet (PBUH) continued to face their opposition and persecution.' He would look towards the heaven, sometimes, and pray to God to turn their hearts towards Islam, so that the people of Mecca, for whose reformation he was initially sent, could be saved from the final doom. The holy Prophet (PBUH) was fully conscious of the Quranic edict that "if some one saved someone else from a catastrophe, he almost saved the entire mankind. But the Divine knowledge encompassed who would receive the guidance and who would not. Therefore, the holy Prophet (PBUH) was advised not to feel depressed at the attitude of the people of Mecca:

> "But if they are averse, We have not sent you as a warder over them. Thine is only to convey the message." (Al-Shura-48)"

Further, knowing that the holy Prophet (PBUH) had a soft corner for his own people of Mecca, the Divine command came:

> "Therefore, O, Prophet! Do not treat them with favour, as you are not to blame at all."

This was by way of consolation to the holy Prophet (PBUH) that he had done his duty, and if the polytheists of Mecca did not listen to his preaching, he should leave them alone;

> "Leave Me to deal with those who falsify thy preaching. We shall lead them on by steps from whence they do not know.
>
> And yet I bear with them, but My scheme is firm". (Qalam 41-45)

Again, Allah tried to explain to the holy Prophet (PBUH) in Sura Muzammil:

> "Leave Me to deal with the deniers who are enjoying ease and comfort (of this life) and give them respite awhile"

The holy Prophet (PBUH) was now fully conscious of the fact that the last warning from the Lord had been served on these unlucky folk, as had happened earlier in the case of the deniers of the Prophets of God, but his attitude was quite different from that of the other Prophets. For example, Prophet Nuh appealed to God, in similar circumstances:

> "O, Lord! Do not leave even a single of the infidels safe on this earth."

Thus, the entire nation of Prophet Nuh was drowned in the deluge, including his own son who belonged to the group of his detractors.

Similarly, Prophet Hood warned his people that if they failed to respond to his call, God would impose some other people over them. And this is exactly what happened, as those who had accepted the Prophet's message were saved and the rest perished.

Again, the people of Thamud, who were a wicked lot, were completely destroyed when they did not listen to the preaching of Prophet Saleh, who was sent to reform them.

## Peace for All

But, in identical conditions, when the people of Mecca made it almost impossible for the holy Prophet (PBUH) to live with security and when the people of Taif behaved brutally with him, he stayed the Divine punishment as he was sent as a "mercy for all mankind."

It was in the 13th year of Prophethood, during Hajj season, when people from all over Arabia had assembled in Mecca, that four Muslims of Medina, who had not seen the holy Prophet (PBUH) before, were very eager to have a glimpse of him, and after great secrecy and caution lest the infidels of Mecca do them harm, enquired about the holy Prophet's (PBUH) address from some one who was, perhaps, a Muslim. They were Uwaim bin Saeda, Saad bin Khasima, Maan bin Adi and Abdullah bin Jubayr. They had not seen the holy Prophet (PBUH) before, but recognised him at first sight because of his special prophetic features and captivating appearance and bearing. Picking up courage and collecting their senses, they saluted the holy Prophet (PBUH) which was duly acknowledged. Thereafter, they enquired:

> "When will your goodself meet the people of Medina?"

The holy Prophet's (PBUH) uncle Hadrat Abbas, with whom he was staying at that time, enquired from the Ansar:

> "Have the polytheists of Medina also accompanied you people?"

They answered in the affirmative. They were advised to keep the meeting a guarded secret until the pilgrims started journeying back after Hajj. The holy Prophet (PBUH) fixed the slopes of Aqba as the meeting place and night fall as the time of the meeting.

The holy Prophet (PBUH) also advised them not to awaken any one who might be asleep and not to wait for one who might be absent. He had given similar instructions to Baraa bin Maroor and Kaab bin Malik when they had met him in the precincts of Kaaba.

At the appointed time and place, 71 men and 2 women of the Ansar of Medina, one by the name of Nasiba bint Kaab Umme Ammara and the other a courageous lady Asma bint Amroo, met the holy Prophet (PBUH).

It may be pointed out here that when the false prophets like Musailama Kazzab, during the caliphate of Hadrat Abu Bakr, raised their heads, Umme Ammara and her son, Abdullah took part in the campaign against Musailma and she lost one arm and suffered twelve grievous injuries. Prior to this Musailma had chopped off one limb after another of her son, Habib, who refused to acknowledge Musailma as a true prophet.

The holy Prophet (PBUH), accompanied by his uncle Hadrat Abbas, was already there at Aqaba when the Ansar, who were extremely eager to cast a glance at the holy Prophet (PBUH), arrived there. The holy Prophet, (PBUH) at the outset, advised them to be brief in expressing their views, as the detectives of the polytheists might be on their trail. Then, his uncle addressed the 73 Ansar in a low voice:

> "O, people of Khazraj! I need not tell you in what high esteem we hold Muhammad (PBUH) and the entire clan of Banu Hashim has been at his back to protect him from his enemies. But now he has decided firmly to migrate to your city. Therefore, if you can fulfil your promise and can support him against all odds, then he can go with you, otherwise you may leave him alone."

A representative of theirs undertook to discharge all possible responsibilities in respect of the holy Prophet's (PBUH) protection and offered to declare it on any kind of oath.

Then, the holy Prophet (PBUH) verses from the holy Quran and spoke:

> "I obtain your oath of fealty that you will protect me in the same manner as you would do your own children."

Therefore, Bara bin Abul Haisan bin Altihan stood up and assured the holy Prophet (PBUH) of full protection the way he wanted, but Abul Haisan, at the same time posed the question:

> "O, Prophet of God! Should we rule out the possibility of your deserting us and joining your people of Mecca when you get the upper hand and become victorious?"

The holy Prophet (PBUH) smiled and assured:

> 'Never, never will it so happen. I shall live and die among you. I am yours and you are mine. Whoever is your enemy is my enemy and whoever is your friend is my friend."

This assurance cheered them up and all of them took the oath of fealty at the holy Prophet's (PBUH) hand. This was the last oath of fealty at Aqba.

Hadrat Bara bin delivered a very impassioned speech on the occasion pledging all support for the cause of Islam.

It may be borne in mind that the Ansar of Medina were not providing a kind of refuge to the holy Prophet (PBUH) taking him as a helpless displaced person but recognising him as their leader for whom they could lay their lives if the occasion arose. In fact, they considered it a great honour to play host to the holy Prophet (PBUH).

According to the 'Tabaqat', the holy Prophet (PBUH) asked them to elect 12 representatives from among them who should be dependable and responsible persons in their respective tribes and according to Ibne Ishaque, the holy Prophet (PBUH) cited the example of Prophet Jesus's helpers. Out of the twelve representatives, who were unanimously elected, nine belonged to the tribe of Khazraj and three to Aus.

Hardly had the 73 Ansar who had taken the oath of fealty at Aqba, retired to their camps that the polytheists of Mecca got wind of it and they contacted the Ansar in their camps and protested against their offer of refuge to the holy Prophet (PBUH) in Medina. The polytheists of Medina, who had no knowledge of this oath of fealty denied that any such offer had been made, and by daybreak they left for 'Medina'. The polytheists of Mecca went in hot pursuit after them and succeeded only in getting hold of Saad bin Ibada, who also got free shortly afterwards and returned to Medina. These 73 converts of Medina broke all the idols in their city, except a few.

***End of Idolatory Days :*** At that time, Baalma's Chief Umroo bin Jamoo, who wielded great influence in Medina was lying prostrate before the beautifully carved wooden idol of Manaat in his house, as the night before this idol had been removed from its pedestal and dumped on garbage outside his house. He had, somehow, succeeded in recovering this 'desecrated' idol the same night; but when he went to the idol's chamber in his house, the next morning he found the idol missing again and he discovered it again lying on the heap of litter outside his house. He again restored it to its pedestal and hung an unsheated sword in its neck supplicating it to defend itself against the intruder. But the next morning, the idol was again missing and was found in a dry well with a dead dog tied to its neck in place of the sword. In the meanwhile, came his son Maad bin Umroo, who had turned a Muslim, accompanied by youths of his tribe, who explained to him the monotheistic message of Islam, driving home the point that if a life-less idol could not protect itself, it was sheer folly to expect of it any kind of help and assistance.

The disconcerting news of the spread of Islam in Medina had unnerved the polytheists of Mecca and they intensified their persecution of the Muslim converts of Mecca, making it impossible for them to continue living in their place of birth.

Among the heart-rending incidents of their oppression is the tale of Hadrat Umme Salma wife of the holy Prophet's (PBUH) aunt Barra bint Abdul Muttalib. She and her husband had decided to migrate from Mecca to Medina alongwith their children. Hardly had they mounted the camel with their belongings loaded on it, that Bani Mughira, to which tribe Umme Salma belonged, forced the wife and the girl child to dismount. They took both of them back to their tribe. Learning of this, the tribesmen of the husband appeared on the scene and took away their son just as the wife's tribesmen had taken away their daughter. Hadrat Umme Salma was so badly aggrieved that she spent most of her time in Mecca lamenting her separation from the husband and the son. One day, one of the notables of Bani Mughira chanced to witness the wailing and mourning of Hadrat Umme Salma and he was so affected by it that he prevailed upon his tribesmen to let Hadrat Umme Salma go to join her husband and she, accordingly set out for Medina and got united with her husband at Quba, on the outskirts of the city.

According to Ibne Ishaque, the holy Prophet (PBUH) permitted all the Muslims of Mecca to migrate under the circumstances, and soon family after family set out for Medina severing all connections with their native place and leaving their hearths and homes.

But the persecution was not restricted within the confines of Mecca alone. The polytheists even raided the approaches to Medina and arrested the emigrants whenever they could. One such case pertaining to the arrest of Hadrat Ayyash whom Abu Jahl and Harith bin Hisham arrested through deceit and brought him to Mecca lashed on camel back scorning and jesting and inciting the people of Mecca to follow suit.

But the distinctive way in which Hadrat Umar migrated from Mecca was eminently different from that of others. He openly sought the holy Prophet's (PBUH) leave, circumambulated the Kaaba, offered prayers there and declared aloud that he was migrating-to Medina and if one had the courage or strength to stop him from doing so, he should come forward. None did so, and he left in a procession of twenty riders in day light accompanied, among others, by his brother Zaid bin Khattab, brother-in-law Sayed bin Zaid. According to their plan, Ayyash bin Ali Rabeeya and Hisham bin Aas bin Wael had to meet them at a place ten miles away from Mecca; but Hisham was caught on way and Ayyash succeeded in reaching Medina. However, shortly, thereafter, Abu Jahl and Harith bin Hisham reached Medina and, through a perfidy, returned to Mecca, despite Hadrat Umar's advice to the contrary. Hadrat Ayyash was the cousin of Abu Jahl and Harith. How the two behaved with him after bringing him to Mecca in chains, like a prisoner, we know.

The holy Prophet (PBUH), Hadrat Abu Bakr and Hadrat Ali stayed on in Mecca:

> Hadrat Abu Bakr, when he sought leave to migrate, was advised by the holy Prophet (PBUH) to tarry a little as he hoped that he would himself be given Divine permission to migrate. Hearing this, Hadrat Abu Bakr's joy knew no bounds. It is related, on the authority of Hadrat Ali, that Gabriel had informed the holy Prophet (PBUH), in advance, that Hadrat Abu Bakr would be his companion and comrade during migration.

***The Meetings :*** The notables of Quraish were upset at the situation in Mecca and were holding secret sessions in the 'house of consultation' - Damn - Nadwa. They anticipated that in case the holy Prophet (PBUH) also left for Medina, he would be able to secure a strong foot-hold there, gifted as he was, with the power of persuasion and ability of guidance and organisation. What they apprehended most was the danger that the nascent Muslim power in Medina, which lay on the trade route for Mecca to Egypt, Syria and other Roman possessions, would pose a serious threat to their trade with these countries. At the instigation of Abu Jahl, they decided that each tribe should select one youth and they should jointly attack the holy Prophet (PBUH) and kill him. In that case, the holy Prophet's (PBUH) tribe will not be in a position to avenge his death and they will have no option but agree to accept ransom money for the death of the holy Prophet (PBUH). The proposal was adopted with extreme secrecy and the executants of this nefarious plan had also been selected. But nothing could remain hidden from Allah, Who revealed their secret plot to the holy Prophet (PBUH).

According to Ibne Ishaque, the holy Prophet (PBUH), hooding his face, came to Hadrat Abu Bakr's place at an unusual time of mid-day and disclosed to him that he had been permitted by the Almighty to migrate and also that Hadrat Abu Bakr would be his companion during the journey. Hadrat Abu Bakr had already made arrangements of two dromedaries for the journey, one of which was purchased by the holy Prophet (PBUH) then and there from his companion despite the latter's protestations to the contrary. The holy Prophet (PBUH) promised to pay the actual price of the she-camel to Hadrat Abu Bakr.

Thereafter, the holy Prophet (PBUH) sent for Abdullah bin Al ariqat, who was known for his expertise as a guide in the desert. Though a polytheist, he was a dependable man. This is the fellow whom the holy Prophet (PBUH) had sent to Matam bin Adi' as his personal envoy on return from Taif. Both the she-camels were made over to Abdullah bin Ariqat with instructions to reach the appointed site whenever advised.

Only Hadrat Ali had to stay on in Mecca and that too for returning the things deposited by the Meccans as trust with the holy Prophet (PBUH). He had to leave for Medina thereafter. The polytheists had deputed detectives around the holy Prophet's (PBUH) house to keep an eye on his movements and advise the killers of the opportune time.

While the holy Prophet (PBUH) was busy preparing with a heavy heart to leave his home for good and be away from Kaaba for almost an uncertain time, he approached Uthman, the key-bearer of Kaaba, a sworn enemy of Islam and an opponent of the holy Prophet (PBUH). He requested him to open the door of the Kaaba for a short while so that he could have a last look at it.

Uthman, who had persecuted his cousin Musab bin Umair most inhumanly, was not the type of person to oblige the holy Prophet (PBUH). However, the holy Prophet (PBUH) left Kaaba saying to Uthman:

> "Remember, a time will come when I will entrust this key to a person from whom no power can ever withdraw the key."

And, the day dawned after the conquest of Mecca when Uthman was standing in front of the holy Prophet (PBUH) hanging his head in disgrace. No one anticipated to whom the holy Prophet (PBUH) would entrust the keys of Kaaba. But, what a surprise, when the holy Prophet (PBUH) entrusted the key to the same Uthman who had not only been always disrespectful to him but one of the worst enemies of Islam. Uthman was so swayed by emotion that he fell on the holy Prophet's (PBUH) feet and embraced Islam.

On the day, the polytheists had planned to assassinate the holy Prophet (PBUH), he did not come out of his house. This assured them that the holy Prophet was inside his house. So, they surrounded his house near Safa. The holy Prophet (PBUH) sent for Hadrat Ali and gave him his green cloak advising him to wrap himself up with that sheet of cloth and sleep on his bed so that the enemies might be under the impression that their quandary was in the house. He also instructed Hadrat Ali about the details of the articles held by him in trust and to return them to their owners. After nightfall, the holy Prophet (PBUH), reciting the opening verses of Sura Yasin, came out of the house and went unnoticed by the would be assassins who stood around his house with their weapons of death. He took Hadrat Abu Bakr alongwith him and crossed the limits of Mecca before day-break.

In the morning, the killers peeped into his house and discovered that it was Hadrat Ali who was lying on the holy Prophet's (PBUH) bed. They got hold of Hadrat Ali and enquired about the holy Prophet's whereabouts. But since the former did not actually know where the holy Prophet (PBUH) was at that time, he could not tell them anything.

They beat him and locked him up in the precincts of Kaaba. But when they learnt that the articles kept in trust with the holy Prophet (PBUH) by many of them were in Hadrat Ali's custody, they released him.

The polytheists searched and searched on the routes leading to Medina but could not find any trace of the holy Prophet (PBUH), who had taken refuge in the Cave of Thaur which falls in the west on way to Yemen. None of them suspected that he would have travelled to Yemen. According to Ibne Hisham, the polytheists, in sheer disgust and great anger reached Hadrat Abu Bakr's house, led by Abu Jahl and enquired from Hadrat Asma bint Abu Bakr about her father's whereabouts, and finding no satisfactory reply, Abu Jahl slapped her on the face.

The holy Prophet (PBUH) stayed in the cave of Thaur for three days, looking towards Kaaba which was built by his ancient ancestor, Prophet Abraham with supplication to the Almighty to send a Prophet in Arabia from his progeny. Hadrat Abu Bakr had first closed the various holes in the cave and cleaned it and then asked the holy Prophet (PBUH) to set his foot inside. On one of the holes, he put his heel to keep away serpents or other creeping animals from harming the holy Prophet (PBUH).

It was a dark night, and two holy persons, the holy Prophet (PBUH) and Hadrat Abu Bakr, were trudging along continuously in the hilly terrain in the dim light of the stars. Sometimes, Hadrat Abu Bakr walked ahead and sometimes behind the holy Prophet (PBUH), to protect him from any one either attacking him from the front or from the rear. Hadrat Abu Bakr had already instructed before hand his son Hadrat Abdullah, after disclosing him in confidence that they would travel via Yemen and take rest in the Cave of Thaur to keep an eye on the movements of the polytheists in day and inform him about their plans and activities by visiting the cave at night. At the same time, he had instructed his freed slave Hadrat Aamir to bring the goats for grazing near the cave so that the holy Prophet (PBUH) could get milk regularly.

One day, while still in the Cave, they heard the voice and sounds of footsteps close to the cave. These belonged to the polytheists of Mecca who had succeeded in tracing their whereabouts with the help of experts of foot prints of men and camels.

Hadrat Abu Bakr whispered to the holy Prophet (PBUH):

> O, Messenger of Allah! If any one of them would look below his feet, he might he able to locate us."

The holy Prophet (PBUH) consoled him:

> "We are not two of us here. Allah is the third Being with us."

In the meantime, the voices grew louder. The expert of foot-prints, Alqama Khazai, was telling the pursuants that no foot-prints were discernable beyond the cave. Some one suggested:

> "Let us enter the Cave and see".

But Umayya bin Khalaf laughed at the idea saying:

> "There is a large spider's web on the mouth of the cave which is perhaps, there from before Muhammad was born."

Thereafter, they all went back. This was purely Divine power that misled them and they returned unsuccessful.

The holy Quran refers to this incident in these words: (Tauba: 40) "If you did not help him, Allah still helped him when the disbelievers drove him forth, the second of the two, when they two were in the cave, when he said to his comrade: Grieve not as Allah is with us. Then Allah caused His peace of reassurance to descend upon him and supported with hosts you can not see and made the word of the disbelievers low while it was Allah's word that became uppermost. Allah is Mighty, Wise."

## Beginning of New Age

These few words sum up, in a nutshell, the history of Islam's victory over the whole of Arabia. This verse, according to the various authorities on Quran being a part of Sura Tauba, is believed to have been revealed in Zeeqad of 9th A.H. the period when the holy Prophet (PBUH) had thrown the gauntlet against the world's super power at that time and preparations were afoot for the battle of Tabuk. This sura calls the Muslims to wage war against the disbelievers and condemns those who, on account of their lack of faith or weakness, shirk their responsibility to participate in the efforts for Allah's cause, and promises Divine help in case the hypocrite Muslims do not come forward to hold the banner of faith aloft. By referring to such Divine help against the enemies of the holy Prophet (PBUH) while the latter was taking refuge in the Cave, Allah made the believers firm in their faith in similar help in future in case they fought for the cause of Islam.

The disappointed polytheists, after their unsuccessful attempt to apprehend the holy Prophet (PBUH), announced a reward of 200 camels for any one who could arrest or assassinate the holy Prophet (PBUH) and his companion, Hadrat Abu Bakr.

After staying in the Cave for three consecutive nights and days, when the polytheists had given up further attempt to trace him, the holy Prophet (PBUH) sent for Abdullah bin Ariqat, the man with the she-camels, to come to the Cave on the fourth day. Hadrat Abu Bakr's daugther, Hadrat Asma brought with her food and ration for the journey but forgot to bring the strapped pouch (Kajawa') in which such articles are loaded and hung on the camel's back. She tore her waist band in two and tied with it the container of food and provisions and hung it on the camel's harness. Since then she was nick-named as the" lady who tore her waist band in two."

In the latter part of the night, the small caravan of two camels, led by Abdullah bin Ariqat left for the destination—Medina—the holy Prophet (PBUH) and Hadrat Abu Bakr each riding a camel with Hadrat Aamir bin Fahira sitting behind Hadrat Abu Bakr on the same camel.

According to Qastlani, this momentous journey of migration commenced on Monday, as the holy Prophet (PBUH) had spent the night of Friday, Saturday and Sunday in the Cave of Thaur. The caravan kept on moving till afternoon of the next day. Hadrat Abu Bakr, finding the comforting shade under a protruding rock laid a carpet under it and suggested to the holy Prophet (PBUH) to rest a while. Hadrat Abu Bakr got some milk from a shepherd boy who was grazing his flock in the nearby pasture and offered it to the holy Prophet (PBUH) to drink. When the sun's heat subsided, they set out on the journey ahead. But, suddenly, when the camels led by Ariqat stepped out of the hilly terrain and came on a plain tract, Hadrat Abu Bakr noticed a horse-rider approaching them.

Hadrat Abu Bakr got worried and spoke:

> "O, Messenger of Allah! The pursuer has come quite close."

"May Allah make him fall from horse-back", the holy Prophet (PBUH) prayed. And instantly, the rider fell from the horse, but he again jumped on horse-back and started pursuing. The holy Prophet (PBUH) prayed and the rider's horse sank chest-deep in the sand. Now the rider was evidently perplexed and he drew a lot to ascertain whether his pursuit would be successful. The result was in the negative. This disheartened him completely and he thought to himself that the holy Prophet (PBUH) would succeed in escaping from him. Therefore, he loudly shouted in a trembling voice giving out his name as Suraqa bin Josham and swearing that he should be allowed to be heard as he would do no harm. He came near and informed the holy Prophet (PBUH) of the reward for his head announced by the polytheists of Mecca. He apologetically said to the holy Prophet (PBUH):

> "O, Messenger of Allah! Kindly command me to do whatever you want me to do. You will find me obedient."

But the holy Prophet (PBUH) only asked him to keep his whereabouts during this journey a guarded secret and to prevent any one from pursuing him.

On Suraqa's request, the holy Prophet (PBUH) asked Aamir bin Fahira to write on a piece of leather that the former had been pardoned and granted protection in future. Thus, it was again a Divine marvel that the man who had come to assassinate the holy Prophet (PBUH) turned into a protector telling others not to go in the direction of his small caravan as he had searched the entire area and there was no trace of the holy Prophet (PBUH).

The holy Prophet (PBUH) kept on journeying toward Medina till the sand dunes of Quwaid became visible an the sun's heat became less oppressive and its rays acquire a yellow hue like that of dried grass, and the shades in the foot-hills grew bigger and bigger. Just in front lay the tent of Umme Maabad where something to refresh the wear travellers could be hoped for. The holy caravan inched forward and reached the tent. What happened there, had already been narrated in the opening part of this book.

The real destination was Medina, at a distance from Quwaid, where the Ansar (Helpers) and Muhaji (immigrants) were awaiting the arrival of the holy Prophet (PBUH) most impatiently with extreme anxiety about his welfare. Every morning, a group of theirs looked for him on the approaches to Medina and they returned to the homes in the evenings in despair.

But tomorrow was going to be that auspicious day when they will not return in despondency, because who will enter the limits of Medina, on the coming day would belong to them for good. The Ansar and the Muhajirs were figuring out by calculating the normally taken on journey from Mecca to Medina, after arrived at the conclusion that the holy Prophet (PBUH) should have reached by then. Since their expectations had not materialised according to their earthly calculations, they were all visibly worried and over-anxious on account of that person, who was more dear to them than their own children and their personal possessions.

No one should misconstrue their deep devotion to the holy Prophet (PBUH) because they had reposed unswerving belief in his Prohethood, but because they were also enamoured of his personal qualities of head and heart, his spotless character, moral conduct, noble precepts, pious deeds, truthfulness and trust-worthiness, benevolent disposition, kindness to the kindred, sympathy for the oppressed, generosity towards the indigent, distinctive personality, noble temperament and stainless example of human behaviour.

If one scans, the 40-year life of the holy Prophet (PBUH) prior to Prophethood and analyses all the facets of his career from any angle of a biographer, no one would find any blindside in his personality.

You have already read how the holy Prophet's (PBUH) slave, Zaid bin Harith refused to go with his parents and continue to live with the holy Prophet (PBUH) only because he was so charmed by the nobility of his character and personality that he completely ignored his parental love and affection.

***Acts and Operations :*** The holy Prophet's (PBUH) pious life is a practical demonstration of the teachings of the holy Quran. This underlines an extremely important aspect of Islam— it stresses first on practice and action than on mere principles and preachings. The holy Prophet's (PBUH) forty-year career before Prophethood preceded, as a practical example, the maxims and laws of Islam as enunciated in the holy Quran. Therefore, the practicability of this religion remains unchallenged.

Is there a man, in human history, who can stand beside the holy Prophet (PBUH) and can match him in any way from the standpoint of the multitude of persecuted and oppressed persons who stood firm in their faith in his Prophethood and the truth of the words uttered by him and falsehood of the claims of his detractors.

Divine blessing can be attained only through true and perfect love for His last Prophet (PBUH). And, if one were to observe the love, respect and high esteem for the holy Prophet (PBUH) that his followers have for him, one has only to look at the dedication and strong emotional attachment of those devotees who enter the limits of Medina, where the Noblest Prophet (PBUH) rests peacefully.

10

# Law and Order

## Prophet's Words

***Sources of Law :*** Notwithstanding the fact of Shatibi's juristic views unfortunately remained external to the mainstream of Islamic legal thought, the principle of Masla was suggested to be the essential point for the convergence of all enquiries about the nature and purpose of legal obligation, social and legal change and the method of legal reasoning. It was also thought to provide the culmination for the search of desirable unity underlying the diversity of rules in Islamic Law.

The theological objections against the principle were satisfied with the argument that Divine will at the legislative level, in contrast with its manifestation at the level of the creation, allows man's will for freedom to act and holds him responsible for his acts. The translation of human freedom and responsibility in modern terminology will reflect the concept of legal obligation, with the logical derivation of Divine commands to remain within man's capability for compliance, and their necessary intelligibility which cannot be without the inclusion of rational considerations. A collective assessment of all these factors would emphasize the requirement for the explicit or implicit occasioning reasons (ila) for the commands in order for their understanding, generalization and extension to like situations.

The law is recognized to reflect the "soul" of the society to be a social reality, and without coming upto the aspirations of a society and its demands for new adjustments, law can only remain less than a living force. For these reasons law cannot be studied for its own sake as an "introspective science." The decline in the legal development of Islamic Law after the establishment of legal schools, in particular, due to its characterization as "scholastic law," is explainable against this perspective. This realization is underscored by the understanding that the primary sources of Islamic Law are a code of life, however, any claim to their being a final code of law is unsustainable.

The conceptual adequacy of law as reflected in the harmony of legal principles is a recognized criterion of evolved law. In this setting, it is a common presumption that the legal principles are mutually interrelated and the outweighing of one principle in relation to others is violative of this criterion. A survey of the legal development of Islamic Law is demonstrative of the fact that no such requirements were particularly maintained.

The incompletion and insufficiency of law remain a known issue and the primary sources of Islamic Law do not lend any presumption of substantive corpus juris, and its judicial provisions are inadequate as a statement of Muslim personal relations and some of the basic institutions of Islam are not even mentioned in it. This argument, however, is to favour the idea of the Quran being a set of super-eminent principles which should have formed the basis for the deduction of rules and development of law. Some of the more prominent legal inadequacies in Islamic Law are the law of civil obligations, wide arbitrary powers vested in political sovereign under the Shariah doctrine of deterrence or "tazir" as a part of less than developed constitutional law in particular, and public law in general, and law pertaining to the status of women in society as a result of unsatisfactory interpretations.

A survey of the Islamic Law is demonstrative of the lack of imaginative harnessing of full potentials of the Quran as a source of law, because the ground for the law resided in its explicit provisions. In the making of law, reliance was placed upon rules rather than on standards, and ideals were not utilised in the law. This observation is also substantiated by the outlining of some of the more prominent legal inadequacies in the previous section. According to Hart, the question of law concerns the society and the constitutional law is positive morality merely, thus the primary source of Islamic Law could have yielded a prodigious material for law-making. For the same purposes, the far-reaching and wide connotations of Islamic legal "norms" whose value in the modern legal literature is acknowledged beyond doubt," were not beneficially used.

The Muslim legal thought has typically come to be identified with the Islamic laws of inheritance and succession. Similarly, the rights of inheritance in Islam have come to be the facsimile reflection of the social values. The considerations of customary laws prevalent in the Arabian society on the advent of Islam, especially the patrilineal nature of social set-up, the revealed law furnishing vital directions divergent from the customary practices, the critical issue of the revealed standards not accorded any preponderant role in the law-making in relation to the revealed canons, are credible indications of essential Islamic legal thought remaining dormant.

In this respect, the issue whether the pre-Islamic customary law underwent replacement or merely modifications following the Quranic legislation is of proximate relevance. The concurrence with Coulson's view is but unavoidable, for the promulgant or customary law was neither entirely supplanted nor superseded by the revealed tenets, as the latter were merely instrumental in that law's reformation in certain particulars. As an illustrative instance, in the patriarchal social configuration of the tribal pattern of society, male agnate laid claim to the succession as well as the patrimony.

The apportioning of legal share in the financial inheritance for the female was the Quranic modification of the customary law whose substitution could only have been the consequence of the legal development in Islam. However, in addition to the factors already stated, this legal transformation remained unattained due to the essential nature of "Jurists' law" in Islam, for the academic law lacked the apprehension of factual situation and human circumstances, and this observation can find assertion due to the available benefit of retrospection.

Similarly, the attitude of vehement religious trust in the invocation of Divine name during the course of legal matters and morbid fear of sin are the factors traceable in the lack of development of the law. The reliance upon the force of religious belief, such as was not in legal consonance with the practical circumstances of law and legal proceedings, is reflective of the exercise of religious idealism in a basically academic approach towards law of evidence. The realization is of fundamental significance that the ascribed idealism cannot be held without deficiency in fulfilling the criteria of objectiveness in religion, as is exemplified by the inadmissibility of circumstantial evidence in legal process, notwithstanding of the fact that the occurrence of deliberate hiding of the silver pale in the ration of grain, as a later pretext of involvement and incrimination, cited in the chapter of Joseph in the Islamic Scripture, would have served as an adequate instance to introduce the validity of circumstantial evidence.

The zeal to benefit the great belief-system, by subscribing to the notion that the unflinching obligation of the society is to maintain judicially unprocessed primary ethico-legal "rules" in the provided form, is misconceived, for the ordinary religio-ethical outlook is incapable to encompass the intricacies of law and its making. Fundamental problem facing Islamic Jurisprudence in the contemporary era bears essential resemblance with the one that existed in the past-the need to define the legal standards available in the religion and their interrelationships with the vital social factors which influence society. As a matter of critical differentiation, while law in the modern knowledge is viewed to reflect the soul of a society in order to be a "living force," however, in Islam, the law due to its religious origin is the "animating force" for the soul of society. This aspect is of such fundamental significance in Islam that without designating the pivotal social system as Nomocracy—where "nomo" is Greek for law—the claim to essential Islamic character of society cannot be made convincingly.

If the same crucial aspect is considered from another viewpoint, wherein the religion is upheld as the basis of comprehension and implementation of the Divine purposes for the Islamic society, then, necessarily the Islamic Law is to be assigned the role of the medium for the attainment of those objectives. Now the emphasis is laid upon the use of reason in the Islamic Scripture, and the intricate yet subtle prerequisite for the possession of understanding is indicated therein for its intended subjects. Thus, in the deliberately patterned texture of the Islamic Law, the warp and woof of the Divine revelation and human reason are to be inseparably interwoven. The observation, that rational justification should have been adopted as the essential religious injunction in respect of law, has sound basis.

Accessible to the Muslim legists were the records of antedating Roman and Greek Civilizations, with the respective legal systems prevalent during their politically ascendant periods as models for comparative study, and so was available the precedent of Canon Law. Evidence to the contrary is available in the instances of Islamic constitutional and other categories of public law, which do not reflect the benefits of such a comparative study. Now recourse to comparison of laws is an indispensable part of legal scholarship and unavoidable in the determination of superior form of political constitution and, therefore, a paradigm of political community. Aristotle studied a large number of constitutions concerned with Greek and other cities in his treatise, Politics. In drafting the Athenian Laws, Solon (640-558 B.C.) proceeded on similar course.

Further, the drawing up of the law of the Twelve Tables for Rome was preceded by the enquiries in relation to comparative law concerning the legal systems in the Greek cities. In later periods, the comparative studies of Canon and Roman Laws were conducted and their respective advantages compared. Montesquieu (1689-1755 A.D.) attempted through comparison to penetrate the spirit of laws and, thereby, to establish common principles of sound government.

Due to the essential differentiation that exists between the doctrines of "Kalam" and the principles of "Usul," its mitigation during the interpretation of the rules is undesirable. The leading original Muslim legists possessed a theological inclination which permitted an excessive devotion to the letter of law, making it an end *per se,* independent of its underlying purpose. In accordance with the modern legal terminology, such an interpretation earns the designation of "grammatical." As a result, the inter-relationship of rules, vital for the development and efficiency of law, is not satisfactorily maintainable.

Besides, such interpretative outcome may cast some aspersions upon the legal system and, upon the translation of this observation into Islamic terms, the implementation of such a rule may result in the besmirching of Islam in the final analysis, an occurrence of which should not allow such a rule to remain any more cherishable. Additionally, the result of this particular interpretative method is not likely to cause the reinforcement of necessary link between the law and society. And, above all else, the underlying principles, functional throughout the law, comprising its spirit as derived from Islam, that perform an important role in the fostering of fundamental values in the society, are unable to leave their desired impact. Now, in order to give full effect to law, its intention must also be interpreted in the light of certain fundamental legal doctrines.

The real meanings of the legislative texts cannot be provided elucidation without taking into account the whole of the system and principles by which the legislative policy is unquestionably guided. This particular interpretative approach is designated as "logical." Approximately related issue to this interpretative approach is the spirit of the laws, derived from Islam and enshrined in its Supreme Fundamental Principles, which is indispensable to the concept of the "soul of society."

***Methodology of Law :*** Appropriateness of a legal system in meeting the challenge of social change is basically dependent upon its philosophical and methodological adequacy and, in the instance of Fiqh, Shatibi had emphasized these aspects. This approach was a precedence of the Fuero, or Spanish Christian, system of law wherein reliance was placed upon the exposition of the shortcomings of the system and the effecting of the renaissance of the Roman Law, in bringing about its reformation. In this process of the systematization of Roman Law, the ascertainment of reasons for the rules marked the advent of the philosophy of law in modern legal systems.

The proponents of dynamism in Islamic Law considered "Masla" as a principle of adaptability, in contrast with the immutability of the law upheld by the theological and idealistic proponents, and it conveyed a distinct implication of modification in adjustment to emerging social conditions, with the added significance of the expansion of law. The immediate concern of adaptability with social change is not related to the latter resulting from the transformation of society, but due to its happening as an outcome of social needs. The distinction in regard to praiseworthy and condemnable "bida," or innovation in Islamic Law consequent to the adoption of Masla, was maintained. These measures were deemed necessary, for the methodological issues concerning Shariah as to the application and extension of law to new situations, the interpretation of law in accordance with the principles of jurisprudence developed in the past several centuries, and the eradication of difficulties existing in the then prevalent law had remained undefined.

Any satisfactory outcome of those issues was hampered due to adherence to the theological viewpoint concerning the denial of cause in legal reasoning, which was a notion in contrast with that subscribed by the proponents, including Shatibi, of command or edict not to be without some motivating cause. The fact in this respect is of more than passing historical interest that Suarez initiated similar improvements in the philosophy of law in the 16th century A.D., which were to influence the fundamental legal developments in Europe. As a tribute to Shatib's legal genius, the ironical instance of Rashid Rida is mentionable, who succeeded in blunting the popularity of his views in the 19th century A.D., with the undeserving epithets of conservative, crusader against innovation and traditionalist, which is as notice worthy as it is instructive.

The search for the principles, such as are the essential point at which all enquiries about the nature and purpose of legal obligation, social and legal change and the method of legal reasoning converge, besides providing the basis for the unity that underlies the diversity of rules in Islamic Law, is indicative that the complete identification of those principles remained unattained in Islamic Law. The justification for this view is available in the modern concept of legal system to constitute a unity, and Kelsen proposed basic norms pertaining to each system. The definition of the relationship between these principles, mandated by the religio-legal system of Islam, and the dynamic forces which activate society, is an unfulfilled requirement of the Islamic jurisprudence. The lack of complex congruent practice of a legal system is its recognized malfunctioning. Kelsen presented a related view in the idea of the law as a "hierarchical structure" which rendered it perpetual self-creativeness. On the other hand, Fuller presented a theory, maintaining the implicitness of certain principles in the concept of law and to the extent these principles are violated, the law is lacking, hence, a consideration to be viewed as a matter of degrees. A survey of Islamic Law is suggestive of the non-contribution of these latter-day concepts in the development of the legal system.

Religious idealism characterized the early Islamic jurists, and the concurrence is due Coulson in the observation of the Islamic jurisprudence that began as the formulation of a scheme of law, rather than the formation of an envisioned society. The theological approach to law is considered to "denaturalize" the legal science, for the object of the law, which is intended to be obtained, may be lost in the literal interpretation of the text. The Quran was unquestionably the primary source of law, however, the juridical provisions provided therein were not an all-embracing law, and the possibilities of interpreting the source of law in Islam gradually diminished due to the theological influence and a want of the evolvement of a comprehensive methodology for the development of Law.

The other non-legal influence upon Islamic jurisprudence, in its formative period, was the prevalent social traditions, and the legal interpretation in the area of the status of women, in particular, bears its evidence. It is a reflection of the inadequacy in legal methodology, and not of the want in the content of law specifically, which underscores the necessity for the formulation of a methodology for the fruitful adaptation of Islamic Law to an ascendant social order.

The period between the middle of 7th to the abolition of Khilafat in the initial quarter of the last century in the Islamic calendar is identifiable with the juristic phenomenon of "Taqlid," which is another way of suggesting the recession of "Ijtihad," whereby sapping of the intellectual vitality and inducing the immobility of the legal system are noticeable. In Shariah the meaning of the term "Taqlid" is to follow the decisions of a jurist without the demand for the arguments. The jurists of the period followed the views of the founders of the respective schools of law. The development and systematization of the legal work of the founders of schools constituted main juristic activity, with the exception of dealing such cases as were not evaluated by the founders.

The adoption of this legal doctrine of blind orthodoxy was to become the precursor for the "closing of the door of Ijtihad" in the 10th century A.D., and it generally assigned the responsibility of the curtailment of creative force immanent in the Muslim jurisprudence. Similarly, it is not difficult to trace its non-creative influence upon the legal method of analogical reasoning which, translated in present-day terms, resembled with the "distinctions" drawn during juristic decisions, but with the striking difference that the created rules failed to find further application.

Now, adherence to the legal orthodoxy is violative of the fundamental truism applicable to the world: Its complete characterization according to a definite, preset number of features is not feasible. Hence, the legal provisions cannot be made available in advance for every imaginable likelihood, for no expression will then be provided to creative elements in the legal concepts. In sum and substance, the result will be the mechanical application of law which invariably proves inimical to legal development.

The shortcoming of a literal interpretation is the theoretical possibility of the binding application of a rule with pernicious tendency and, on the basis of empirical criterion available in the legal systems, such a rule is treated as void. The Islamic concept of "riba" has been extrapolated to exclude any form of interest on a capital loan or investment. Basically a prohibition of usury, the legal concept of riba was coupled with the rules concerning the general prohibition on gambling transactions, with the connotation of chance or unpredictable earnings, in accordance with the meanings of their literal interpretation. Including in its legal ambit all speculative transactions, the law has thus excluded from its validity such contracts and business transactions as may ensure the prosperity of commercial and economic system.

No different is the issue of the husband's basic rights of polygamy and repudiation of spouse, an illustrative instance of a literal interpretative technique without consideration for the empirical tendency of the related law. A sound method placing reliance upon recognized legal criteria is likely to demonstrate those rights as an outcome of misinterpretation. Now, irrespective of the actual incidence of the exercise of the mentioned rights on the part of husbands, even if due to social censure and economic impracticability, the recognized existence of those rights in Islamic Law constitutes an adequate basis for the socio-psychological hindrance, from a practical stand-point, to the advancement of Muslim society. As a consequence, for an unaccountably long duration, the basic and prominent Islamic religio-legal principle of the interaction of reciprocal duties, a foundation of social interdependence leading to social solidarity, has been held in abeyance.

## Rapid Growth

***Failure to Make Law :*** The impasse faced by the Islamic jurisprudence in the 14th century A.D. was furnished a resolution and Shatibi is credited with it, however, the legal ingenuity of an outstanding intellect remained unavailed in the final analysis. Interestingly enough, this situation arose after the four Islamic schools of law were fully established and independent exposition of law gradually dwindled. The result, obviously, was the immobility of law, which is a testimonial, albeit negative, to the absent framework for legal development. An ongoing process, in the form of juristic inquisition, for future development of law, should have been mandatorily available and, additionally, it was required to embody the vital principle of rapid development. These developmental deficiencies in the legal system, however, were to deprive it of the "open" character with a potential for the constant discovery of new rules. On the contrary, the kind of automatism utilised in the application of established law was to paralyse its evolution.

The view, that Islamic Law is essentially rigid and immutable, takes its roots in the two equally unjustifiable misconceptions: its incapacity to accommodate legal change, and the misunderstanding about the comprehensiveness of Divine legislation in the sense of not embodying coverage in all its variety and detail. Recognition is to be granted in this regard to the early Islamic jurists' self-imposed terms of reference. And the tendency of the mechanical observances of the incidents of a legal rule, rather than designed purposes of the rule, is also a factor. Notice worthy is the fact, a legal method which incorporates the remedial steps even for these shortcomings, can allay the stationary character of the Law of Islam.

***Law of Schools :*** In addition to the reasons for the decline in the development of Islamic Law-literal interpretation, "taqlid" and the exercise of "Ijtihad" becoming defunct-a communalism in law on the basis of established schools of law further compounded this hindrance. Juristic disciples from respective schools, in extolling the virtues and authority of the particular master genius almost to the extent of canonization, became devotedly adherent to its legal expositions. Its one logical consequence was the ratification of the Shariah doctrine within each school of law, and the other eventually culminated in the invaluable legal notion of independent juristic enquiry or Ijtihad coming to stagnate. In consequence, the creative potential of

Islamic jurisprudence was to undergo curtailment. In time, this led to the functional assumption that the material sources of revealed legislation were fully utilised in law-making, and their contents finally determined, which bred legal complacency- the anathema to the science of law.

***Religious vs. Legal Outlook :*** Coulson draws distinctions in the essential nature of legislations on the basis of comparison between the attitudes of religious prophet and political legislator. The concern with the consequences of an act or omission is common to both, however, if the one views such consequences in terms of the attainment of merit or fault in the sight of God, then, the other considers those as practical sanctions enforceable by human agencies. The social problems are viewed by the political legislator in terms of the effects of an individual's behaviour upon his neighbour or upon the community as a whole. In contrast, religious law considers the effect that actions may have upon the conscience and eternal soul of the one performing the acts.

In brief, the primary purpose of one is to regulate relationship of man with his fellow beings, and of the other is their regulation with the Creator. The author further observed that the legal verses, or the regulations which are more specifically of a legal tone, cover a great variety of subjects and "often have the appearance of *ad hoc* solutions for particular problems rather than attempts to deal with any general topic comprehensively." Now, the appropriateness of the observations is unexceptionable as to the practical distinction between religion and statutory law is concerned. However, Islam is to be viewed as a composite of these two general categories, and the *ad hoc* nature of revealed rules of legal value remains no more than an appearance once these rules are viewed as juridical guidelines, for the revealed legal injunctions, in purport, cannot be considered as a compendium of law. Nonetheless, in relation to the Islamic religious laws, the issue of *ad hoc* nature of legislation carries significance, for then alone the relevance of the intent of legislation, history of legislation and the law or customs prevailing in the society immediately antecedent to revelation, appear of legal utility. But, more importantly, the necessity for the consideration of the particular modalities of interpretation of the revealed laws and legal application of the vital conception of Supreme Fundamental Islamic Principles, in distinction from the regulatory rules, only then arises.

Realization is due to the fact that any hiatus or deficiency of juristic merit, in the legal methods, introduces difficulty in maintaining legal relationships in the formulation of legal situations, and hampers legal development, as exemplified by the dormancy of the principle of Ijtihad and the subscription to the approach of "taqlid" in traditional Islamic jurisprudence, respectively. Nowhere else, perhaps, than in the sphere of religious law the relevance of the observation made by Mill is evident that the political institutions, in every stage of their existence, are the result of human voluntary agency.

With the apprehension of this political truism, and within the concept of self-binding force of legislation, whereby, making of law presupposes the existence of certain rules which govern the process, the necessity, on the one hand, for the application of the Supreme Fundamental Islamic Principles of legal value and, on the other, for the predominant activity of lawmaking in Islam, becomes obvious. A legal method entailing the application of the fundamental principles is described in the subsequent discourse.

The failure to make law is epitomized by the lack of identification of these principles in view of the fact that direct access to revealed law has ceased as a result of the finality of Prophethood in Islam, and the available source of law must have provided the universal principles against legal status and immobility.

*Other Causes :* In the enumeration of the causes for failure of law-making, Fuller describes inability to provide effective remedies for non-compliance of law, and to maintain minimal literacy conditions in society required for legal compliance. In the survey of Islamic Law, the maintenance of these causes is conspicuous and, particularly, the Muslim family laws and the laws of inheritance do not impose any other than social censure as the legal requirements for the compliance of various provisions. The observation is justifiable that a certain level of general and legal literacy is a requisite for the Muslim law as a part of "nomocracy", where "nomo" is law in Greek-in Islam. Additional cause for failure to make law is the deficiency in the requirements of "natural justice," such as the judicial impartiality and a right to a hearing, so that, disrespect for law becomes common.

In this perspective, restoration of the reverence for law is an inviting issue that resides at the core of a successful legal system, with its foundations in the revealed source of law. It is the social effect that acquires relevance in this context. And excessive use of law in the controlling of human beliefs and passions is another notice worthy cause from the viewpoint of the subject under review, which brings to apt attention the ramifications ensuing from an exercise of overzeal in law-making.

***Rights and Duty :*** The rights prescribed in a body of law are the partial constituents of its "spirit," and the formalism of law remains devoid of reality without the proper inclusion of rights. In Islamic Law, remedy for any shortcoming in this sphere resides in the investigation of the real nature of its legal theory and the requisite rectifications. In the adjacent half millennium, Shatibi appears outstanding amidst those whose juristic pursuits were dedicated to such an undertaking. As a matter of legal history, guaranteeing of the various types of rights in the law-making of Islam would have been of the fundamental significance, as it would have obviated the subsequent authoritarian tendency in the statecraft. This inadvertent exclusion on the part of Islamic Law was the misdirection in orientation of the law concerning the origin of all interests and concerns.

The want of juristic, social and political equality not consonant even with the implication of Islam, was its undesirable outcome. Apart from moral and ethical considerations of the results of this legal slant in Islamic humanism, an equitable society has become a political pre-condition for religious ascendancy and national independence, without which the vision of national security, social development and political stability may remain an illusion. As an illustrative instance of legal methodology through which the legal development in Islam remained deficient in those desirable objectives, on evaluation in retrospect, the analogy of the Habeas Corpus Acts can be cited.

These Acts declare no principle and define no rights but, from a practical standpoint, represent the constitutional guarantee for individual liberty, that is, to provide means for giving legal security to the rights declared by the constitution. The primary sources of law in Islam are replete with such means *par excellence* and, simultaneously, ensure the full-functioning of those rights even in the theoretical instance of the suspension of the relevant constitutional provisions.

In a developed legal system the concepts of rights and duties form a pivotal part in the legal structure, and are proximately allied to the performance of its social functions. The legal connotations of justification and entitlement are conveyed by the concept of right within the framework of a legal system, and it is facilitative of the adherence to a legal order. The legal notions of obligation and right are an essential component of a system of law and, more important, are logically interconnected in the efficiency and development of the system. Pertinent is the fact that the set of rights and the legal framework for their satisfactory fulfillment, in contrast with the gamut and nature of legal obligations, constitute the legal distinction and political identification of a society.

Traditional Muslim Law is assessed to center upon the legal obligations rather than on lawful rights, and to place reliance upon the religious principles that become inoperative in the instance of non-Muslims.' However, a conscientious and meticulous evaluation of the Islamic Law will demonstrate its subtle legal distinction from the original source of law, due to the self-imposed terms of reference that have found applicability in the former instance. The inference is available that the rights are to be emphasized in the Islamic Law in conformity with the requirements of the original source of law. The methodology of legal change, incorporates the invaluable suggestion for the satisfactory inclusion of the legal rights and the adaptability of the Islamic Law in the event of its application upon the non-Muslims in symmetrical conformity with the requirements of Islamic religio-legal principles.

The delineation of the causative factor for shortcomings in law, in relation to the crucial legal issue of the actual scope of rights, entailing distinction between original limitations of law in granting and the default of society in securing the rights, is an aspect of extraordinary legal and ideological significance. As a prototypical example, the rights of Muslim women, within the jurisdiction of traditional Muslim laws, are not uncommonly deemed to have been abridged especially relative to their Muslim counterparts. The characteristic construction of the relevant provisions in the primary source of law notwithstanding, the customary status of women in society in conjunction with their general inability to clearly understand the valid scope of their legal rights, and the perpetuation of nearly patriarchal pattern of society, are substantive contributory factors in an historic lack of implementation of the legal rights of women within the proper jurisdiction as provided in the primary source of law. This discrepancy in the availing of rights, pertaining to Muslim women, is explainable as the responsibility of society due to custom and socio-political constraints. With this in perspective, a legal methodology, founded upon the fundamental principles available from the primary source of law, which would demonstrate such rights of women as are consonant with the religious purposes and legal meanings of Islam and, hence, restore the legal balance due in favour of the rights, will establish a credible proof of its usefulness.

From among the three verses in the Quran whose misinterpretations have caused misconceptions with an historic consequences, ".... obey those in authority" is one such verse. An out of context interpretation was construed to also refer to jurists of all ages and, hence, was misapplied in support of "taglid, " with lamentable consequences to the Islamic Law. This misconstruction evidently exemplifies an out of context interpretation, notwithstanding of the fact that the legal concept of "taqlid" is deviant from the fundamental Islamic precepts whose foundation is the idea of "individual responsibility." The undesirability of taqlid according to essential Islamic principles and empirical results of its application are a part of legal history.

Another and far more serious drawback emanating from the out of context interpretation of the aforementioned Quranic verse is the distortion in the politico-legal notion of social contract, to adopt the description according to modern terminology, to the extent it contains the idea of the correspondence of rights and obligations between the rulers and the populace. The obligation of allegiance to political authority represents the concurrent demand for the supremacy of Islamic Law to be satisfied by the latter, with the implication of contractual reciprocation and to the exclusion of the "sovereign and subject" politico-legal arrangement. As a matter of history ripe with invaluable lessons, in this correlation of right to the rule of Islamic Law and the obligation of allegiance to political authority, the disruption of the contractual harmony, whereby obligation superseded the right, was the verifiable cause of the consequences to developmental shortfall in the legal and political systems.

The vital scriptural injunction as the epitome of the requirement for the observance of revealed law, and it will be referred repeatedly in this discourse, is quoted here: "O ye who believe! obey Allah, and obey the Messenger and those of you who are in authority; and if ye have a dispute concerning any matter, refer it to Allah and the Messenger if ye are (in truth) believer in Allah and the last day. That is better and more seemly in the end." Notice worthy is the scale of sovereignty and any lack of adherence to the specified sequence is a fundamental breach of the revealed injunction. The evaluation of this Quranic verse in terms of law makes manifest the primary sources of Islamic Law to supersede the political authority as a matter of legal obligation.

The dual conceptions of consummate juridical significance and revolutionary political connotation in the tenet are the equalization of the fundamental religious ideas pertaining to faith with the objective notion of law and the contingency of the allegiance to the political authority upon its compatibility with the sovereignty of Islamic Law. The importance of these observations is summarily describable as the fact that their complete realization into definite social institutions has eluded the Islamic Civilization during the course of its history. The conversion of religious obedience into legal obligation is the key factor in the practical realization of the substantive implications which are conveyed in the revealed precept, and this is inferable from the commentaries by other learned sources. To recognize the obligation towards the observance of Islamic Law constitutes the essential measure in this approach, which has been made manifest in numerous other revealed precepts.

The phraseology of religious commentators, whose representation is provided in the expressions such as "obedient to Allah," "ultimate authority rests in Allah," "cornerstone" of Islam, and "no independent obedience to men in authority," is translatable in modern juristic terms of the sovereignty of law. A meaningful elucidation of this instrumental concept, with its practical significance in view, will be the content of this discourse at appropriate junctures. If Islamic Law is in quest of itself and Islamic Civilization is in search of a definite direction for the realization of its an historic destiny, then, the implementation of these basic ideas will prove a turning point in the attainment of those objectives.

***Constitutional Law-General View :*** Constitutional law generally includes all the rules which directly or indirectly effect the distribution and the exercise of the sovereign power in the state. As a part of public laws, it is distinguished by the superior importance of the subject therein treated." The constitutional law in Islam remained underdeveloped and the constitutional limits upon the ruler were neither well-defined nor the means and laws for their implementation were made available. The legal interpretation of the critical Quranic verse, elucidated earlier, was adopted out of context of the verse itself and other legal parameters of the constitutional law in the Scripture.

These scriptural parameters included the Quranic requirement of council in managing the affairs, the meritorious attributes for aspiring to the position of public authority, and the Quranic concept of the emancipation of man as a derivative from the precept of the equality of men underwritten by the idea of Oneness of the Creator. In accordance with the expression of the last determining legal standard, no individual was to be subservient to another except through the legal notion of the equality before law. Translated in terms of the constitutional measures, the same legal concept of the rule of law amounted to constitutional limits upon the authority of political ruler and, as a vital legal deduction from the verse (iv : 59); it was to be the evolvement of the constitutional framework for lending security to the society's prerogative to effect change of rule under specific conditions of the infringement or breach of those constitutional limits. Such a constitutional framework could be constructed through the comparative study of the constitutions ever since the Greek Civilization, and the characteristic vision of the particular society and the state, entertained by the jurists, would have become a political reality. The preceding observations serve as an illuminating instance of the necessity for the development of law from the original sources, which remained unutilized in the area of constitution-making due to the want of methodological approach.

***Caliph—Requirements of Law*** **:** The historical circumstances of the early part of Islam, bordering upon the "right-guided" Caliphate era, had bequeathed the political tradition of the appointment of the Caliph by consent of the representatives of the community. The Ummayad rule, however, left the legacy of the rule of dynasty and, subsequently, the august office of the Caliph remained unstamped by the valuable procedure of the rule with the political consent, but with rare exceptions. If the constitutional framework for the settlement of the issue of the highest executive office in Islam was not in effect, then, the requirements of the qualifications for the same could not be constitutionally satisfied. Therefore, the effective promulgation of the Shariah law was at the discretion of the *de facto* ruler."

The conditions for the office of the Caliph, as a matter of consensus among all schools of law, comprised of piety of character and ability to ascertain and understand the revealed law. Discretion of political power is a natural result of such a constitutional set-up, and arbitrariness follows unavoidably in its wake. The political view of "sovereign and subject" expresses only one aspect of the relationship between state and individual under these political circumstances, and the political distinguishing mark of such a legal relationship is the unquestioning reception of orders." This aspect contrasts with the issue of the meticulous observance of law by the political authority, and brings into sharp focus the imperativeness of the accessibility to the constitutional security, provided to the society's prerogative to effect change of rule within the meanings of the Quranic verse of prototypical significance, already alluded. No surprise, therefore, is to be evinced on the reversal of the order of allegiance in that verse and, with the passage of time, the ruler had become the effective object of obedience.

To chronicler, a subject of interest, to philosopher, a matter of natural result emanating from the circumvention of law, to a jurist, a legal issue replete with invaluable constitutional instructions for the future, and to a believer, an occasion for lamentation as an historical opportunity was squandered for the political ascendancy over time, the political rulers in era subsequent to the right-guided Caliphs assumed powers which the law did not concede to them and, in their political conduct, abridged or isolated the Shariah law's vital principles.

The deterrent punishment or "tazir" is discretion made available to the ruler in Islamic Law under the doctrine of "Siasa Shariah." The basic premises of the doctrine are the sound order of the state and considerations of public interest; and within the meanings of these broad principles, sufficient discretion for the law-making through ordinances, as an addition to the rules of Shariah, is retained.

***Siasa Shariah :*** The public law lacked comprehensive form and, as its component, the law did not comprise of any complete system of constitutional law." Naturally, additional jurisdiction was necessitated in the domain of public law, and the legal doctrine of "Siasa Shariah" was evolved to satisfy this legal demand. Under the provisions of this doctrine, generous discretionary powers were available to the ruler for the law-making as a supplement to the Shariah law, under the need of the maintenance of state and requirements of public interest. As a reflection of the deficient constitutional law, the doctrine was simultaneously indicative of the non-availability of the law for the ascertainment of the qualifications as an Islamic prerequisite for the rule. For the maintenance of the required order of precedence in the Quranic injunction (iv:59) God, Messenger and ruler-a self-regulatory judicial system was required, and such legal requirements were in obvious conflict with the demands of the Siasa doctrine. The discretionary powers available to the ruler were the signal of the *basic drawback* in the legal system. Fundamental problem facing Islamic jurisprudence since is essentially the deficient legal framework for the implementation of Islam, which is a nomocracy, wherein the conscientious judicial system, a demand approximately represented in the latter-day legal notion of the separation of powers, is indispensable.

The settlement of the issues of moral worth and justness of the legal rule should be interrelated with the criteria for its validity. Thomas Hobbes sought to argue that the decrees of the law are synonymous with morality. However, Bentham adjudged the moralness of law according to the dictates of his prominent principle of utility. The essential advantage claimed for this method was the clarity of thinking it imparted in distinguishing between legal and moral obligations. Legal philosophers, however, provided no response to the issue whether the citizen is entitled to disobey a law appearing morally condemnable.

In the Islamic conception of the rule of law, in accordance with the requirements of the important verse with substantive connotations on interpretation (iv : 59), the individual is granted the exercise of this choice, once morality is considered in Islamic religious context. This crucial privilege with far-reaching legal implications did not secure due recognition in the Islamic legal system, notwithstanding of the fact that it constituted another of the vital requirements of the Islamic rule of law. This aspect is intimately interlinked with the substantive legal issue of the discretion provided to the ruler without the definite constitutional framework.

## The Ideology

***Purpose of Law*** : The subject of the purpose of law is intricately related to the concept of law as an activity, with the emphasis upon its functions, rather than as an entity, with the importance of its nature. Purposive character of law generates principles that regulate the creation and administration of law. These principles amount to an "inner morality" of law because of their implicitness in the concept and nature of law. Shatibi defined "Masla" as the purpose of Islamic Law, and its assimilation into the Islamic legal theory would have freed its operation from a number of factors of determinism, rigidly arising out of theological and methodological considerations.

The pivotal point in the legal philosophy of Suarez was the exposition of the end of law which, according to him, was the "common good of the community." Notwithstanding of the fact that an interval of approximately three centuries separated Shatibi and Suarez, the similarity in their approach towards law and its end is notice worthy. And, if the latter contributed towards the development of law in Europe, then, the former's juristic expositions did not cross the stage of legal scholarship.

To reiterate, the reformation of the Spanish Christian system of law entailed the measures of the exposition of its shortcomings and the renaissance of the Roman Law. This approach consisted of the systematization of the Roman Law in accordance with the Aristotelian method in the light of Christian doctrine, which also comprised the ascertainment of the reasons for the motivation of its rules. This trend was to mark the beginning of the philosophy of law in the Western legal system, and it had the far-reaching effects on the evolution of law. Shatibi was involved in the investigation of the philosophy of law and this vital pursuit, associated with the shaping of the concept of law, became inconspicuous afterwards.

It is of no passing interest then, that the philosophical inadequacy of law has the causative role, in conjunction with the legal methodological insufficiency, for the developmental shortfall in the Islamic Law ("fiqh"). This basic concept in legal philosophy was considered an obstacle in the method of legal reasoning, while contrastingly acceptance was given to placing an excessive reliance upon the theological principles in the application of the law.

Irrespective of the evaluation of the laws of inheritance under the Shariah doctrine, as the general functions of law or the relationship between law and morals, which are the concerns of the legal philosophy among other subjects, for those laws to retain their moral nature in Islamic Law, as their infringement did not occasion legal sanction, is one illustrative instance of the inadequate legal development in Islam." The critical differentiation between law viewed as a fixed entity and law considered as an activity was not maintained, and with the general functions taken as the expression of law is also evident.

***Particular Concerns :*** Values resulting from the application of certain laws may lie external to the intended objectives of relevant law, however, their concern is within the purview of the philosophy of law, such as the conceptions of justice and limits of law. The instances of such resultants are not rare, and the values of equality in relation to status, right and opportunity pertaining to the women in a Muslim society, have born such influence as to be the manifest concern of legal philosophy. The consideration for existential interdependence of law and the engendered values raises the issue of the limits of the law. The possibility is entertainable that the beneficial objectives of the law are transferable into their antithesis and, in effect, law ceases to be the original entity. Within the meanings of these estimations, the behaviour of citizens as the outward expression of the internal accompaniments in the form of psychological states, is a consideration not to face omission.

The legislative and judicial justifications, as a concern of the legal philosophy, view the lack of internal consistency of law anathematical to its "inner morality." The requirements of the same justifications are the indications that a legal system which, not unlike an issue or an approach, may be fundamentally misconceived due to the erroneous definition of its objectives. Understanding of the law is also influenced unless its purpose is evident. The failure to separate conceptual issues from those of straightforward facts cannot be deemed out of bounds, within the purview of this concern, of religious laws. Austin's elucidation of legal rule, employing the notions of command and habitual obedience, poses an obstacle in its unquestioning adoption in view of the concept of justice, in addition to the aforeoutlined concern of legal philosophy. And this legal aspect in canonical laws taxes the juristic subtleties to the maximum.

Legal philosophy cannot remain unconcerned about the issues of adaptability of laws, legal concepts, and changing social order. The revealed law itself visualizes a changing social order. And a legal theory falters if the included legal methods are inadequate in encompassing these demands of legal, conceptual and social change.

Judicial justification is instrumental in the jurisprudential reconstruction of the legal system. Definition of the role of jurist in the legal system and the judicious direction for the juristic efforts are its antecedents. As an ensuing step, display of characteristic judicial virtues, with the special appropriateness to legal decisions in this perspective, is an explanation for not designating this judicial activity as "legislative," especially in the Islamic legal context. The guideline furnished by the Prophet of Islam to a newly appointed judge, in regard to the exercise of personal judiciousness, in legal matters lacking, in effect, appropriate rules and directions from the primary source of law, is citable in support of this assertion. In addition, the juristic principles provided in the original sources of Islamic Law, with the capacity of functioning as a definite legal framework, in conjunction with the adequacy of legal methodology which is an onus of this treatise, are to transform the judicial activity into "finding," rather than "making," of law.

Due to the crucial significance of the subject of appropriate rules and directions in the original sources of law, in particular, the comprehensive ascertainment of those, a formulation to this end is essential.

*Role of Religion*

***Theological Considerations*** : Any interest in a religious law is the marked inclination to extend the attitude of worship, or "tabbad," to the revealed legal injunctions. The fundamental error introduced into law in this approach is the assignment of value in jurisprudence relative to theological beliefs, rather than to the proven legal principles identifiable with a particular system of law. The reductionist impulse, invariably associated with the theological attitude, imparts its unavoidable influence upon the process of law-making. The characteristic perceptions of reality, whose determinant normally is the current situation, leave their impact upon the shaping of the legal order.

Historically, theological and legal composition in Islam was reflected in the combined office of the "qadi" and "mufti," which could not have been devoid of certain difficulties. The differentiation between two kinds of obligations—absolute and not subject to change, relative and subject to changes-necessitated according to legal criteria, which can resolve some important legal issues, was not maintained. Similarly, a vital legal issue of "mixed obligations," wherein the observance of two related but variant rules is a mutually conflicting obligation, which in a religious law can retain a theological solution, however, a legal solution would prefer a legal framework of reference to establish the preponderance of one of the obligations. For instance, the injunctions pertaining to the equal rights and economic parity between two sexes are a source of mixed obligations, relative to the rules concerning the repudiation of marriage and inheritance of property.

The explanation for this variance in legal obligations resides in the divergence between the "siprit" and the "letter" of the law, and this perspective induced Shatibi to favour the "meanings" of the law as a predominant measure towards the intelligibility of Shariah. To imagine the issuance of divergent obligations as the intention of the lawgiver is without justification and, therefore, the formulation of a legal method for the reconciliation of the seeming legislative duality is a substantive step. Notice worthy is the fact that these factors can prove impediments in the organization and evolvement of an enduring legal system.

***Deficient Jurisprudential Approach*** : A crucial discriminating concept of law is the distinction to be drawn between the question essentially pertaining to law, morals or religion. This is necessitated on the basis of cautious evaluation and understanding of the conditions prevalent in legal thinking. The Quranic prohibition of gambling was merged with the revelational demands for usury or "riba," to assign the latter an extensive legal scope that included any chanceful and unearned capital gain, not based upon its precise estimation in advance. An outcome of reliance placed upon subjective belief and personal reasoning, rather than the acknowledged principles of Islamic jurisprudence, the law was to perform a critical function in the designing of the Islamic economic system. Similarly, religious law, not unlike natural law, encouraged obedience to established rulers.

However, there was nothing inherent in religious law which compelled allegiance to the existing rulers. And, in resemblance with natural law, the legal notion of certain fundamental rights, possessed by the individual, could not have been absent from the source of religious law. But the demands of religious faith, largely misconceived as imposing duties and prohibitions, were allowed to hold overwhelming precedence over the jurisprudential dictates of individual right to the "rule of law," with the legal implication that makes this obedience conditional upon that right.

In subsequent times, Locke proposed the terms of social contract, whereby the political authority was conceded only on trust, and the infringement of the fundamental rights of the people by the ruler was an evident breach of the same. The distinct change in emphasis from imposition of duties and obligations, previously misconceived as derivatives of natural law, to the source of fundamental democratic rights—or individual political liberty in society—as a restriction upon the absolute political authority of the ruler, was brought according to the suggestions of the social contract. As an instructive happening of legal history, Islamic Law, under the influence of religious belief, in substitution of the legal requirements, adopted a legal course that evolved law in a direction ironically opposite to the valid dictates of revealed law.

The political authority in Islam is a trusteeship of God and, hence, of people, conceded only in accordance as well as in acceptance of the Islamic code of law and its observance, simply translatable in latter-day terminology as the rule of law. Due to the contractual basis of the conceded trust, the Islamic rule of law is a right of people and, as a counterbalance against the tendency of absolute political authority of the ruler, the socio-political system in Islam, therefore, must be designated as "Nomocracy" This legal situation is in contrast with the fundamental democratic rights of the people as a restraint against the assumption of the absolute authority by the political ruler, as envisioned in the original Lockian concept.

The juristic interest notwithstanding, the concept of Islamic "social contract," to adopt a latter-day terminology, with its derivation reposed in the complete corpus of revealed law and epitomized in the Quranic verse aforementioned, establishes a general resemblance with the Lockian social contract, with the difference of rule of law as the fundamental Islamic right in substitution of the fundamental democratic right envisaged in the latter instance. In contrast, Rousseau proceeded from premises different from those of Islam as well as Locke. Natural law, in this case, rather than creating imprescriptible natural rights in favour of individuals, conferred absolute and inalienable authority upon the people as a whole.

Thus, the people *en mass* were regarded to constitute the entity of "general will," which was a legal authority in the state, assignable to a ruler through delegation alone. A matter of intellectually engaging legal distinction, the primary Islamic source of law is the equivalent of "general will" in Rousseau's "social contract," and essentially external to the scope of delegation. Nevertheless, social contract defined by Rousseau, enacted an historic role, because the French Revolution adopted this doctrine for promulgation in the wake of its victory. Islamic legal development sustained a shortfall and, indeed, Islamic Law became virtually stationary due to the deficient jurisprudential approach. This vital aspect is described by Ibn Khaldun in an insight imparting way, who deserves to be quoted at some length, given the importance of the subject: "The school doctrine of each authority became, among his adherents, a scholarly discipline in its own right.

They were no longer in a position to apply independent judgment and analogy. Therefore, they had to make reference to the established principles from the school doctrine of their authority, in order to be able to analyze problems in their context and disentangle them when they got confused. A firmly rooted habit was required to enable a person to undertake such analysis and disentanglement and to apply the school doctrine of his particular authority to those processes according to the best of his ability. This habit is what is meant at this time by the science of jurisprudence."

***Shariah for Muslims*** : The word 'Muslim' is the subject noun of the word *Aslama* which means 'he became obedient and submissive' to his (Creator and his Lord). In this sense, the word Islam, applies to the submission of the whole universe to Almighty Allah. The messages and missions of all the Apostles of Allah were also in obedience to the Commands of Allah.

> The Holy Quran says: "Seek they other than the religion of Allah, when unto Him submitteth whosoever is in the heavens and the earth, willingly, or unwillingly, and unto Him they will be returned'.
> (III: 83 ).

> And again: "Who forsaketh the religion of Ibrahim save him who befooleth himself, Verily we chose him in the world, and lo! in the Hereafter he is among the righteous. When his Lord said unto him: Surrender: I have surrendered to the Lord of the worlds. The same did Ibrahim enjoin upon his sons, and also Jacob (Saying): O my sons! Allah hath chosen for you, the (true) religion; therefore that not save as men who have surrendered (unto Him). Or were ye present when death came to Jacob, when he said unto his sons: "What will ye worship after me?' They said: "We shall worship thy Allah and the Allah of thy father of Ibrahim, Ismail, and Ishaq the one (true) Allah to Him we bow (in Islam)". (II: 130-133).

> Allah mentions the prayer of His Apostle Joseph in these words: "O my Lord: Thou hast given me (something) of sovereignty and hast taught me (something) of the interpretation of events—creator of the heavens and the earth! Thou are my Protecting Friend in the world and the Hereafter. Make me to die submissive ( unto Thee), and join me to the righteous". ( XII: 101).

It must be borne in mind that the decrees of Allah consist of the following common points:

(1) Allah's worship with sincere devotion.

(2) Humble prostration before Him.

(3) Accepting His commandments cheerfully.

(4) Strict observance of what has been enjoined and abstention from what has been prohibited by Allah.

These points were the integral part of every *Shariah* although the means and the nature of revelations differed. It has been narrated in a Tradition of the Holy Prophet (peace be upon him): "We, the community of Prophets, are like brothers. Our religion is one".

With the Prophethood of Muhammad, Islam has become a symbolic name to denote the *Shariah* of Allah and a title which represents its followers. No man is allowed to transgress the limits imposed by the religion of Islam which was revealed by Allah to the Prophet who conveyed it to the world.

> ***The Surrender :*** Says the Quran; "Lo! religion with Allah (is) the surrender (to His will and Guidance). Those who (formerly) received the Scripture dittered only after knowledge came unto them, through transgression among themselves. Whoso dis-believeth the revelations of Allah (will find that), lo! Allah is swift at reckoning. And if they argue with thee (O Muhammad), say: I have surrendered my purpose to Allah and (so have) those who follow me. And say unto those who have received the Scripture and those who read not: Have ye (too) surrendered? If they surrender, then truly they are rightly guided, and if they turn away, then it is their duty only to convey the message (unto them). Allah is seer of (His) bondmen." (III: 19-20).
>
> "And whose seeketh as religion other than the surrender (to Allah) it will not be accepted from him, and he will be a loser in the Hereafter."
>
> (III:85).

"O ye who believe! Observe your duty to Allah with right observance, and die not save as those who have surrendered (Unto Him)." (III: 102).

"And whomsoever it is Allah's will to guide, He expandeth his bosom unto the surrender, and whomsoever it is His Will to send astray, He maketh his bosom close and narrow as if he were engaged in sheer ascent. Thus Allah layeth ignominy upon those who believe not". (IV: 126).

In a Tradition regarding Jibbrail the Prophet has interpreted the word "Islam" as follows:

"Islam is that thou shall bear withness that there is no god but Allah and that Muhammad is the Messenger of Allah and (that) thou keep up prayer and pay the *Zakat* and (keep) fast in *Ramadan* and perform pilgrimage to the House, in case you have means."

In another Hadith, the Messenger of Allah said :

"Islam is based on five things: the bearing of witness that there is no god but Allah and Muhammad is the Messenger of Allah and the keeping up of prayer and the payment of *Zakat* and the pilgrimage and fasting in *Ramadan* ". At another place the Prophet explained the meanings of *Iman* (faith) in the following words: "Faith is that you believe in Allah and His angels and His books and His messengers, in the Hereafter and in the divine decree to good and evil".

Whenever a mention of Islam and faith is made simultaneously, as has been mentioned in the Tradition regarding Jibbrail, the word Islam indicated outward actions, whereas faith implies inner beliefs or convictions; and when their mention is made separately, each of these words would mean actions as well as inner beliefs or convictions.

Islam is another name for belief and action, religion and the world, and a code of life. Sheikh-ul-Islam Muhammad bin Abdul Wahab has defined Islam as follows: "Islam means bowing before Allah with firm belief in His Oneness, and prostration before Him in complete submission, and abstinence from ascribing partners unto Him".

A true Muslim is one who by the grace and favour of Allah embraces Islam, acts upon it and affirms his faith in it by convictions, actions and practice so that he acquires unshakable trust and confidence in it.

The bases of Islamic *Shariah* are the revelations of Allah which He vouchsafed to the Prophet. The purpose of these revelations was to bring the people out of darkness into light. These are intact even today in the form of the Holy Quran. There is no question of interpolation or distortion in it from any side. The other source of the *Shariah* is the *Sunnah* of the Prophet which is an interpretation and elucidation of the Quran.

The Book of Allah and the *Sunnah* of the Prophet are co-related with each other just as the bearing of witness to the truth that "there is no god but Allah", and the affirmation of the truth that "Muhammad is the Messenger of Allah", are inseparable from one another. A further probe would reveal that the foundation of Islamic *Shariah* is based on the following two unique and fundamental principles :

(1) Worship is due to none but Allah who has no partner, may he be an angel or an apostle. Says the Quran: "And the places of worship are only for Allah so pray not unto anyone alongwith Allah". (LXXII: 18). It has been mentioned at another place: "Say: LO! my worship and my sacrifice and my living and my dying are for Allah, Lord of the worlds. He hath no partner. This am I commanded, and I am first of those who surrender (unto Him)". (VI: 163-164).

(2) The second fundamental principle is that Allah must be worshipped as has been enjoined in the Quran and according to the *Sunnah* of the Prophet. The Quran says: "And whatsoever the Messenger giveth you, take it. And whatsoever he forbiddeth, abstain from it". (LIX : 7).

At another place it has been said: "Say: I am only a mortal like you. My Lord inspireth in me that your God is only One God. And whosoever hopeth for the meeting with his Lord, let him do righteous work, and make none sharer of the worship due unto his Lord". (XVIII : 110).

Hafiz ibn Kathir while interpreting the phrase 'righteous work', writes that it denotes the actions which are in conformity with the decrees of Allah and are performed only to please Allah. There are only two basic conditions, the fulfilment of which make the actions agreeable to Allah. The first condition is that they should be done with the sole intention of pleasing Allah and the second is that these actions should be in accordance with the *Sunnah* of the Prophet. It has been reported by Hadrat Aishah that the Holy Prophet said: "He who made an innovation in our matter *(Sunnah)* is condemnable".

Allah has embodied all goodness and virtue in the Islamic *Shariah* so that it has reached its culmination. It has an all-embracing and universal position and has become eternal. So far as the question of its excellence and its being free from all sorts of errors is concerned, the Quran itself affirmed: "This day have I perfected your religion for you and completed My favour unto you, and have chosen for you as religion Al-Islam". (V : 3).

Explaining this verse, Hafiz ibn Kathir states that it is the greatest favour and bounty of Allah on the Muslim *Ummah* that He has perfected the religion for them. Now it stands in need of no other religion or code of life. This is the reason why the Prophet was exalted to the eminent position of the last of the Prophets. What he declared lawful is lawful and what he forbade is unlawful. The only true religion is that which he preached and the only truth is that of which he gave the knowledge.

It is free from all errors and blemishes and there is no question of disputing about it. Says the Quran: "The words of your Allah are complete as regards Truth and Justice". (VI : 116). That means the events which have been related are based on truth and the verses which enjoin and prohibit certain things and actions are based on justice and equity. With the completion of the religion, the blessings and favours of Allah have reached at the highest. The Muslims should express their delight that the choicest religion of Allah has been sent down for them and this religion has been revealed to the Prophet who handed it down to them through the most exalted divine book, the Holy Quran.

As regards universality, it must be borne in mind that it is incumbent on every Muslim to abide by the all-embracing and universal *Shariah* and none is allowed the slightest deviation from it. So it is essential that every Muslim realise that he is to mould his life according to its behests so that he may earn the blessings and favours of Allah and refrain from incurring His displeasure and wrath.

Says the Quran:

> "And it becometh not a believing man or a believing woman, when Allah and His Messenger have decided an affair (for them), that they should (after that) claim any say in their affair; and whoso is rebellious to Allah and His Messenger, verily he goeth astray in error manifest." (XXXIII: 36).

It is not the only place where such a course has been recommended. I quote below some passages from the Quran where this idea has been emphasised very clearly and unequivocally :

> "And whatsoever the Messenger giveth you, take it. And whatsoever he forbiddeth, abstain (from it). And keep your duty to Allah. Lo! Allah is stern in reprisal." (LIX : 7).
>
> "And let those who conspire to evade orders beware lest grief or painful punishment befall them." (XXIV : 63).
>
> "Follow that which is sent down unto you from your Lord, and follow no protecting friends beside Him. Little do you recollect." (VII : 3).
>
> "So tread thou the straight path as thou art commanded and those who turn (unto Allah) with thee, and transgress not. Lo! He is seer of what ye do." (XI : 112).
>
> "So hold thou fast to that which is inspired in these. Lo! thou, art on a right path." (XLIII :43).
>
> "And (He commandeth you, saying): This is my straight path, so follow it. Follow not other ways, lest ye be parted from His way. This hath He ordained for you, that ye may ward off evil)." (VI : 154).
>
> Say, (O Muhammad, to mankind): It ye love Allah, follow me, Allah will love you and forgive you and your sins. Allah is forgiving, Merciful. Say: Obey Allah and the Messenger. But if they turn away. Lo! Allah loveth not the disbelievers (in His guidance)." (III : 31-32).
>
> Obey Allah.
>
> "The saying of (all true) believers when they appeal unto Allah and His Messenger to judge between them

is only that they say: We hear and we obey, and such are the successful. He who obeyeth Allah and his Messenger, and feareth Allah, and keepeth duty (unto Him): such indeed are the victorious."

(XXIV: 51-52).

"O ye who believe! Obey Allah and obey the Messenger and those of you who are in authority; and if ye have a dispute concerning any matter, refer it to Allah and the Messenger if ye are (in truth) believers in Allah and the Last Day. That is better and more seemly in the end." (IV : 59).

"But nay, by thy Lord, they will not believe (in truth) until they make thee judged what is in dispute between them and find within themselves no dislike of that which thou decidest, and submit with full submission."

(IV : 65).

"Whoso judgeth not by that which Allah hath revealed: such are disbelievers." (V : 44).

"Let the people of the Gospel judge by that which Allah hath revealed therein. Whoso judgeth not by that which Allah hath revealed; such as evil-livers. And unto thee have We revealed the Scripture with the truth, confirming whatever Scripture was before it, and a watcher over it. So judge between them by that which Allah hath revealed, and follow not their desires away from the truth which hath come unto thee. For each We have prescribed divine law and traced out way. Had Allah willed, He could have made you one community. But may try you by that which He hath given you (He hath made you as ye are). So vie one with another in good works. Unto Allah yet will all return, and He will then inform you of that wherein ye differ. So judge between them by that which Allah hath revealed and follow not their desires, but beware of them lest they seduce thee from some part of that which Allah hath revealed unto thee. And if they turn away, then know that Allah's Will is to smite them for some sin of theirs. Lo! many of mankind are evil liver. Is it a judgement of the time of (pagan) ignorance that they are seeking? Who is better than Allah for judgement to a people who have certainty (in their belief)?"

(V : 47-50).

"Shall I seek other than Allah for judge, when He it is who hath revealed unto you (this Scripture) known that it is revealed from thy Lord in truth. So be not thou (O Muhammad) of the waverers. Perfected is the word of thy Lord in truth and justice. There is naught that can change His words. He is the Hearer, the Knower." (VI : 115-116).

***Preach Truth :*** Success, honour, prestige, victory over the enemies and peace and stability of the Muslims depend on acting upon the *Shariah.* If the condition of the Muslims be reversed to that which has been stated above or, in other words, they become indifferent to the *Shariah,* only loss, ignominy and disgrace would fall to their lot. We must keep this fact in mind that the Almighty Allah has observed, swearing by the age, that all men are in a state of loss save those who affirm belief and do good deeds and preach truth and perseverance.

There are many statements in the Divine Book and in the *Ahadith* of the Holy Prophet (peace be upon him) which bear testimony to this fact. Moreover, history also affirms the fact that real honour and respect lie in submission to Allah and he who disobeys Him nothing but disgrace is in store for him. The Holy Quran affirm this fact at a number of places, such as :

"He who holdeth fast to Allah, he indeed is guided unto a right path." (III : 101).

"And those who strive hard in Our cause We shall guide them to Our right path. Verily, Allah is with the grateful." (XXIX : 69).

"O ye who believe! If ye help Allah, He will help you and will make your foothold firm."
(XLVII : 7).

"Verily, Allah helpeth one who helpeth Him. Lo! Allah is strong, Almighty—those who, if We gave them power in the land, establish prayer and pay *Zakat* and enjoin kindness and forbid iniquity and Allah's is the sequel of events."
(XVII : 4041).

"O ye who believe! Shall I show a commerce that will save you from a painful doom? Ye should believe in Allah and His Messenger, and should strive for the cause of Allah with your wealth and your lives. That is better for you, if ye did but know. He will forgive you, your sins and bring you into Gardens underneath which rivers flow, and pleasant dwellings in Gardens of Eden. That is the supreme triumph."
(LXI : 10.12).

"O ye who believe: If ye keep your duty to Allah, He will give you discrimination (between right and wrong) and will rid you of your evil thoughts and deeds, and will forgive you. Allah is of infinite Bounty." (VIII : 29).

"Allah hath promised such good deeds that He will surely make them to succeed (the present rulers) in the earth even as He caused those who were before them to succeed (others); and that He will surely establish for them their religion which He hath approved for them and will give them in exchange safety after their fear. They serve Me. They ascribe nothing as partner unto Me. Those who disbelieve henceforth, they are the miscreants. Establish prayer and pay *Zakat* and obey the Messenger, that happily ye may find mercy." (XXIV : 55-56).

***Attainment through Reason :*** The Law in Islam is not comprehensively in revealed form and the need of law is attainable through its ascertainment with reason. Some legal methods have acquired the recognized status of the sources of law, while other methods have remained juristic principles. Deficiencies in the development of the area of legal methods have cast a reflection upon the law. In the view of Mahmasani, foundations of the modern renaissance in Islamic legal thought were laid in the 14th century by the Muslim jurists who wrote on the legal methodology and the end of law.

These writings no doubt were the precursors of the modern legal philosophies in the West, however, the Islamic Law *per se* remained substantially unbenefitted, for those legal conceptions stayed without assimilation into Islamic legal thought as a matter of an historic irony. Response of legal theory to social changes, development of law and the completion of the objectives of law were adversely influenced as a result.

***Consensus of Opinion (Ijma) :*** The implications of Ijma are the consensus of opinion of Islamic community on a legal issue, the consensus of persons competent for Ijtihad, or the unanimous agreement of the jurists of the community in a particular age. Consensus of all Muslims on essentials and of the Muslim scholars on points of detail are the distinguishing features of the "unanimity of opinion." Some eminent jurists also consider the majority of all Muslims to constitute Ijma as well.

The present-day definition of Ijma places reliance upon an agreement of the Muslim jurists in a particular age on an issue of law. The four Sunni Schools of Law uphold it as a valid source of law. However, in this perspective, a proper apprehension of the meaning of Ijma is lent by considering it as a natural process of the crystallization of viewpoints into agreement. With wide awareness of the Islamic history, Hurjronge's observation of Ijma as the "foundation of foundations and the moveable element in law" demands attention.

In the opinion of Gibb, Ijma is described as the third source of revelation, erected with a theory of infallibility. Ascribable advantages to Ijma in a sympathetic view would include the resolution of conflicts due to divergent opinions and authentication of the rules of law, formulated by the jurists, and their elevation to a status of law. An aspect of more than academic interest, legal history of Ijma takes the juristic curiosity to conclude that its validity should be dependent upon the consonance with the text, general spirit and objectives of Shariah. Ijma has been an ongoing process, for rules and decisions based upon it may change with the alterations in time and conditions. Nevertheless, as an inductive principle of fundamental import, the construction of Ijma as popular voluntary consensus, obtained in advance of the implementation of the legal measure, and not a sovereign viewpoint which can arrogate to itself the unique authority for overwhelming legal preponderance, remained unutilized in the Islamic constitutional law.

In the opinion of McDonald, the famous Muslim jurist, Shafii, is rightly credited with the extension of the principle of agreement and its erection into a formal source of law. According to him, the absolute form of the principle-whatever the community of Islam has agreed upon at any time, is of God-is notice worthy." The ramifications of this principle upon the political unity of Islam and the critical evolution of Islamic Law is a subject suited to the evaluation for vital legal insight. Now, in conformity with Ijma as a material source of law, the constitutional requirement for the office of the Caliph could have been the consent of the representatives of the ruled, in consonance with the agreed practice of "baiya" during the era of the "right-guided" Caliphs.

The omission of this constitutional practice from the subsequent political course in Islam, especially, after the enunciation of the principle of consensus, is the expression of the maxim, "what is potent for the good, can also be good for the evil," whose practical manifestations are deceptively rare in life. The principle of agreement must have been of avail in the authentication of the legal tradition of Caliphs assuming political powers which were not sanctioned by Islamic Law. Hence, the substantive issue, whether the common political error can be authenticated by the method of Ijma, is of extraordinary relevance. Obviously, then, the principle of consensus in legal authentication is to be intimately associated with the settled merit of reasons.

The substantive aspects of the utilization of lawmaking potential of Ijma in the present-day constitutional set-ups, the avoidance of the shortcomings such as become apparent from the evaluation of its utility from the Islamic history, and the preservation of the politically unifying role of Ijma in Islam will be addressed during the ensuing course of this treatise.

***Logical Reasoning (Ijtihad) :*** Independent intellectual striving or Ijtihad is based upon the premise that on all problems, which confront the Muslims, there is either a binding decision or an indication of the right solution that is to be sought. The implication of reasoning is involved in the exercise of Ijtihad, which is based on Islamic criteria, and its Islamic desirability is demonstrated by the emphasis laid repetitively upon the measures of "thinking" and "understanding" in the original source of Islamic Law. As an accepted juristic principle, it is considered to make the legal system of Islam dynamic, and its development and evolution in the changing circumstances possible.

In the view of Schacht, the opinion of expert on questions of fact is a parallel of Ijtihad, while Coulson describes it as the process of juristic endeavour to ascertain the terms of Shariah law. Shatibi thought of it as a process of adaptability and, among one of its four functions, deduction of the basis of the rules of Shariah law, also called reasoning by analogy, was included. And, most importantly, he considered Ijtihad as a necessary duty of Muslims, and suggested that its use should not contradict the objectives of Shariah.

The deductions of a jurist, in the course of Ijtihad, do not ipso facto attain the status of law, which is consequent to the consensus or Ijma of the jurists, and its wide popular acceptance. Now as an inglorious chapter in the Islamic legal history, the "closure of the doors of Ijtihad" in the 10th century A.D. curtailed the legal usefulness of analogous reasoning, for it is considered as synonymous with Ijtihad by Shafii and many other Muslim jurists, and severely eroded the basis of Ijma. Thus, the result was destined to reflect as the marked decline in the Islamic legal development. Against this perspective of Islamic legal history, the reintroduction of Ijtihad as a process of legal development will depend upon the prerequisite of a functional Islamic legal system, considered strictly according to the accepted denotation of this term, and this treatise is an endeavour in that direction.

***Analogy (Qiyas)*** : Analogous reasoning or "Qiyas" was adopted by the Muslim Jurist, Hanifa, as a source of law-making. A review of relevant literature demonstrates this juristic method as a process, by which the rules of law embodied in the Quran, Traditions and Ijma are extended to cases not covered by their texts. The jurist Shafii considered analogous reasoning to be synonymous with Ijtihad, and to the extent that the former is a part of the latter, it is a dependable view. The legal authority as a binding precedent in the instance of analogous reasoning is, however, lent by the consensus of jurists in this regard.

The crucial issue of the role of human reason ("ray") in relation to revealed law was addressed by Shafii to the satisfactory settlement of the controversy, concerning the divine and human elements in law, that surfaced in the 8th century, A.D. This fundamental conflict of principle in Islamic jurisprudence was resolved with the two specified elements, finding accommodation in a complementary relationship, in the process of reasoning by analogy. This juristic accomplishment was, no doubt, the partial basis for the title of the "father of Muslim Jurisprudence," which was bestowed upon him. Another eminent Muslim legist, who succeeded Shafii by several centuries, Shatibi viewed analogical reasoning or deduction as a systematic mode of Ijtihad, wherein the human reason is assigned the role of discovering the "ila" of the text.

In turn, this is extended to analogical cases and situations which though are not covered by the language of the text, however, the reason employed therein serves as the coverage. The "ila" is definable as the fact, circumstance or consideration underlying the law embodied in the text, as related to the lawgiver. Extension of the law of text is the function of analogical reasoning. In another opinion, the application of the "effective cause of the law" in a text upon new cases and situations is the essence of analogical reasoning.

***Principles of Juristic Reasoning*:** From among other juristic principles, "Istihsan" or juristic preference is a legal argument contrary to the apparent analogy. The controversy arose due to the arrogation of legislative privilege, perceived in the application of this principle, and Shafii was proponent of such a view. However, Maliki jurists defined it in the sense of the attention to public interest and justice. In this perspective, it appears as a juristic and not personal preference, in conformity with its adoption as a doctrine of equity.

The same legal attribute is ascribable to another juristic principle of "Istislah," and the Muslim Jurist, Malik, favoured it as a legal modality for the deduction of law, based upon the consideration of public interest. The Islamic legal conception of public interest does not carry unlimited or unrestricted connotation, for it is conceived within the scope of Shariah law. The recommended conditions for the applicability of the legal notion of public interest excluded matters of religion, and included concerns of transactions.

The precepts of Shariah law and its objectives did not come in conflict with the considerations of public interest. And the demands of public interest were of the essential and necessary type, and included the preservation of life, religion, reason, progeny and property, as also the betterment of life. Considered from another viewpoint, "Istislah" is a mode of Ijtihad, which upholds public interest such as is envisaged by Shariah law to be paramount. Although this juristic principle should have developed into the legal concept of adaptability in law, a view ably proposed by Shatibi later, but remained unassimilated into Islamic legal theory, however, in actual application, it succumbed to the theological and idealistic limitations. The idealism of literal emphasis in law, without making legal theory in conformity with the principles of jurisprudence, was a causative factor which hampered the development of the principles of 'adaptability in Islamic Law."

The juristic principle of "Istidlal" is the deduction of a rule, with the use of reason and logic, on the basis of another rule. The absence of "ila," or common cause for the basis of reasoning, is its differentiating feature from the analogous reasoning. This principle relies upon juristic exposition and leads to legal development. The juristic principle of "Istishab" literally means "permanence," and denotes the existence or non-existence of a state which is not proved to have ceased from the past. In the description by Ibn Khaldun it is "the attempt to associate the present legal situation with the past by judging the present in the same way as the past is judged, with the result that the legal situation is left as it had been, for no evidence to change it has been found."

"Siasa Shariah" was denoted to administer justice in conformity with the spirit of Islamic Law. According to this legal doctrine, the deficiency in law was no doubt compensated, however, the arrogation of legislative prerogative to the political authority, under the mis-perceived scriptural precept of sovereignty being Divine ordained, compromised the development of constitutional law and independence of judiciary. At this juncture, it is suited to the occasion to enunciate the preceding precept as one of the misinterpreted revealed injunctions whose adverse consequences upon the Islamic polity have been no less than substantial.

The principle of "selection" was adopted to choose between variant opinions recognized in jurisprudence as equally authoritative. And the principle of "need or necessity" was viewed as different mode of reasoning, resulted in an exception of rule to accommodate the change in imperative circumstances, and it was not generally considered to be a source of law. In legal writings by Malik, considerable stress was laid upon the maxim that necessity makes prohibited things permissible.

The subject of juristic preference, in the interpretation of law, cannot be completely separated from the interpretative ad hocism, and an opportune selection for a mode of reasoning. A strict conformity with the fundamental principles of Islam, underlying the Shariah law, and constituting its spirit, reinforced with the principle of authentication by Ijma, is necessitated in the use of the juristic principles and modes of legal reasoning.

However, due to the disuse of the principle of Ijtihad, these juristic principles would not have been of much usefulness as methods of legal development and change. Therefore, concurrence is affordable to Schacht's observation that these methods were not adopted as principles of change, but were rather employed to interpret and justify the already existing rules of Islamic Law.

# Bibliography


Adams, C.C. : *Islam and Modernism in Egypt,* Oxford University Press, New York, 1953.

Ahmad, Bherhan : *The Mujaddid's Conception of Tauhid,* Feroz Pub., Lahore, 1940.

Ahmad, Imtiaz : *Divorce and Remarriage among Muslims in India,* Manohar Publishers, New Delhi, 2003.

Ahmad, K. N. : *Muslim Law of Divorce,* Kitab Bhavan, New Delhi, 1988.

Ahmad, Manzuruddin : *Islamic Political System,* Kitab Bhavan, New Delhi, 1991.

Ali, Chiragh : *The Proposed Political Legal and Social Reform under Muslim Rule,* Popular Prakashan, Bombay, 1883.

Badrul, S. : *Muslim Behaviour,* Kitab Bhavan, New Delhi, 1991.

Bahedur, Kalim : *The Jamaat-i-Islami of Pakistan,* Progressive Books, Lahore, 1978.

Baksh, S. K. : *Politics in Islam,* Kitab Bhavan, New Delhi, 2003.

Bawer, Raymond : *The New Man in Soviet Social Psychology,* Oxford, New York, 1990.

Berger, M. : *Islam in Egypt Today : Social and Political Aspects of Popular Religion,* MacMillan, London, 1970.

Bernier, Francois : *Travels in the Mogul Empire,* MacMillan, London, 1916.

Bukhsh, S. K. : *Contribution to the History of Islamic Civilization,* Kitab Bhavan, New Delhi, 2000.

Charles, Howard : *The Constitutionalism,* Great Seal Books, New York, 1947.

Chave, F. : *Islamic Histroriography,* Cambridge University press, New York, 1990.

Davids, Waines : *An Introduction to Islam,* Cambridge University Press, New Delhi, 1995.

Durrani, F.K.K. : *Muhammad (PBUH) the Prophet,* Oxford, New York, 2001.

Enayat, Hamid : *Islam in the Political Process,* Cambridge University Press, Cambridge, 1993.

Engineer, Asghar Ali : *A Rational Approach to Islam,* Gyan Books Pvt. Ltd., New Delhi, 2001.

————: *Islam : Challenge in Twenty-first Century,* Gyan Books Pvt. Ltd., New Delhi, 2004.

Guillaume, A. : *The Traditions of Islam,* Khayats, Beirut, 1966.

Hassan, Ali : *Observations on the Musulmauns of India,* Macmillan & Co., London, 1832.

Helmut, Reifeld : *Islam in South Asia : Adaptation, Accommodation and Conflict,* Social Science Press, New Delhi, 1999.

Houtsma, T. : *Encyclopaedia of Islam,* Macmillan, London, 1934.

Irfan, Habib : *The Agrarian System of Mughal India,* Popular Prakashan, Bombay, 1963.

Jafar, Sharif : *Islam in India,* Oxford, New Delhi, 1972.

James, Burges : *The Muhammadan Architecture of Ahmadabad,* Bernard Quaritch, London,1900.

Jha, V. : *Indian Society: Historical Probings,* Rawat Pub., Delhi, 1974.

Joseph, and Bosworth, C.E. : *The Legacy of Islam,* Oxford University Press, New York, 1979.

Karl, Jaspers : *Man in the Modern Age,* Routledge & Kegan Paul Ltd., London, 1997.

Katharine, Scarfe : *Perception of the Islamic Word,* Cambridge University Press, New Delhi, 1992.

Lewin, Roger : *In the Age of Mankind,* Simithsonian Books, Washington, D.C., 1956.

Lewis, Richards : *Universe,* Harmony Books, New York, 1973.

Martin, Lings : *A Sufi Saint of the Twentieth Century,* Century Pub., London, 1971.

Mirza, Waheed : *The Life and Works of Amir Khusrau,* Kaveri Pub., Calcutta, 1935.

Mortimer, Edward : *Faith and Power, the Politics of Islam,* Oxford, New York, 2002.

Muhammad, Iqbal : *Six Lectures on the Reconstruction of Religious Thought in Islam,* Royal Pub., Lahore, 1930.

Nabith, A. : *The Foundations of the Articles of Faith,* Feroz Pub., Lahore, 1963.

Nasr, Seyyed H. : *An Introduction to Islamic Cosmological Doctrines,* Cambridge, 1964.

Nicholson, R.A. : *Literary History of the Arabs,* Kitab Bhavan, New Delhi, 1994.

Nusservanji, D. : *Zoroastrian Civilization,* Oxford, New York, 1922.

Oage, Charles H. : *The Society,* Macmillan & Co., London, 1959.

Padwick, C.E. : *Muslim Devotions,* MacMillan & Co., London, 1960.

Phillips, O. Hood : *Reform of the Constitution,* MacMillan & Co., London, 1970.

Pierce, R.A.: *Russia in Central Asia, 1867-1917,* University of California, Berkeley, 1960.

Qadir, Abdul, : *Criminal Law of Islam,* Kitab Bhavan, New Delhi, 1999.

Qazi A. Qadir : *The Changing World of Islam,* Royal Pub., Lahore, 1992.

Rizvi, Hasan Askari : *Islami Reassertion : a Socio Political Study,* Progressive Publishers, Lahore, 1981.

Robert, D. : *Exploring our Living Planet,* National Geographic Society, Washington, 1989.

Saukat, S. : *Human Rights in Islam,* Kitab Bhavan, New Delhi, 2001.

Sharma, Arvind : *Women in World Religion,* New York Press, New York, 1990.

Syed, M. H. : *History of Muslims in India,* Anmol Publications, New Delhi, 2003.

———— : *Islamic Terrorism : Myth or Reality,* Gyan Books, New Delhi, 2002.

Tarn, W. W. : *The Greeks in Bactria and India,* Cambridge, London, 1938.

Thomas, Arnold : *The Legacy of Islam,* Oxford University Press, New York, 2000.

Thompson, H.R. : *Sculptures and Inscriptions of Darius the Great on the Rock of Behistan,* Oxford, London, 1907.

Tritton, A.S. : *The Caliphs and their Non-Muslim Subjects,* Oxford, New York, 1930.

Tutsch, Hans E. : *Facets of Arab Nationalism,* Wayne State University Press, Detroit, 1965.

Underhill, E. : *Mysticism : a Study in the Nature and Development of Man's Spiritual Consciousness,* Oxford, New York, 1956.

Usmani, J.M. : *The Authority of Sunnah,* Kitab Bhavan, New Delhi, 1998.

Von, Edmund : *Modern Islam,* University Press, Los Angeles, 1952.

Von, Grunebaum : *Unity and Variety in Muslim World,* Oxford, New York, 2003.

Waheed, Akhtar : *Sufi Approach to the Problem of Alienation,* Wilson & Co., New Delhi, 1975.

Weiner, Myron : *Sons of the Soil : Migration and Ethnic Conflict in India,* University Press, Prineton, 1978.

Williams, Michael : *Outlines of World Military History,* Oxford, New York, 1996.

Wilson, Lambron : *Traditional Modes of Contemplation and Action,* University Press, Tehran, 1977.

Wolfson, H.A. : *Glimpses of Medieval Indian Culture,* Popular Pub., Bombay, 1959.

Yahanan, Friedmann : *Tolerance and Coercion in Islam : Interfaith Relations in the Muslims Traditions,* Cambridge, New York, 1990.

Yazbeck, Haddad : *Islamic Values in the United States,* Oxford, New York, 1997.

Zaehner, R.C. : *Hindu and Muslim Mysticism,* Oxford, London, 1960.

Zahid, Malik : *Subjects of Quran,* Kitab Bhavan, New Delhi, 1998.

Zahurul, Hasan : *Tarikb-i-Sufiya-i-Gujarat,* Jamil Academy, Ahmadabad, 1981.

Zaki, Azam : *The Ideas of Arab Nationalism,* Cornell University Press, New York,1956.

# Index


## A

Abu Bakr, 22, 27, 51, 52, 88, 89, 97, 101, 137, 174, 179, 181, 183, 195, 241, 243, 270, 275, 276, 277, 278, 279, 280, 281.

Allah, 61, 63, 65, 67, 76, 77, 80, 81, 82, 85, 86, 87, 94, 98, 104, 235, 303, 315, 316, 317, 318, 319, 320, 321, 322, 323, 324.

America, 7, 137, 162.

Authority, 8, 11, 13, 33, 43, 49, 65, 66, 69, 72, 77, 79, 81, 86, 97, 99, 116, 125, 126, 127, 137, 157, 163, 167, 173, 175, 183, 184, 190, 203, 275, 296, 302, 303, 304, 305, 313, 314, 322, 326, 328, 331.

## B

Baghdad, 117.

Brotherhood, 17, 18, 19, 25, 65, 76, 84, 104.

## C

Caliphate, 4, 8, 9, 10, 11, 15, 270, 305.

Christianity, 29, 46, 47, 108, 162, 166, 196, 197, 235.

City of the Prophet, 76.

Concept of Fraternity, 84.

Concept of State, 1, 3, 55, 56, 57, 87, 104.

## D

Discrimination, 60, 114, 165, 324.

## E

Economic Policy, 73.

Egypt, 9, 80, 88, 100, 275.

Exemplary Behaviour, 52.

## F

Force, 33, 38, 40, 54, 57,

59, 60, 65, 71, 80, 90, 117, 128, 129, 130, 132, 139, 145, 166, 204, 222, 236, 240, 247, 286, 288, 289, 298.

Fraternity, 17, 42, 65, 74, 76, 79, 84, 86.

Fundamental Liberties, 66.

## G

Guiding Principles, 71.

## H

Hadrat Ali, 85, 89, 90, 92, 181, 183, 275, 276, 277.

Holy Prophet, 171, 172, 173, 174, 175, 176, 177, 178, 179, 180, 181, 182, 183, 184, 185, 186, 188, 190, 191, 192, 193, 194, 195, 196, 199, 200, 201, 205, 267, 268, 269, 270, 271, 272, 274, 275, 276, 277, 278, 279, 280, 281, 282, 283, 284.

Human Society, 36, 40, 41, 42, 209.

Hungary, 117.

## I

India, 9, 85, 109, 112, 235.

Iran, 81, 108, 110, 114, 137, 262.

Iraq, 88, 89.

Islam, 2, 3, 8, 9, 10, 11, 12, 19, 23, 24, 25, 26, 27, 28, 29, 30, 31, 33, 35, 36, 37, 39, 40, 42, 43, 45, 48, 49, 50, 52, 53, 55, 56, 57, 59, 61, 62, 63, 64, 65, 66, 67, 68, 69, 70, 71, 73, 75, 76, 77, 80, 81, 84, 85, 86, 87, 90, 93, 95, 99, 101, 102, 103, 104, 110, 111, 113, 114, 115, 116, 117, 118, 123, 124, 125, 127, 128, 130, 140, 141, 142, 145, 146, 147, 150, 152, 157, 159, 165, 167, 169, 180, 181, 184, 185, 186, 187, 188, 191, 206, 211, 227, 228, 233, 234, 235, 237, 239, 242, 243, 244, 245, 246, 247, 251, 252, 253, 254, 255, 256, 259, 263, 264, 267, 272, 273, 276, 277, 283, 287, 288, 289, 290, 291, 293, 296, 297, 298, 299, 300, 302, 304, 305, 307, 309, 311, 313, 314, 315, 316, 317, 318, 319, 325, 326, 327, 331.

Islamic Principles, 298, 302.

Islamic State, 3, 8, 20, 55, 56, 57, 59, 61, 64, 65, 66, 67, 68, 69, 70, 71, 72, 73, 74, 75, 82, 85, 86,

96, 99, 101, 103, 104, 106, 116.

## J

Jizya, 70, 85, 95.
Jurisprudence, 10, 11, 289, 292, 293, 294, 295, 298, 311, 314, 329, 331.

## K

Kaaba, 171, 173, 175, 179, 191, 192, 194, 199, 227, 246, 247, 248, 249, 252, 255, 256, 270, 274, 276, 277, 278.
Khalifa, 80, 88, 89, 90, 91, 92, 93, 95, 97, 98, 99, 100, 101, 146.

## L

Law in Force, 145.
Legal System, 67, 290, 291, 292, 293, 294, 296, 299, 300, 307, 308, 309, 310, 312, 327, 328.
London, 140, 160.

## M

Mecca, 15, 17, 21, 27, 28, 39, 75, 79, 90, 119, 123, 124, 125, 126, 127, 131, 132, 138, 139, 141, 158, 173, 175, 177, 178, 179, 180, 188, 190, 191, 194, 195, 196, 199, 200, 201, 205, 216, 227, 230, 231, 232, 237, 239, 240, 242, 244, 246, 248, 250, 252, 253, 254, 255, 267, 268, 269, 271, 272, 273, 274, 275, 276, 277, 279, 281, 282.
Medina, 13, 17, 18, 21, 22, 27, 75, 77, 78, 79, 83, 84, 86, 87, 88, 89, 90, 97, 118, 119, 120, 123, 124, 125, 135, 136, 137, 142, 148, 158, 163, 164, 167, 172, 175, 184, 185, 186, 188, 189, 190, 192, 229, 230, 231, 232, 233, 235, 236, 238, 239, 240, 241, 242, 250, 260, 261, 262, 263, 267, 269, 270, 272, 273, 274, 275, 276, 280, 282, 284.
Muhammad, 14, 15, 16, 18, 19, 21, 22, 23, 24, 25, 27, 28, 56, 69, 72, 105, 107, 111, 116, 127, 137, 138, 140, 141, 143, 144, 162, 166, 167, 172, 179, 187, 192, 206, 207, 210, 212, 214, 215, 216, 217, 218, 219, 222, 223, 224, 226, 227, 228, 229, 230, 238, 245, 252, 253, 254, 260, 263, 271, 316, 317, 318, 323.

## P

Peninsula, 180.
Political Realm, 4.
Protection, 22, 68, 70, 71, 77, 78, 79, 85, 120, 122, 149, 155, 158, 162, 165, 166, 172, 173, 179, 231, 234, 235, 246, 247, 256, 271, 282.

## Q

Quran, 1, 61, 62, 63, 64, 65, 66, 67, 69, 70, 71.
Quranic Fundamentals, 61.
Quranic Injunctions, 67, 92, 96, 115.
Quranic Principles, 64, 71, 73.
Quranic Verse, , 249, 251.
Quranic Words, 242.

## R

Revisional Jurisdiction, 103.
Rule, 18, 45, 52, 57, 58, 61, 63, 66 75, 82, 86, 90, 99, 118, 119, 123, 164, 165, 235, 259, 271, 290, 294, 296, 302, 304, 305, 306, 307, 310, 312, 313, 330, 331.
Rulers, 3, 90, 159, 160, 164, 165, 183, 302, 306, 312, 324.

## S

Syria, 88, 89, 108, 121, 155, 164, 240, 250, 275.

## T

Town, 2, 39, 41, 127, 186, 231, 239, 248, 263.
Transylvania, 117.

## U

Uthman, 15, 89, 249, 250, 276, 277.

## Z

Zakat, 26, 27, 73, 74, 85, 95, 317, 324, 325.

❑❑❑